The journey to Tahrir

The Journey to Tahrir

REVOLUTION, PROTEST,
AND SOCIAL CHANGE IN EGYPT

Edited by Jeannie Sowers
and Chris Toensing

VERSO

London • New York

This edition first published by Verso 2012
The collection © Verso 2012
The contributions © the contributors 2012
Translation of Chapter 19 © Ann Delehanty 2012

Chapter 4 first appeared in the online magazine *Jadaliyya*.

Chapter 9 is primarily based upon three articles published by MERIP: "Popular Social Movements and the Future of Egyptian Politics," *Middle East Report Online*, March 10, 2005; "Strikes in Egypt Spread from Center of Gravity" (with Hossam el-Hamalawy), *Middle East Report Online*, May 9, 2007; and "The Militancy of Mahalla al-Kubra," *Middle East Report Online*, September 29, 2007. It also draws upon material previously published in the *Nation* and *Foreign Policy*'s Middle East Channel.

Chapter 12 draws from three articles published by MERIP: "Egypt's Paradoxical Elections," *Middle East Report* 238 (Spring 2006); "The Dynamics of Egypt's Elections," *Middle East Report Online*, September 19, 2010; "The Liquidation of Egypt's Illiberal Experiment," *Middle East Report Online*, December 29, 2010. The author would like to express her gratitude to Sayed El-Ghobashy, George Gavrilis, Mandy McClure, and Chris Toensing for very helpful criticism and advice on these articles.

Chapter 17 draws on joint publications by Marsha Pripstein Posusney (1951–2008) and Karen Pfeifer, and from published and unpublished manuscripts written separately by the two authors and collated by Pfeifer for this volume.

1 3 5 7 9 10 8 6 4 2

Verso
UK: 6 Meard Street, London W1F 0EG
US: 20 Jay Street, Suite 1010, Brooklyn, NY 11201
www.versobooks.com

Verso is the imprint of New Left Books

ISBN-13: 978-1-84467-875-4

British Library Cataloguing in Publication Data
A catalogue record for this book is available from the British Library

Library of Congress Cataloging-in-Publication Data
The journey to Tahrir : revolution, protest, and social change in Egypt, 1999-2011 / edited by Jeannie Sowers and Chris Toensing.
    p. cm.
"This book is a collective effort by the contributing authors to Middle East Report."--Acknowledgements.
Includes bibliographical references.
ISBN 978-1-84467-875-4
1. Egypt--Politics and government--21st century. 2. Egypt--Social conditions--21st century. 3. Protest movements--Egypt--History--21st century. I. Sowers, Jeannie Lynn, 1967- II. Toensing, Christopher J.
DT107.87.J68 2012
962.055--dc23
                              2012001432
A catalog record for this book is available from the Library of Congress

Typeset in Minion Pro by Hewer Text UK Ltd, Edinburgh
Printed in the US by Maple Vail

For Egypt's activists

Contents

Acknowledgements

This book is a collective effort by several contributing authors to *Middle East Report*, whose original essays provided such rich material for this collection. The authors graciously supported this project from the outset and provided timely revised submissions in the midst of the momentous political change sweeping across the Arab world.

The advice and prompt assistance of our commissioning editor at Verso, Sebastian Budgen, and the managing editor, Mark Martin, made working with Verso a pleasure. Michelle Woodward, the photo editor for *Middle East Report*, found the wonderful pictures that open each section of the volume. Sasa Tang helped format the typescript with care. Amanda Ufheil-Somers, assistant editor of *Middle East Report*, took on extra duties so that Chris Toensing might work on this project.

Jeannie Sowers thanks the College of Liberal Arts, University of New Hampshire, for supporting research in Egypt during the summer of 2011. She is also grateful to her husband Ben Chandran and son Evan for their support and humor during this project.

CHAPTER ONE

Egypt in Transformation

Jeannie Sowers

At sunset on June 6, 2011, Egyptians once again demonstrated their creativity and tenacity in staging public protests. Activists stood motionless on Cairo's Qasr al-Nil bridge, shoulder to shoulder, facing each other across four lanes of choked traffic, garbed in black. A few talked in quiet voices, others held signs, but most kept silent with folded hands as taxis, microbuses, and cars filled with passengers crawled past. Occasionally a young man came down the line, reminding participants they would soon move across the bridge, through the streets near Tahrir Square, and assemble in front of the Ministry of Interior, the government authority responsible for the detested internal security forces.

This silent stand-in was in memory of Khalid Sa'id, a twenty-eight-year-old man beaten to death on an Alexandria sidewalk by security forces exactly one year before. The brazen brutality had galvanized citizens across the country, coordinated anonymously through the "We Are All Khalid Sa'id" Facebook page and other social media, to take to the streets. On July 23, 2010, activists mounted the first in the series of stand-ins. To avoid the draconian restrictions on public gatherings enshrined in Egypt's Emergency Law, organizers in Alexandria and Cairo asked participants to stand a few meters apart, facing the sea or the Nile if possible, in quiet contemplation or prayer. The novel form of protest attracted unexpectedly large crowds, prompting one commentator to wonder if "the thunderous silence on the Nile" in the summer of 2010 presaged greater civil unrest.[1]

And indeed it did. In early 2011, after Tunisia's long-standing dictator fled in the face of a mass uprising, millions of people turned out on the streets of Cairo and other Egyptian cities to demand that President Husni Mubarak step down. The Qasr al-Nil bridge, like other thoroughfares, became the site of some of the most visible clashes between state security forces and protesters during the January 25 revolution, as it is known in Egypt. Defying the black-clad conscripts of the regime's Central Security Forces, protesters tried to make their way across the bridge to converge on Tahrir Square. They encountered tear gas, bullets, water cannons mounted

---

1   Adel Iskandar, "Thunderous Silence on the Nile," July 26, 2010, huffingtonpost.com.

on armored vehicles, and phalanxes of state security. As captured on videos posted on the Internet and viewed around the world, however, the protesters regrouped, pushed forward behind improvised barricades, and sometimes broke through as the security forces retreated in disorder.

The battles on the Qasr al-Nil bridge were only some of many attacks on protesters across Egyptian cities, often at night, in places with far less media coverage. The courage and determination of many ordinary Egyptians to stay in the streets forced the military to remove Mubarak from office and assert direct control over the country after a mere eighteeen days. Those who participated in the uprising were not simply out to end Mubarak's thirty-year hold on power. Like their counterparts in Tunisia, protesters wanted to create a political regime that would respect dignity, rights, and justice, not trample upon them.

Embedding such principles in any political system, even consolidated democracies, is an ongoing challenge. But it is a particularly difficult task when the key institutions and personnel of the *ancien régime* are entrusted with revolutionary goals. Egyptians were initially grateful that the military eased Mubarak out of power, preventing an escalation of the repression and atrocities that unfolded in Syria, Bahrain, Yemen, and Libya. By the summer of 2011, activists became frustrated by the military council's refusal to repeal the Emergency Law, restructure the security services, or make concrete preparations for elections. The military, a pillar of the Mubarak regime, continued to employ many of the techniques of control and repression that security forces had used in previous years. The Supreme Council of the Armed Forces (SCAF) criminalized protests and strikes through new laws issued by decree, arrested protesters and tried civilians in military courts, and detained individuals on vague and often questionable charges of subversion, espionage, and treason. Some pro-democracy activists bravely questioned these tactics in blogs, TV interviews, and the press, and were then "invited" in for questioning by the military council. At the same time, however, the public trials of former President Mubarak and his former interior minister went ahead as announced, an unthinkable event just six months earlier, while there is no indication that the SCAF has retreated from its commitment to hold substantive parliamentary and presidential elections.

The January 25 revolution has thus already reshaped the political landscape of Egypt in new and profound ways. The significant gains made by the protesters, and their tenacity in returning to the streets, open up possibilities for systemic institutional transformation in the months and years to come. Success in creating a more accountable, inclusionary political system is far from assured. But for those who took to the streets, and those who did not but watched their compatriots persevere, the uprising has already wrought substantial changes. These can be summed up as the dissolution of fear and its replacement with willingness to challenge practices of political control and hierarchy. As one Egyptian engineer put it, "We feel that a great weight, the weight of *zulm* [oppression], has been lifted. We know what we are capable of. We can go to the streets again."[2]

This lack of fear has concrete roots in victories achieved through peaceful protest and pitched battles like those on the Qasr al-Nil bridge and elsewhere. The old regime inadvertently helped create collective assertiveness and self-sufficiency when it pulled the security and police forces in their entirety off the streets during the January uprising. This decision, like those to unleash gangs of thugs and to free criminals from prisons, proved to be self-defeating, part of a desperate bid to create insecurity and turn public opinion against the protesters. Instead, local watch committees (*ligan sha'biyya*) emerged in every neighborhood to address the threat of armed thugs, looting, and disorder. Streets and neighborhoods were self-organized and self-policed. Cairo, a metropolitan area of approximately 22 million people, continued to function, without the traffic police, the security forces, or any other external apparatus of coercion. City streets, it turned out, were not just spaces of protest, but of participatory self-governance.

UNDERSTANDING EGYPT'S UPRISING IN CONTEXT

This book situates Egypt's January uprising in terms of the key trends in Egyptian society and economy of the past decade. It also covers the unfolding of the January 25 revolution and the initial impact of the revolution on Egypt's politics and economy. The volume originated as essays published in *Middle East Report*, a quarterly journal providing independent, in-depth analysis of the region's political economy since 1971. Many chapters have been reworked and updated to include recent developments; others are reprinted as originally written, to capture a particular historical moment.

The contributors to the volume have all lived, worked, and conducted research in Egypt, and include some well-known Egyptian activists and civil society organizers. The authors hail from a range of academic disciplines, including anthropology, history, sociology, and political science, and their work provides original, empirically grounded knowledge of past trends and unfolding developments in Egypt.

---

2   Interview with the author, Cairo, May 25, 2011.

In compiling such a volume, we do not claim that the January 25 uprising was either inevitable or anticipated. No one was more surprised at the escalation of the protests than the youthful organizers themselves; they did not foresee, any more than did the regime, the extent to which the protests would escalate. "The miracle of the Egyptian revolution," recalled one middle-aged professional who strolled to Tahrir Square on the first day with all of his coworkers, "was that we all decided simply to walk in the streets (*mashawir fi shawari'*). It was such an ordinary thing to do, but when millions of us did it, it was extraordinary."[3]

While the uprising seemed spontaneous even to participants, veteran activists had rethought their protest strategies in light of the Tunisian success. Rather than announcing protest locations in advance, allowing security forces to overwhelm discrete demonstrations, activists dispersed to various streets and neighborhoods, gathering crowds as they went along and converging on major thoroughfares, bridges, and squares.[4] A series of miscalculations by the regime and its supporters in the National Democratic Party (NDP) also contributed to rapid escalation and growing public support. These included sending thugs to attack protesters in Tahrir Square for twelve hours during the infamous "Battle of the Camel," without any interference from the security forces or the army. Carried live on satellite television, the camel-borne assault placed the contempt of the regime for Egyptian citizens on full display.

While the January uprising was not predictable, momentum for significant political change was building during the 2000s.[5] The Mubarak regime was widely viewed as out of touch, corrupt, and heavy-handed. During the 1990s and 2000s, the ruling clique expanded the reach of the internal security and intelligence agencies, employing hundreds of thousands as informants, thugs, police officers, and other personnel to conduct ever more extensive monitoring of the citizenry. Human Rights Watch and local human rights organizations chronicled the systematic use of torture, widespread illegal and indefinite detentions in police stations across the country, and

---

3   Interview with the author, Cairo, June 5, 2011.

4   "I Want a Democratic Egypt," interview with Israa Abdel Fattah, *Cairo Review of Global Affairs* 1/1 (Spring 2011), p. 76.

5   For works in English, see, for instance, Rabab El-Mahdi and Philip Marfleet, eds, *Egypt: Moment of Change* (Cairo: AUC Press, 2010); Nicholas Hopkins, ed., "Political and Social Protest in Egypt," *Cairo Papers in Social Science* 29 (2006); and the collected articles of Alaa Al Aswany in *The State of Egypt* (Cairo: AUC Press, 2011). Several volumes in Arabic have compiled newspaper articles from independent and opposition papers that highlight the mounting economic, social, and political tensions in Egypt prior to the revolution. See, among others, Wahid 'Abd al-Magid, *January 25 Revolution: The First Readings* (Cairo: al-Ahram Center for Publishing, Translation, and Distribution).

even cases of abductions and disappearances.[6] Once limited to targeting political opponents and Islamists, these tactics now spread as a routine use of state power.[7] In a prescient 2006 essay, Robert Springborg outlined how these policies, designed to forestall the possibility of mass protest, instead undermined its ability to gauge public opinion and react appropriately.[8] In other words, the Mubarak regime became progressively less capable of governing during the 2000s, as its reliance on security agencies overshadowed its limited avenues of engagement with political and civil society.

THE JANUARY 25 REVOLUTION: TAHRIR AND BEYOND

As Mona El-Ghobashy argues in Chapter 2, during the 2000s the police and security forces came into direct confrontation with increasing numbers of Egyptians across class and communal lines. She notes that "by January 25, 2011, every protest sector had field experience with police rule . . . but no population group had come close to shifting the balance of resources in its favor." All this changed in the first four days of the January 2011 street battles, she argues, as the police encountered an unprecedented, cascading situation. Protest, strikes, and vigils diffused rapidly through cities across the country, and protesters returned to the streets in ever greater numbers despite extensive and often lethal police violence. The protesters also literally destroyed key parts of the hated police and security infrastructure, storming and burning police stations, armored vehicles, and government party headquarters in the capital and the provinces.

The epicenter of the protests quickly became Tahrir Square in downtown Cairo. In Chapter 3, Ahmad Shokr chronicles from firsthand experience how the days and nights spent in Tahrir transformed participants and their expectations. When people recall their time in Tahrir, many describe living in a utopia where they felt freed from their own circumscribed identities as well as from fear of the regime. As the protesters repeatedly fought to hold Tahrir in the face of attacks by police forces and hired thugs, and organized the routine tasks of sustaining everyday life, such as providing food, shelter, and medical care, staying in the square became far more than a political demonstration. As Shokr observes, the square "became a tent city where people of every political stripe and social class gathered to exchange views about everything."

---

6   "Rights Group Threatens to Release Secret Arrests Record," *al-Masry al-Youm*, June 22, 2011.

7   Aida Seif Al-Dawla, "Torture: A State Policy," in Al-Mahdi and Marfleet, *Egypt*, pp. 120–35.

8   Robert Springborg, "Protest Against a Hybrid State: Words Without Meaning?" in Hopkins, *Cairo Papers*.

Many participants felt that they were collectively involved in creating a political community for the first time. Jessica Winegar, in Chapter 6, shows how this sense of community persisted when young people embarked on cleaning up Tahrir and other urban spaces in the aftermath of the protests. She sees efforts at collecting garbage, painting, and sweeping the streets as part of a broader reclaiming of public space by marginalized youth.

Patriotism, communal purpose, and joy: all these were facilitated in Tahrir and elsewhere by protest leaders leading crowds in chants and slogans. After January 2011, protest in Tahrir and other public spaces continued, hoping to push forward the goals of the uprising in the face of a recalcitrant security state. The most talented sloganeers kept the crowds engaged with satire, humor, and wordplay worthy of a talented rap artist.[9] As Elliott Colla demonstrates in Chapter 4, Egypt has a long and rich history of sloganeers, poets, and songwriters galvanizing and sustaining street protest and social movements. Colla illustrates how the political poetry of Tahrir poked fun at officials and kept fear at bay even as chants also conveyed the serious political demands of the demonstrators.

Another critical factor sustaining street action during the uprising was the nonstop media coverage provided by Al Jazeera and other media outlets, which kept Egyptians all over the country informed of developments despite the campaign of state-run media to discredit the protesters. Ursula Lindsey chronicles in Chapter 5 how the uprising was not simply a contest for control of the streets, but for public opinion more broadly. The independent, private, and foreign media provided staunchly supportive coverage of the protesters and their aims, in stark contrast to government-owned outlets. Lindsey shows how young activists also used social media, cell phones, and interviews on privately owned satellite stations to counter the regime's propaganda.

STREET PROTEST AND POLITICAL MOBILIZATION UNDER MUBARAK

Part II of this volume places the January uprising in the context of intensifying, contentious street politics across Egypt during the 2000s. In Chapter 7, Asef Bayat argues that the "Arab street" is not only a physical space of contestation, but also "an expression of the collective sensibilities, shared feelings, and public judgment of ordinary people." Bayat argues that with

---

9   Cheers, jokes, and slogans have been collected and published in small paperback books in Egypt. In Arabic, see "The Egyptian People," in *The People Want . . .* (Cairo: al-'Arabi for Publishing and Distribution, 2011).

the increased policing of streets and public spaces during the 1980s and early 1990s, Islamist and leftist activists moved to informal mosques, universities, and professional associations. Activists returned to street protests in the 2000s, however, to demonstrate in support of the Palestinians (2002), oppose the US invasion of Iraq (2003), and support democracy and labor demands.

Street protest in Cairo against the 2003 Iraq war looked much like a dress rehearsal for January 2011, as Paul Schemm shows in Chapter 8. Protesters occupied Tahrir Square and fought pitched battles with battalions of riot police in the surrounding streets. Popular criticism of Mubarak's foreign policies escalated when Egypt helped Israel seal off the Hamas-controlled Gaza Strip after 2007. Ursula Lindsey, in Chapter 10, shows how public anger mounted against Egypt's blockade of Gaza, a policy that included building a subterranean steel wall on the Egyptian–Gazan border with American assistance.

In parallel with the revival of street protest, labor activism also intensified. Joel Beinin argues in Chapter 9 that workers felt threatened on several fronts by accelerating economic reforms. As the state restructured state-owned enterprises for privatization, many workers were laid off. Wages in the public and private sectors failed to keep pace with rising prices for food and other basic commodities, while employers often arbitrarily withheld pay and bonuses.

As a result of these increasingly difficult conditions, labor leaders launched approximately 2,623 collective actions involving over 1.7 million workers between 1998 and 2008, while the number of strikes, sit-ins, demonstrations, and campaigns accelerated in subsequent years.[10] The government responded to major strikes not only with police repression but also with strategic concessions on bonuses and wages. Thus, despite draconian laws and government-controlled unions designed to contain activism, workers quickly learned that direct action was effective. After the fall of Mubarak, as strikes spread, the SCAF issued a new law criminalizing work stoppages. With strikes and sit-ins showing little sign of abating, however, there is little indication that Egypt's workers will be so easily intimidated.

---

10   Joel Beinin, "A Workers' Social Movement on the Margin of the Global Neoliberal Order, Egypt 2004–2009," in Beinin and Frédéric Vairel, eds. *Social Movements, Mobilization, and Contestation in the Middle East and North Africa* (Stanford, CA: Stanford University Press, 2011), pp. 188–90.

CONTESTED RULES AND INSTITUTIONS

Part III moves from the domain of street protest and civic activism to analyze the dynamics of contention over the rules and practices of formal political institutions. The Mubarak regime appeared for years to have the upper hand in managing participation in formal political life through a combination of patronage, elaborate legal restrictions, and coercive power to divide and punish opposition forces. The 1990s and early 2000s, however, saw cumulative efforts by lawyers, judges, human rights activists, opposition parties, and others to promote competition and accountability within existing political institutions and laws.

At the center of some of these legal battles was the Egyptian constitution. As Mona El-Ghobashy shows in Chapter 11, reforming Egypt's 1971 constitution emerged by 1999 as an issue that unified opposition groups from across the ideological spectrum. Judges, lawyers, leftists, and opposition party figures converged in their demands that the constitution be revised to limit executive power over the parliament and judiciary.

Constitutional debates have only intensified since Mubarak was deposed. In March 2011, the military put forward a package of constitutional amendments for popular vote in a yes/no referendum. Among other measures, the referendum called for a rapid electoral timetable, after which a popularly elected parliament would undertake constitutional reform. Liberal opposition groups staunchly opposed this provision, concerned that Islamist parties and the individuals associated with the government's dissolved party, the NDP, would win a parliamentary majority given their existing organizational capacities, and produce a constitution that did not sufficiently constrain the executive or protect the rights of minorities and women. They called upon the military to convene a committee to put forward a "bill of rights" enumerating basic principles and rights that could not be abrogated in later revisions to the constitution. In contrast, the leadership of the Muslim Brothers and other Islamist parties argued that only a democratically elected parliament could be delegated to undertake constitutional reforms and enumerate basic rights.

The military's referendum passed by 77 percent of the popular vote in the spring of 2011, but by the summer the military announced that it would consider convening a constitutional committee in advance of elections. This announcement prompted Islamist organizations, including the Muslim Brothers, to organize their own Tahrir protests to oppose such a committee, where protesters chanted, "We want it [the constitution] Islamic."

During the Mubarak period, such debates over constitutional reform were largely confined to professional associations and opposition parties.

This was not the case, however, in hotly contested electoral competitions for parliament in Egypt's cities and rural areas, which involved far greater numbers of people. As Mona El-Ghobashy shows in Chapter 12, the Mubarak regime routinely rigged elections by establishing rules that limited competition, engaging in blatant fraud at voting booths and polling centers, and intimidating voters through the use of state security forces and thugs. Yet she argues that opposition activists turned the conduct of elections into something much more than an exercise in authoritarian domination. In particular, judges and activists sought to strengthen judicial oversight of elections through court cases, documentation of violations, and direct action. These efforts were partly successful, producing expanded judicial oversight over parliamentary elections by 2005. El-Ghobashy goes on to show how the regime closed this opening by canceling provisions for judicial oversight in advance of the 2010 elections. But the victory was Pyrrhic, to say the least: the absence of trusted monitors reduced the already limited credibility of the electoral process among Egyptian citizens to zero. The Mubarak regime's legitimacy was thus further eroded.

In Chapter 13, Issandr El Amrani chronicles the results of the landmark 2005 parliamentary elections. In order for judges to monitor the many polling stations, elections were spread out over several weeks. In doing so, the regime's blatantly illegal actions to win races came under greater scrutiny. Despite massive cheating and obstruction, the NDP secured only 149 out of 444 seats. The party eventually claimed a supermajority of 316 seats, attained only when independent candidates joined the party after they had won.

As El Amrani points out, the Muslim Brothers were widely considered to be the biggest winners of the 2005 election. Candidates affiliated with the Brothers captured an unexpected eighty-eight seats, despite the fact that the organization was formally banned. In Chapter 14, Joshua Stacher and Samer Shehata examine how the Brothers moved from an organization focused on social reform and proselytization toward a greater role in electoral politics and in parliament. Their chapter illustrates how the newly elected parliamentary bloc took their representative roles seriously, coordinating their positions on political reform measures and working on concrete issues important to their constituents. The Brothers also used their seats under the rotunda to mount their own response to public health and other crises, showing Egyptians that such leadership did not have to be the sole domain of an unaccountable executive branch.

With the fall of Mubarak, political and generational divisions among the Brothers have become clearer. The senior leaders created a new political party, the Freedom and Justice Party, but tried to allay liberal fears by pledging that the organization would not field a presidential candidate. When ʿAbd al-Munʿim Abu al-Futouh, a popular reformist figure, announced he would run for president, he was expelled from the Brothers' ranks. This act, and the old leadership's inconsistent positions on civil rights for minorities and women, prompted some of the younger members to leave the Brothers and announce that they would form their own political party.

The end of the Mubarak era also emboldened the Gamaʿa Islamiyya and other radical Islamist groups espousing visions of an Islamic state. These groups had been at the forefront of a violent insurgency to overthrow the regime in the early 1990s, providing both the impetus and the victims for an expanded internal security apparatus. These groups have begun to claim a public role in politics. One the first two political parties approved in the post-Mubarak era, for instance, was the Nour Party, founded by *salafi* groups from Alexandria.[11] In Chapter 15, Ewan Stein examines the evolution of the Gamaʿa before and after the fall of Mubarak, drawing on his interview with one of the leading spokesmen of the group, Najih Ibrahim, among other sources.

The increasing political visibility of the Brothers and other Islamist groups is partly a product of two decades of "Islamization" of cultural and social life in Egypt, from below by social movements and from above by the state. The Muslim Brothers are only one of many organizations that constructed welfare associations, community organizations, mosques, and social service centers across the urbanizing peripheries of Egyptian cities and towns.[12] This social infrastructure supported the spread of an increasingly narrow, often exclusionary construction of Muslim identity. The Mubarak regime sought to co-opt the Islamist message with ever larger doses of "Islam" on state-run television and radio, often in programs hosted by state-sponsored preachers.

As Mariz Tadros shows in Chapter 16, Egypt's Coptic Christian community, estimated at around 10 percent of the population, has found its communal security more precarious as a result of these social changes. Both the Mubarak government and the SCAF tolerated escalating violent attacks on Coptic villagers, churches, and shops. Security forces and military forces typically failed to respond quickly and were directly implicated in some attacks. The military, like the Mubarak regime before it, has relied largely on "reconciliation committees" that focus on placating "both sides"

---

11   "Egyptian Authority Approves First Non-Islamic Party Since Revolution," *al-Masry al-Youm*, June 27, 2011.

12   One of the best accounts of the Egyptian Islamic movements remains Carrie Rosefsky Wickham's *Mobilizing Islam* (New York: Columbia University Press, 2002).

in sectarian disputes, including the instigators of violence, rather than prosecuting crimes. Egypt's pro-democracy activists continue to call for guaranteed civil and communal rights for the Coptic population, and this issue remains central to whether a more liberal political regime emerges in Egypt.

PEOPLE, LAND, AND CAPITAL

In Part IV, we examine some of the long-term changes in Egypt's economy, environment, and demography that underpinned momentum for political and social change. Faced with a large, inefficient state-owned sector and recurrent fiscal crises, the government embarked on structural adjustment programs designed by the IMF and World Bank by the early 1970s under then-President Anwar al-Sadat. As Chapter 17 by Karen Pfeifer shows, neoliberal economic reform during the 1980s and 1990s provided state subsidies and other incentives for investors to focus on sectors such as finance, real estate, construction, tourism, and raw materials extraction and processing. Private investors, foreign and domestic, as well as consortiums involving state-owned enterprises, were given cheap land, cheap natural gas and oil, and extensive tax and customs exemptions. Large plots of land were carved into free zones where Egypt's regular regulatory regimes did not apply, while state-owned enterprises were increasingly privatized and new labor laws favoring employers enacted. The result was aggregate economic growth without commensurate employment expansion or wage increases. Pfeifer shows how while Egypt's market reforms and privatization programs were touted as success stories by international financial institutions, these reforms concentrated profits chiefly in the hands of large-scale foreign and domestic capitalists.

Timothy Mitchell in Chapter 18 analyzes some of the financial underpinnings and spatial consequences of such "undisciplined" capitalism. During the 1980s, state and private banks alike increasingly catered to a small stratum of wealthy businessmen and state-owned enterprises. The costs of non-performing loans were shifted onto public finances when the state bailed out the banking sector and stock market in 1990–91. During the 1990s, wealth continued to accumulate in the hands of well-known family business conglomerates and regime officials, in ventures producing goods and housing affordable only to a few. The reemergence of a wealthy elite was increasingly evident in the proliferation of luxury gated communities reaching into the desert west and east of Cairo, such as Dreamland, as well as in the construction of upscale malls, vacation homes, and coastal resorts.

The increasingly uneven distribution of wealth combined with ongoing population growth poses profound developmental challenges for Egypt. In

Chapter 19, Eric Denis reports on Egypt's demographic trends using the 2006 national census. Although the rate of population growth has slowed, it has done so very gradually. Between 1996 and 2006, the growth rate was 2.05 percent, while for the previous decade it was 2.08 percent. As Denis observes, these growth rates mean that Egypt's population now outstrips that of Iran and is set to overtake that of Turkey in the next decade.

The sluggish decrease in Egypt's population growth rates, Denis argues, stemmed not only from cohorts of girls entering childbearing age from the earlier population boom, but also from economic policy decisions. Privatization limited public-sector employment opportunities for women, while government budgets for education remained stagnant. The state's dwindling social safety net, reduced subsidies for basic commodities, and loss of public-sector jobs informalized much of the labor force. Low-wage jobs in the service sector and nonpaid family labor increasingly constituted employment for even educated young people. Respectable national growth rates thus masked the impoverishment of many in the lower and middle classes, and women accordingly had more children in order to secure family livelihoods. These realities, stemming from national economic policy decisions, ironically undercut the state's efforts to encourage family planning and birth control.

Rapid urbanization has transformed not only Egypt's metropolitan centers, but also its villages, hamlets, and secondary towns. Most Egyptians live in densely populated urban and peri-urban areas in the Nile Delta and Nile Valley. Only some informal areas have adequate access to sanitation services or good quality water, despite rosy official statistics.[13] Agricultural and urban land is in high demand, often claimed by the military and state-owned entities. Small farmers have steadily seen their access to, and control over, lucrative agricultural land rolled back, as the Mubarak regime reversed Nasser-era land reform and tenancy laws. Ray Bush and Amal Sabri document in Chapter 20 how fisheries and grazing areas on Egypt's northern coast, once used in communal rotation by local communities, are increasingly "enclosed" by private investors and industrial enterprises, many of which are partially state-owned.

Pollution loads are also unequally distributed. Significant air and water pollution afflicts most Egyptian cities and villages, but is most dire where concentrated industrial activity and transport combine with inadequate sanitation and solid waste systems. In Chapter 21, Sharif Elmusa

---

13   Neda Zawahri, Jeannie Sowers, and Erika Weinthal, "The Politics of Assessment: Water and Sanitation MDGs in the Middle East and North Africa," *Development and Change* 42/5 (2011).

and I analyze the largest environmental protest movement to emerge under Mubarak, a campaign in the port city of Damietta against a proposed fertilizer plant. The campaign was notable in that it united groups in the province across class and ideological lines, invoking local economic priorities to contest the central government's investment plans.

In the aftermath of the revolution, some of the "crony capitalists" most closely associated with the Mubarak regime were charged with corruption. Those who held official positions in the government and the NDP, like Ahmad 'Izz, head of one of Egypt's largest steel enterprises, were among the first to be charged and imprisoned. The government also began to review a large number of privatization agreements and renegotiate land concessions with private investors. The Ministry of Investment was officially abolished, and the privatization program halted.

There is little doubt that Egypt needs more equitable development policies that generate employment and improve wages. As shown in this volume, the unequal accumulation of wealth under neoliberal reform was official government policy, not simply some version of "private" corruption in the absence of a capable state. Yet the SCAF's emerging anti-privatization stance holds its own pitfalls. Most of Egypt's state-owned enterprises have been sustained only through ongoing borrowing from state-owned banks, pension funds, and other government entities. They require either significant public investment or privatization to become financially viable. Furthermore, as periodically done by the Mubarak regime, the SCAF has selectively targeted leading businessmen with allegations of corruption.

If the interim government shifts toward the economic statism of earlier decades, it will simply delay much-needed progress in constructing more "disciplined"—that is, regulated—forms of capitalism. As Beinin points out in Chapter 9, the Muslim Brothers and other emerging political forces have traditionally been hostile to working-class organizations and extensive state ownership. It remains to be seen if Egypt's mobilized workers can create a credible labor party. If upcoming elections produce more representation of diverse political forces, at least one can expect more open, contentious discussions about economic policy than those that took place within Mubarak's closed circles of decision-making.

THE POLITICS OF IDENTITY, GENDER, AND YOUTH

The chapters in Part V explore how norms of fashion, marriage, sexuality, and youth are socially constructed in contemporary Egypt. Linda Herrera analyzes the cultural phenomenon of "downveiling," or women wearing less conservative forms of Islamic dress, in Chapter 22. During the 1980s and early 1990s, Islamic movements for religious revitalization reshaped public notions of women's dress, and various styles of conservative "Islamic" attire spread rapidly in Egypt. By the mid-1990s, however, Herrera observes that women chose more form-fitting, colorful, and stylish ways of wearing the *hijab* (headscarf) and *khimar* (a cloak that covers the arms and upper torso). She traces downveiling to several factors: the Mubarak regime's bans on conservative Islamic attire in schools, the emergence of new fashion styles, such as "Islamic urban chic," women's preferences for less hot, more practical clothing, and policies at elite private universities that discouraged conservative dress.

In Chapter 23, Hanan Kholoussy turns to the social construction of marriage and courtship as she analyzes the book *'Ayiza Atgawwiz* (I Want to Get Married) by the popular blogger Ghada Abdel Aal. Abdel Aal's satirical postings on Egyptian courtship rituals and marriage customs became an instant hit in Egypt, spinning off into not only a book but also a TV serial aired over the nights of Ramadan in 2010. Kholoussy situates Abdel Aal's writing in broad, long-running debates about a "marriage crisis" in Egypt. Many observers attribute the trend of deferred wedlock in Egypt to the rising costs of acquiring the accoutrements of middle-class marriage, such as a flat and furniture. Abdel Aal's blog reveals that some women simply choose not to get married right away. Kholoussy points out that Abdel Aal's popularity stems in part from her class position; as a thirty-something pharmacist living in the industrial city of Mahalla al-Kubra with a father who is a small-time state employee, Abdel Aal appeals to many young women who share her modest, non-elite background. Similarly, she writes in a familiar idiom, the funny, smart, street language of Egyptian colloquial Arabic rather than the formal standardized style.

Hossam Bahgat, in Chapter 24, directs our attention to forms of sexuality and courtship other than sanctioned heterosexual marriage. Bahgat chronicles the unpredictable and erratically abusive policies of the Mubarak regime toward homosexuals and homosexuality. In 2001, the regime's state security services embarked on a series of raids, arrests, and prosecutions of tourist boats, nightclubs, and other places thought to be gay hangouts. The Egyptian media showed no hesitation in publishing sensational, unsubstantiated claims made by the security forces, such as allegations that the men involved were members of Satanic cults. Bahgat suggests that the regime's sudden targeting of gays may have been intended to distract the public from pressing economic problems and position the government as the guardian of "Islamic values." He observes that many Egyptian human rights organizations were unwilling to protest the regime's behavior, since the suspects were described as homosexual. As if to prove his point, Bahgat was fired from his position at the Egyptian Organization for Human Rights two days after this chapter was originally published in *Middle East Report* on July 23, 2001.

He went on to found the Egyptian Initiative for Personal Rights (EIPR), which continues to press for the rights and bodily safety of all Egyptians, regardless of their gender, religious affiliation, or sexual orientation. EIPR has been at the forefront of the Egyptian organizations speaking out against the SCAF's arbitrary restrictions on freedom of speech and assembly in the wake of the January 25 revolution.

It is fitting that the last chapter in this volume looks at notions of "youth" in Egypt and the Middle East. As the main force catalyzing the uprisings in Tunisia, Egypt, and elsewhere, Middle Eastern youth have again become of great interest to outsiders—although in 2011 they tend to be regarded as democratic agents of change, rather than as potential recruits for radical networks as they were often portrayed after the September 11, 2001 attacks. In Chapter 25, Ted Swedenburg examines how regimes in the Middle East framed the youthful populations as a problem. The average age in Egypt is slightly over twenty-four, and youth are more likely to be unemployed or underemployed than any other group. Swedenburg argues that official and public discourses often depicted youth as in need of guidance by parental and state authorities to avoid a host of temptations—variously identified as moral corruption, Westernization, materialism, Islamism, and radicalization. Little did officials realize that come the spring of 2011, youthful, educated activists in Egypt would destabilize a paternal, patriarchal, and patronizing regime literally run by old men.

LOOKING FORWARD: SECURITY REFORM
AND LOCAL GOVERNANCE

In conclusion, I want to call attention to two important issues outside the scope of this volume but which are critical to whether Egyptians succeed in creating a more accountable political regime. The first issue is whether newly elected political leaderships will document and prosecute past and ongoing violations of human rights by state security forces, and create clear distinctions between a civil police force, the military, and domestic intelligence services. After Mubarak was deposed, the SCAF announced the dissolution of the State Security Investigations (usually known simply as State Security, Amn al-Dawla), and promptly reconstituted it under a new name, the National Security Agency (Amn al-Watani), with a seemingly minor reshuffling of officers.[14] In March 2011, amidst reports that state security offices were burning and shredding incriminating documents, protesters broke into state security

---

14   Egypt's activist-bloggers attempted to track these reappointments at high levels, but there has been no publicly established process of investigation for officers.

compounds in Nasr City, Alexandria, Sixth of October, Minya, Asyut, Marsa Matruh and other cities. They found mounds of shredded paper, charred piles of documents, destroyed computers and files, underground detention cells, and torture implements, as well as intact documents. Army forces prevented protesters at some locations from taking documents, and announced that all documents should be returned to the military on national security grounds.

The role of the military in reinforcing the prerogatives of the security state here is instructive. The council of generals had no experience in dealing with a mobilized civil society, and little capacity for governing the country transparently. Amidst mounting concern that the old generals of the SCAF were obstructing real political change, protesters took to the streets and city squares again in the summer of 2011. In the sweltering heat of midsummer, activists returned to camping out in Tahrir Square and staging large rallies on successive Fridays. The central slogan of the January uprising—"The people want the fall of the regime"—returned in new variations, such as "The people want the fall of the marshal," referring to the head of the SCAF, Field Marshal Muhammad Husayn Tantawi. Tantawi had been a key figure under the Mubarak regime, having held the position of minister of defense and military production since 1991.

To date, calls from activists and human rights groups to devise mechanisms for independent oversight of the Ministry of Interior have been ignored. Systematic reform of the institutions that perpetuated abuses depends on the outcome of parliamentary and presidential elections—and on whether the political parties that survive the electoral process take such reforms seriously. Given the entrenched institutional position of the military, it will be even more difficult for newly elected civilian leaders to gain oversight over the military's opaque budget, extensive land ownership, economic activities, and other privileges. As in Turkey, this process will likely unfold over decades, punctuated by reversals and periods of conflict over the role of the security forces and the military in the political system.

A second critical issue is whether and how political power will be devolved to local governments and whether local civic associations will be allowed to participate fully and without interference in community organizing and activism. Despite frequent announcements that the government was going to decentralize administrative functions, in practice the Mubarak regime showed no interest in devolving power to lower levels. Instead, the regime deepened already extensive controls over municipalities and provinces (muhafazat). It appointed governors drawn largely from the military and police forces, and maintained centralized control over revenue collection and expenditures. To make matters worse, elected local councils at the city and neighborhood levels were little more than appendages of the government's party, the NDP. For voluntary organizations, multiple legal restrictions—nominally supervised by the Orwellian-named Ministry of Social Solidarity and in practice overseen by State Security—severely limited their autonomy and effectiveness.

As suggested at the outset of this chapter, the experience of the January uprising has generated a sense of collective empowerment, at least for the present. As one scholar who interviewed members of the popular committees in both poor and rich neighborhoods found, participants felt that they could finally speak out for better treatment and services.[15] Some activists have tried to scale up the popular committees so that they can participate more actively in local and municipal affairs. Others have focused their efforts on calling for the dissolution of the old regime's local councils, a step that was finally decreed by an administrative court in June.[16] At present, however, residents of neighborhoods and cities have few legitimate opportunities to participate in local affairs. On this issue, like many others examined in this volume, it remains to be seen whether the activists who led the January 25 revolution can bring about substantive changes in governance.

July 2001

15   Jennifer Bremer, "Leadership and Collective Action in Egypt's Tahrir Revolution: Emergence of Civic Activism in Response to Repression," paper presented at the annual meeting of the International Association of Schools and Institutes of Administration, Rome, Italy, June 13–18, 2011.

16   "Egyptian Court Dissolves Municipal Council," al-Masry al-Youm, June 28, 2011.

Protesters in Tahrir Square, Cairo, February 6, 2011.
© Remi Ochlik / Bureau233 / Polaris

Part I

THE JANUARY 25 REVOLUTION

CHAPTER 2

The Praxis of the Egyptian Revolution

Mona El-Ghobashy

If there was ever to be a popular uprising against autocratic rule, it should not have come in Egypt. The regime of President Husni Mubarak was the quintessential case of durable authoritarianism. "Our assessment is that the Egyptian government is stable and is looking for ways to respond to the legitimate needs and interests of the Egyptian people," said Secretary of State Hillary Clinton on January 25, 2011.[1] With these words, Clinton gave voice to a common understanding of Egypt under Mubarak. Government officials, pundits, and academics, foreign and domestic, thought the regime was resilient—not because it used brute force or Orwellian propaganda, but because it had shrewdly constructed a simulacrum of politics. Parties, elections and civic associations were allowed but carefully controlled, providing space for just enough participatory politics to keep people busy without threatening regime dominance. Mubarak's own party was a cohesive machine, organizing intramural competition among elites. The media was relatively free, giving vent to popular frustrations. And even the wave of protest that began to swell in 2000 was interpreted as another index of the regime's skill in managing, rather than suppressing, dissent. Fundamentally, Egypt's rulers were smart authoritarians who had their house in order. Yet they were toppled by an eighteen-day popular revolt.

Three main explanations have emerged to make sense of this conundrum: technology, Tunisia, and tribulation. Technological analyses celebrate young people who employed new media to defeat a stolid autocrat. By the second day of the Egyptian uprising, CNN correspondent Ben Wedeman was calling it a "very techie revolution." In the following days, every major news outlet framed the uprising as the work of wired, savvy twenty-somethings awakening the liberating potential of Facebook, Twitter, and the writings of American intellectual Gene Sharp. "For the world's despots, his ideas can be fatal," asserted the *New York Times* of Sharp.[2] A second class of

---

Author's Note: Thanks to Evelyn Alsultany, George Gavrilis, Mandy McClure, and Chris Toensing for sympathetic and tough-minded feedback.

[1]   Reuters, January 25, 2011.
[2]   *New York Times*, February 16, 2011.

explanation credits the Tunisian people's ouster of Zine El Abidine Ben Ali in mid-January with supplying a shining example to follow. Esam Al-Amin notes that the Tunisian revolution "inspired Egyptians beyond the activists or elites."[3] A third theorem focuses on the many tribulations afflicting Egyptians, particularly soaring commodity prices, positing that hardship finally pushed the population to rise up against oppression. "Food: What's Really Behind the Unrest in Egypt," one Canadian newspaper headlined its story.[4]

None of these explanations are false. All of them correspond to interpretations of events forwarded by the participants themselves. And each has an impeccable intellectual pedigree, harkening back to two influential traditions in the study of popular collective action. One is the dramaturgical model, identifying a cast of self-propelled characters, armed with courage and a new consciousness, who then make an uprising. The second is the grievance model, by which an accumulation of social troubles steadily diffuses among the population and finally reaches an unforeseeable tipping point. The two models call attention to distinct but equally important forces: specific actors and generalized complaints. But both are oddly without context. Because aggrieved and heroic people exist under every type of political system, the models do not explain when such people will band together to challenge the conditions they deplore.

Egypt's momentous uprising did not happen because Egyptians willed it into being. It happened because there was a sudden change in the balance of resources between rulers and ruled. Mubarak's structures of dominion were thought to be foolproof, and for thirty years they were. What shifted the balance away from the regime were four continuous days of street fighting, January 25–28, that pitted the people against police all over the country. That battle converted a familiar, predictable episode into a revolutionary situation. Decades ago, Charles Tilly observed that one of the ways revolutions happen is that the efficiency of government coercion deteriorates. That decline occurs "when the character, organization and daily routines of the population to be controlled change rapidly."[5] The organization and daily routines of the Egyptian population had undergone significant changes in the years preceding the revolt. By January 25, 2011, a strong regime faced a strong society versed in the politics of the street. With hindsight, it is simple

---

3 Esam Al-Amin, "When Egypt's Revolution Was at the Crossroads," *Counterpunch*, March 9, 2011.

4 *Globe and Mail*, February 9, 2011.

5 Charles Tilly, "Does Modernization Breed Revolution?" *Comparative Politics* 5 (April 1973).

to pick out the vulnerabilities of the Mubarak regime and arrange them in a neat list as the ingredients of breakdown. But that retrospective temptation misses the essential point: Egyptians overthrew a strong regime.

STRONG REGIME, STRONG SOCIETY

Like his predecessors, President Husni Mubarak deployed the resources of a high-capacity state to cement his power. He summarily eliminated all threats to his rule, from a riot police mutiny in 1986, to an armed Islamist insurgency in the 1990s, to an over-ambitious deputy, Defense Minister 'Abd al-Halim Abu Ghazala, whom he sacked in 1989. He presided over the transformation of the economy, from a command model with the state as primary owner to a neoliberal model with the state as conduit for the transfer of public assets to cronies. He introduced an innovation to the Egyptian authoritarian tradition as well, attempting to engineer the handover of presidential power to a blood relative, rather than a military subordinate. To manage social opposition to these big changes, Mubarak used the political arena to co-opt critics and the coercive apparatus to deal with those who would not be incorporated.

Opposite this wily regime stood an ostensibly weak and fragmented society. Echoing the regime's arguments, workers' protests, rural riots, electoral struggles, and any other forms of popular striving were commonly explained away as economic, not political; local, not national; and defensive, not proactive. The little people had no politics. Thus spoke the political scientist and Mubarak loyalist 'Ali al-Din Hilal to a US diplomat, who in a 2009 cable reported that according to Hilal, "Widespread, politically motivated unrest was unlikely because it was not part of the 'Egyptian mentality.'" Independent academics shared his view: "There could be a poor people's revolt if the state fails to provide food. But we must bear in mind that Egyptians rarely explode and then only in specific cases, among them threats to their daily bread or national dignity."[6]

The reality was that Egyptians had been practicing collective action for at least a decade, acquiring organizational experience in that very old form of politics: the street action. Egypt's streets had become parliaments, negotiating tables and battlegrounds rolled into one. To compel unresponsive officials to enact or revoke specific policies, citizens blockaded major roads with tree branches and burning tires, organized sit-ins in factory plants or outside ministry buildings, and blocked the motorcades of governors and

---

6   Interview with Muhammad al-Mahdi, professor of psychology at al-Azhar University, *Al-Shurouq*, October 15, 2010.

ministers. Take this small event in the logbook of popular politics from January 2001, one of forty-nine protest events that year recorded by just one newspaper. Workers at the new Health Insurance hospital in Suez held a sit-in to protest the halt of their entitlement pay. State Security officers and local officials intervened, prevailing upon the authorities to reinstate the pay and fire the hospital director.[7] By 2008, there were hundreds of such protests every year, big and small. In June 2008, thousands of residents in the fishing town of Burg al-Burullus blocked a major highway for seven hours to protest the governor's abrupt decision to halt the direct distribution of flour to households. Police used tear gas and batons to disperse demonstrators, and ninety people were arrested.[8]

If one classifies Egypt's protests by the type of mobilizing structure that brings people out into the street rather than the content of their claims, three sectors are salient, each with its own repertoire of tactics. The first is workplace protest, including collective action by industrial laborers, civil servants, students, and trade practitioners such as car mechanics and gold traders. The second is neighborhood protest, whether on the scale of a single street or an entire town. Protests by Copts, Sinai Bedouins, and farmers are often organized along residential lines. Associational protest is the third sector. The organizing mediums here are professional associations such as lawyers' and doctors' syndicates; social movements such as the pro-Palestine solidarity campaigns, the anti-Mubarak Kifaya movement and the April 6 youth group; and the youth wings of political parties such as Ayman Nour's liberal Ghad, the Muslim Brothers, the liberal Wafd, the Nasserist Karama, and the Islamist Wasat.

Doing politics outdoors brought citizens face to face with the caste that rules the streets: Egypt's ubiquitous police. Mubarak's was not a police state because the coercive apparatus routinely beat and detained people. It was a police state because the coercive apparatus had become the chief administrative arm of the state, aggregating the functions of several agencies. Police not only deal with crime: they issue passports, drivers' licenses, and birth and death certificates. They resolve local conflicts over land and sectarian relations; fix all national and subnational elections; vet graduate-school candidates and academic appointments at every level; monitor shop floors and mediate worker–management conflicts; observe soccer games and Friday prayers; and maintain a network of local informants in poor neighborhoods, to ensure that dispossession is not converted into political organization. Officers are free to work out their own methods of revenue extraction,

7   *Al-Ahali*, January 3, 2001.
8   *Al-Ahram Weekly*, June 19–25, 2008.

sometimes organizing the urban drug trade.[9] Patrolmen routinely collect tribute from taxi and microbus drivers and shopkeepers, while high-ranking officers partner with landowners or crony businessmen. When there is a riot or a road accident or a natural disaster, Egyptian police personnel are the first responders—not to aid the victims, but to contain their rage.

By January 25, 2011, every protest sector had field experience with police rule, from Helwan University students to villagers in the Delta province of Daqhaliyya to Cairo lawyers to Aswan horse-cart drivers. But no population group had come close to shifting the balance of resources in its favor—with the arguable exception of Sinai's Bedouins, who have been embroiled in fierce battles with police for years, ever since the Taba bombings in 2004 led to massive arrest campaigns targeting residents. The first significant effort to link up Egypt's three protest sectors was easily aborted by the regime. On April 6, 2008, a loose coalition of Mahalla and Kafr al-Dawwar textile workers, town residents, and groups in Cairo's associational landscape coordinated a general strike and national day of protest to demand a minimum wage and an end to corruption and police brutality. Riot police and state security officers dissolved the strike action at the Mahalla textile factory before it could take off. Then they easily broke up irate protests by thousands of Mahalla townspeople, lobbing tear gas canisters into crowds and arresting 150 residents. Smaller solidarity demonstrations in Greater Cairo were also effortlessly managed, and state security's plans succeeded in preventing the spread of protest to other provinces. But the event midwifed the April 6 youth movement, which would be a key organizer of the January 25 action.

Street clashes continued between locals and police in various spots throughout 2010, with some incidents leading to mass arrests and curfews. Although the triggers of these confrontations were particular to place and time, both police and citizens drew upon remarkably similar sets of devices, from Akhmim in Upper Egypt to Rosetta in the Delta to 'Umraniyya in Greater Cairo. Two signal events embedded these local patterns of friction into a national framework. In June 2010, a young Alexandrian named Khalid Sa'id was hauled out of his chair at an Internet café and beaten to death by plainclothes police officers in broad daylight, reportedly in revenge for his posting of a video on YouTube that showed the officers divvying up the proceeds of a drug bust. Sa'id's death galvanized public opinion in disgust at police predation. Google executive Wael Ghonim helped start a Facebook group called "We Are All Khalid Sa'id," and social movements organized several large demonstrations against police brutality at which the

---

9   *Al-Masry al-Youm*, English edition, March 18, 2011.

slogan "Leave! Leave!" was hurled at Husni Mubarak. The second occasion was the national legislative elections. Under complete police management, the elections in November–December 2010 were flagrantly rigged to return 97 percent of the seats for Mubarak's vehicle, the National Democratic Party (NDP). The elections outraged political elites and ordinary people alike, spurring a unified opposition protest on December 12, and leaving behind fresh memories of street battles in dozens of districts across the country.

By the time January 25, 2011 arrived, there was local resonance for the planned national "day of rage" in virtually every corner of Egypt. The political atmosphere was highly charged: public opinion was inflamed by the Alexandria church bombing on January 1, which had led to numerous rumbles between police and Coptic protesters. The Tunisian people's toppling of Ben Ali electrified Egyptians. Riot police corralled a January 16 demonstration outside the Tunisian embassy, where activists had gathered to sing the Tunisian national anthem. Unwittingly, the regime itself provided the calendar date for the "day of rage," having newly designated January 25 a bank holiday to mark Police Day. The holiday freed up citizens for assembly, practically inviting them to convert the official celebration into a popular harangue against police rule. (Several get-out-the-protest clips on YouTube strung together notorious scenes of police brutality captured by cell phone video cameras.) Members of all protest sectors announced their participation, including Mahalla workers, Sinai Bedouins, and civil servants employed by the cabinet. New actors joined in, such as hardcore fans of the two biggest national soccer teams and Khalid Sa'id's mother, who, in an interview uploaded by Nobel laureate Mohamed ElBaradei's reform campaign on January 21, also urged Egyptians to reclaim their rights in the streets.[10] The government felt compelled to counter-organize. State security officers warned Muslim Brothers in the provinces to stay home. NDP parliamentarians branded January 25 the "day of loyalty to the leader," paying for 500,000 posters featuring Mubarak's visage and pasting them in major squares.[11] The Coptic Church, seven tiny opposition parties, the Nasserist party, and Sufi orders spoke out against the protest action.[12]

In the run-up to the "day of rage," a little-noted disturbance prefigured scenes that would soon pop up all over Egypt. One afternoon in the Nile-side working-class neighborhood of Warraq, a brawl erupted between two detainees at the police station. Officers violently put down the fight. The detainees then set fire to the blankets in the lock-up, and the blaze soon

---

10   This interview was available on YouTube.
11   *Al-Shurouq,* January 22, 2011.
12   *Al-Masry al-Youm,* January 23 and 24, 2011.

engulfed the station, injuring the Warraq head detective and his lieutenant. Armored cars and riot police were dispatched to the neighborhood, as
rumors spread that a detainee had died in the fire. Hundreds of residents
and detainees' relatives descended on the station and tried to push their
way in, pelting the building with stones and breaking four window panes.
By 2 am, the standoff had ended. The Giza police chief had arrived to negotiate with residents, allowing them in one by one to ascertain their relatives'
safety. "My brother is wrongly imprisoned. They accused him of stealing a
mobile phone," a resident outside the station told a reporter. "One of the
officers framed him."[13]

VERDICT OF THE BARRICADES

The January 25 protest started as a midsize demonstration and ended as
a massive uprising against autocratic rule. But no one leaving their house
that morning knew that they were stepping into the largest policing failure
of Mubarak's tenure. The uprising was forged in the heat of street fighting,
unanticipated both by its hopeful strategists and its watchful adversaries.
"We went out to protest that day and expected to be arrested in the first
ten minutes, just like usual," recalled Ziad al-'Ulaymi, an organizer with
ElBaradei's campaign.[14] A lieutenant colonel in the riot police, who was
monitoring events from the Cairo operations room, later recalled, "Our
preparations for January 25 were as per usual, and the instructions were not
to molest demonstrators."[15]

Interior Minister Habib al-'Adli and his four lieutenants had met on
January 24 to finalize their strategy. Cairo police chief Isma'il al-Sha'ir
issued stern warnings through the media, threatening protesters with
arrest and invoking the demonstrations law of 1914 requiring a permit for
any public gathering of more than five persons.[16] Giza police chief Usama
al-Marasi deployed twelve riot police trucks on Arab League Street, the
main thoroughfare of Cairo's western half, and eighteen trucks outside Cairo
University, two of the pre-announced protest locations on the Facebook
pages of the April 6 and Khalid Sa'id movements. For good measure,
al-Marasi deployed trucks along the entire stretch of the Warraq corniche.[17]
Outside Greater Cairo, police set up checkpoints along the approaches to the
large Delta towns of Tanta and Mahalla, blocking the entry of delegations

---

13   *Al-Shurouq*, January 12, 2011.
14   *Wall Street Journal*, February 2, 2011.
15   *Al-Masry al-Youm*, March 12, 2011.
16   *Al-Masry al-Youm*, January 25, 2011.
17   *Al-Shurouq*, January 25, 2011.

from Kafr al-Shaykh, Daqhaliyya and Minoufiyya provinces that had been planned by protest organizers. Qalyoubiyya and Suez provinces were placed on high alert. Suez, in particular, had a recent history of troubles. In 2010, a high-ranking police general was assassinated in broad daylight by a former informant, whose trial turned into an exposé of the gendarmerie's brutal methods. And the heavy police hand was evident again during the 2010 elections. "The polling stations are under occupation. Suez has been turned into a military garrison!" cried an irate poll monitor on voting day.[18]

Zero hour, as announced by protest organizers, was to be 2 pm. The stated plan was to demonstrate in front of the Ministry of Interior and then disband at 5 pm. Security forces therefore sealed off all the vital downtown streets leading to and from the Ministry, allowing pedestrians to pass only after checking ID cards. But it was a ruse. On the morning of January 25, organizers used cell phones and landlines to disseminate the real locations of the protests and the actual start time: noon. "The protest locations announced on Facebook and to the press were the major landmarks. The idea was to start marching down small side streets and pick up people along the way, so that by the time demonstrators reached the announced locations, they would be large crowds that security couldn't corral," explained organizer al-'Ulaymi.[19]

The crafty tactic worked in some neighborhoods, but not in others. Envision a sizable Kifaya demonstration walking down a tiny, picturesque lane in the inter-confessional neighborhood of Shubra, calling on residents watching them from the balconies to come down and join. The actor 'Amr Wakid is there, demonstrators are waving Egyptian flags, and the veteran sloganeer Kamal Khalil is providing the soundtrack with his unique sing-song rhymes.[20] By the time this group surged toward the announced rally point of Shubra Circle, they were a thousand strong and police officers had started to chase them. Khalil was arrested, and the other legendary sloganeer and seasoned unionist Kamal Abu Eita just barely escaped. "That's when I realized that Abu Eita runs much faster than me!" said thirty-something activist Ahmad 'Urabi of Abu Eita, who is nearly sixty.

By that point at 2:30 pm, the Shubra people received calls and text messages to say that crowds were filling streets in the working-class neighborhoods of Boulaq, Imbaba, and Bab al-Khalq, and that Arab League Street in middle-class Muhandisin was overflowing with people marching

18   *Al-Shurouq*, November 29, 2010.
19   *Al-Shurouq*, February 18, 2011.
20   This scene was captured on camera and at the time of writing was available on YouTube under the heading "Qik—Shobra1 by Hamdeen Sabahy Campaign."

toward Tahrir Square downtown. So they individually hopped into taxis and headed for the square. Meanwhile, outside the High Court building near Tahrir, middle-aged opposition parliamentarians and tweedy profes- sors were scuffling with riot police. Lawyers from the bar association nearby had broken through the cordon and were approaching, as was a third roving group passing by the Judges' Club around the corner and chant- ing over and over again, "*Hurriyya! Hurriyya!*" (Freedom! Freedom!) The police were disoriented by the convergence of the three formations. State Security officers negotiated with parliamentarians, trying to convince them to persuade the crowds that they could chant as much as they liked but had to remain stationary on the High Court steps. But there was a different logic at work. The bodies gleefully broke through the cordons and rushed toward Gala' Street and from there to 'Abd al-Mun'im Riyad Square abutting the Egyptian Museum, a stone's throw from Tahrir.

While security forces were trying to contain the court demonstration, Ghad party leader Ayman Nour and Wafd party members Muhammad Shurdi and businessman Rami Lakah were fronting an energetic group of Wafdist youth speed-walking from Ramsis Street to the Nile Corniche. A couple-hundred strong, and each member carrying a green party flag, the procession plucked off bystanders as it moved along, making its way to the NDP headquarters where it stopped for some moments to denounce NDP leaders, promising them the fate of the Tunisian ex-president, Ben Ali. Before security forces could pen them in, a large group coming from Qasr al-Nil bridge merged with the Wafdists and, together, they set off for the state radio and television building, completely encircling it for a few minutes with no security forces in sight. From there, they roamed the streets of Boulaq, re-emerging at the intersection of Ramsis and July 26 streets, and headed for Tahrir.

Nearby on 'Abd al-Khaliq Tharwat Street, Khalaf Muhammad Mursi, a seventy-five-year old newspaper vendor, said: "Back in the days of the monarchy, I saw as many demonstrations as there are hairs on my head. Back then, they flipped over the trams and chanted against the king, and some of them wanted [Prime Minister Mustafa] Nahhas back in power. Demonstrating is good. They're marching and not doing anything wrong. The government should let them."[21]

In the provinces, there were also large demonstrations. Police contain- ment varied in intensity, with some brigades tolerating the columns of protesters and others losing control of the crowds, as in Cairo. In Ismailiyya's Firdaws Square, police made rigorous preparations starting the night

---

21   *Al-Masry al-Youm*, January 27, 2011.

before. By early afternoon, rows of riot police were tightly hemming in 600 demonstrators, who were performing the afternoon prayers outdoors and shouting, "Chant it, chant it! Raise your voice high! He who chants will not die!" By 6 pm, more people had joined in, enabling the protesters to break free of the cordon and ramble through the city. The labor stronghold of Mahalla was a different matter, the two demonstrations there having been violently put down, with eleven arrests. Alexandria's squares and landmarks saw several simultaneous, separate protests. Police ringed a large crowd outside the governor's office, chanting for the dissolution of the rigged parliament and demanding an audience with the governor, who refused. In the al-Asafra neighborhood, a procession flowed toward NDP headquarters, fending off the "karate companies," the State Security musclemen who disperse crowds by striking the demonstrators.

Back in Tahrir, shortly before 4 pm, security forces were resisting a two-pronged surge toward the national legislative headquarters. In the square, high-octane crowds led by soccer fans exclaimed "Egypt! Egypt!" in army-like cadence. They repeatedly rushed the thick layers of conscripts blocking the way to Qasr al-'Ayni Street, which leads southwest in rough parallel with the Nile, passing by the houses of Parliament. When the protesters succeeded in breaking through, panicked officers went in hot pursuit, pushing the discombobulated lower ranks in front of them to rearrange them again in a human blockade before the people could reach the People's Assembly, as Egypt's lower house is called. From the other direction on Qasr al-'Ayni Street, a now iconic scene saw light-footed young men sparring with an armored vehicle. In the footage posted online (where it has upwards of 2 million views), one of them then positions himself directly in the path of the moving lorry as it spouts water from a cannon. He stands there defiantly, hands on hips and drenched, as the vehicle brakes and the videographers wildly cheer him on from a balcony above.[22]

By then, something extraordinary was happening. The thousands of demonstrators who had been wending their way through different parts of the city were streaming through all the approaches to the square. Poet and ElBaradei campaign leader 'Abd al-Rahman Yusuf was running from security forces through the labyrinthine streets of chic Garden City, home to the US and British embassies. He and his fellows approached the square from underneath Qasr al-Nil bridge. "It was one of the most profound moments of my life. The sight of the square filled with tens of thousands heralded the long-awaited dawn. As we entered the square, the crowds installed there

---

22   At the time of writing, this scene can be viewed on YouTube under the heading "Egyptian Tank Man."

cheered the coming of a new battalion, greeting us with joy. I wept."[23]

In the orange glow left by a setting sun, a skirmish unfolded outside the upper house of Parliament. Demonstrators had inched their way to that spot by making iterated advances into riot police formations, breaking them apart and gaining a tad more ground each time. Protesters clambered atop a red fire truck, and their jubilant fellows began to sing the national anthem. Tense riot police commanders herded their troops. The black-helmeted conscripts jogged on the spot and emitted the rhythmic grunts of soldiers revving up for close combat. When the order was given, the troops rushed into the crowd. "*Silmiyya! Silmiyya!*" roared the demonstrators, exhorting each other to non-violence and holding their ground as the troops retreated into position. An enterprising civilian knocked over a white-and-blue sentry kiosk. His fellows rushed to help him roll it to their side; a barricade had been made. When hotheads in the crowd started hurling rocks at riot police, a chant rose up from both the front lines and cheerleaders on the sidelines, "No stones! No stones!" In this army, the commanders and the foot soldiers were one.[24]

Night fell, but the people stayed put in the square. Huge speakers were procured from nearby Bab al-Louq, and a people's broadcast service was set up. Angry monologues, poetry couplets, and political demands were read out. A cardboard cutout of a squat dictator hung from a lamp post. News was relayed that two citizens had died in Suez that day, solidifying resolve. Volunteers ranged across the square, collecting garbage in plastic bags. People built fires and danced around their light. Out of nowhere, food and blankets appeared, to the delighted claps and cheers of the encampment. Memories of March 20–21, 2003 flitted through the minds of those who were there that evening, when the square was under the people's control for ten hours to express outrage at the US bombing of Baghdad. But on that occasion, security forces had uprooted them by the next afternoon. Perhaps determined to avoid a reprise, the broadcast rallied everyone to spend this and every night in the square until their demands were met. As they had repeated over and over again throughout the day, they wanted "bread, freedom, social justice!" After sunset, as demonstrators realized their own power, this troika began to alternate with the Tunisian anthem: "The people want to overthrow the regime!" Reporters milled about, collecting stories. Sitting alone was Amal, a young nurse. Her friends had abandoned her,

---

23   'Abd al-Rahman Yusuf, "Diaries of the Revolution of the Patient," *al-Masry al-Youm*, March 7, 2011.

24   See footage from this battle at on YouTube under the heading "Egypt's Violent Day of Anger."

their parents refusing to let them join the demonstrations. Why did not her parents do the same? "My parents have passed away," she explained, "and I support five brothers and sisters. I'm here so that they can live a dignified life. I don't want them to be deprived because they're orphans."[25]

The riot police lieutenant colonel received the order at midnight. "The square had to be cleaned up," he recounted. "Absolutely no one was to spend the night there." The armored vehicles closed in, the riot troops were arrayed and the first tear gas canister was lobbed into the sit-in at 12:45 am. Nearly an hour later, following deployment of 200 vehicles, fifty public buses, 10,000 riot police, and 3,000 special forces troopers, the people were expelled. Before scattering in all directions, knots of protesters encircled the vehicles that barged into the square at breakneck speed. One group ran to the NDP headquarters, where they smashed windows before being arrested. Another headed to the television building and blocked traffic in front of it. And a third group set fire to police kiosks and a police car near the 'Abd al-Mun'im Riyad bus depot. Holding up bloodied hands to the camera, one of the protesters said, "They shot at us! They shot at us! Who are we, the enemy?"[26]

MUBARAK'S WORST FEARS

Habib al-'Adli and his adjutants were concerned by the day's events, especially the synchronized diffusion of protests across the country, the fluidity of crowd movement in the two major cities, and citizens' euphoric sense of the weak points of the police. As the operations room lieutenant colonel recalled, "What we saw on January 25 was an uprising, not a demonstration. A young man standing in front of an armored vehicle, jumping on it to strike it, falling off, and then doing it again? Honestly, there was no fear."[27] Both the Cairo and Giza police chiefs were in the field all day on January 25, and they saw the electrifying empowerment that seemed to course through Egyptians' veins. Both were experienced, hands-on officers who had proved their mettle in dicey situations. Cairo police chief al-Sha'ir won al-'Adli's trust by handily managing the large 2006 protests in support of reformist judges. And Giza police chief al-Marasi had been the head state security officer in Suez, seat of a sparsely populated province with multiple coils of social tension, from labor strife to drug-running to Bedouin tribes with

---

25   *Al-Masry al-Youm*, January 27, 2011.

26   At the time of writing, these moments are recorded on YouTube under the heading "Egypt's 'Unprecedented' Protests."

27   *Al-Masry al-Youm*, March 12, 2011.

serious grievances, all sitting at the southern mouth of the Suez Canal, the country's prime generator of external revenue.

In the early morning hours of January 26, preparations were swiftly made to secure downtown Cairo against another popular takeover. State security instructed all downtown businesses to close before 1 pm on January 26. The two underground Metro lines converging on the major transfer hub at Tahrir announced that trains would not be stopping at the station. Police sealed off four entrances to the station, and three entrances to the July 26 station one stop to the northeast, outside the High Court building. Two thousand undercover policemen fanned out in downtown streets and government installations, and al-Marasi ordered the placement of multiple checkpoints on Nahiya Street, through which thousands of people had streamed the day before onto the Arab League boulevard. Labor commissar Husayn Mugawir, whose job was to control workers through the sole official union federation, instructed all union heads in the provinces to be especially responsive to the rank and file, lest any incipient job action happen to lend the demonstrations strategic depth.[28]

These measures indicated that Mugawir's superiors were feeling the worst fears of an authoritarian regime. For a capable autocrat like Mubarak, large protests are no cause for anxiety. The fears are diffusion and linkage. Indeed, the diffusion of collective action in time and space emboldened Egyptians, signaling the unwillingness or incapacity of the coercive apparatus to suppress demonstrations. The simultaneity of protests across very different locations, especially the filling of streets in neighborhoods entirely unused to such processions, revised citizens' calculations of what was possible and reduced uncertainty about the consequences of action. The second fear is of coordination between the three organizational infrastructures of protest. Indeed, the state security directorate existed to frustrate precisely this bridge-building. It had done so quite successfully with the April 6, 2008 general strike, and had a stellar track record in branding each sector of dissent with a different label: associational protest was "political," but workplace and neighborhood protest were "economic."

The diffusion of protests on January 25–27 shattered both the mental and material divisions between Egypt's three protest sectors, forcing the regime to confront them simultaneously, when for thirty years it had done so serially. In Cairo, there was a spontaneous sit-in on the tracks at the July 26 Metro station, with demonstrators halting the train. In Boulaq, a moving crowd of 1,000 residents fought with police from early afternoon until past 2 am Friday morning, braving tear gas and rubber bullets, and

---

28   *Al-Shurouq* and *al-Masry al-Youm*, January 27, 2011.

setting up barricades on Gala' Street with dumpsters and carefully arranged burning tires. Undeterred by the traumatic routing of people from Tahrir Square, angry demonstrators in their hundreds continued to stride through the streets of downtown.

The picture in the provinces was much the same, with protesters refusing to vacate the streets. Demonstrations in Daqhaliyya, Port Said, and North Sinai demanded the release of those arrested on January 25; in Sinai, residents used their signature tactic of blockading the highway with burning tires. On the third day of protests, a young Sinai protester named Muhammad 'Atif was killed in clashes with police, making him the fourth casualty nationwide. In Alexandria, state security broke up a planned lawyers' protest on the Manshiya court steps, arresting the first twenty people who showed up. The next day, 200 lawyers returned and held their protest. In Qalyoubiyya, 200 lawyers marched down the streets on January 26 inveighing against price hikes and the export of Egyptian natural gas to Israel, so police penned them in the courthouse the next day. And Mahalla was still under lockdown, with security forces importing reinforcements to block renewed attempts by textile workers to start action. Percolating up from these varied locales was a decision to hold another round of protest on the next common-sense date: after Friday prayers on January 28, first dubbed "the Friday of the martyrs and the detained."

The situation in Suez developed rapidly. On January 25, security forces had been especially violent; the fighting resulted in 110 injuries and three deaths, as well as fifty-four arrests. The next day, hundreds of residents flocked to Suez General Hospital to donate blood, finding it so full that the injured were lying on sheets in hallways. Meanwhile, a large group of incensed relatives and citizens had gathered outside the morgue. The authorities insisted on handing over corpses without forensic reports, and security forces besieged the funerals with a ferocity that further enraged residents. "When you see this, you feel like you're in Palestine and Iraq," said the leftist Tagammu' Party parliamentarian for the city. "Security uses bullets and tear gas canisters and water hoses, and the residents can only confront this with stones."[29] But residents escalated their tactics, setting fire to a police post and the municipal council building on January 26, and trying to burn down the local NDP office. On January 27, hundreds of residents and detainees' relatives demonstrated outside the Arba'in police station, chanting, "Enough! We want our kids!" Demonstrators hurled petrol bombs at the station and burned several police cars.

---

29   *Al-Masry al-Youm*, January 28, 2011.

On the evening of January 27, police and protesters each held planning meetings to plot the second act of the confrontation. Police officials devised a comprehensive plan to cut off physical and virtual means of linkage. They ordered a shutdown of Internet and cellular phone service for the next day; cell phones were especially important for demonstrators to spread news of protest diffusion in real time, and to share spot instructions or eleventh-hour location changes. Cairo was sealed off from the provinces and put under lockdown. All of the arteries and bridges leading into Tahrir Square from east and west were closed to traffic—even pedestrians. Additional Metro stops were closed, not just the two nearest the square. And mosques were carefully primed in advance. The 'Umar Makram mosque in Tahrir was ordered to be shuttered. Friday preachers all over the country were instructed to deliver sermons denouncing assembly and disobedience of the ruler. At the Giza mosque where Mohamed ElBaradei was set to attend prayer before joining the protests, the preacher of twenty years was replaced with a government pick. For their part, the youth groups and opposition forces coordinating the protest added new locations and reacquainted themselves with landlines to manage the cellular shutdown. Opposition parties who had sat out the January 25 action—the Tagammu' leftists and the Nasserists—scrambled to join up. And the Muslim Brothers threw their organizational weight behind the action, revising their calculus of risk after seeing the momentous events of the previous three days. The players readied themselves, and the world watched.

On January 28, shortly after noon, a majestic scene unfolded all over Egypt. Grand processions of thousands upon thousands of people in every province made their way to the abodes of the oppressive forces that controlled their lives. Beckoning those watching from their windows, they chanted, "Our people, our people, come and join us!" When the crowds reached town and city centers, they encircled police stations, provincial government buildings, and NDP headquarters, the triad of institutions emblematic of the regime. The syncopated chorus that had traveled from Sidi Bouzid to Tunis now shook the Egyptian earth: "The people . . . want . . . to overthrow the regime!"

In Tanta, 50,000 people blockaded a major highway, encircled the provincial government building and ripped down its billboards. In Kafr al-Dawwar, 25,000 did the same. In Damietta, the people called for the dissolution of Parliament, torching the NDP building and defacing the façade of the governor's offices. In Minya, whose governor had bragged that his middle Nile province had not seen demonstrations on January 25, people ignored the entreaties of the police chief and barricaded the Cairo–Aswan highway, braving rubber bullets to chant outside the NDP headquarters: "Corruption caused this country's destruction!"

Everywhere, the rising of the commons was met with superior force. Police fired tear gas canisters, rubber bullets, and—the ultimate escalation—live ammunition. The goal, to be reached at any cost, was to prevent separate crowds of demonstrators from fusing together in city centers. State security commandeered ambulances to arrest the unsuspecting injured, and hospitals were pressured into falsifying the cause of death for demonstrators who were shot at close range. Residents provided first aid to demonstrators leery of getting into ambulances, and tossed water bottles, vinegar, and onions (homemade tear-gas remedies) to the civilians fighting below. On Ramsis Street in downtown Cairo, as a crowd of 10,000 crashed into a security formation and was hurled back with copious tear gas, a woman cried out from her balcony, "God be with you, men of Egypt!"[30]

Communications between Alexandrian field commanders that day record the shock and awe police experienced in Egypt's second city. "We are still engaging very large numbers coming from both directions. We need more gas," a squadron head radioed to a superior. "The people have barged in and burned a security vehicle. The situation here is beyond belief. I'm telling you, sir, beyond belief," says another. By mid-afternoon, Alexandrians had laid siege to three police stations. In other parts of the city, police had run out of ammunition and resorted to throwing stones. A high-ranking commander got on the line to sternly instruct a field officer, "Stop engaging and secure the police stations! You don't have sufficient forces to calmly engage these numbers. Go and batten down the hatches!"[31]

And Suez? Security forces had isolated the canal town from the rest of the country, closing off all access points. Massive reinforcements had arrived daily since January 25. At 1 am on January 28, the top police brass met at the Arba'in police station, which only a few hours before had been ablaze, to set the plan for the "Friday of anger." The showdown in Suez started after noon prayers. General Ashraf 'Abdallah, commander of the riot police in the Canal Zone, later prepared an internal report:

> After Friday prayers, no fewer than 5,000 people began a procession that was joined by large numbers of citizens from all mosques. The procession grew to 40,000 people, and the police chief ordered that it be allowed to proceed to the provincial capital building. Once there, the numbers exceeded 50,000.

---

30   *Al-Masry al-Youm*, January 30, 2011.
31   The transcripts of these communications were published in *al-Masry al-Youm*, March 15, 2011.

The masses remained outside the building for many hours, chanting hostile slogans. At the same time, large numbers of no less than 20,000 had gathered in front of the Arba'in police station and assaulted the forces with rocks and Molotov cocktails. The forces used only tear gas. Due to the density of the crowds, the forces were unable to deal with them. The crowds burned the station, released the detainees and burned all the police vehicles in the area, among them ten lorries and an armored car belonging to the Ismailiyya force.[32]

In five compact hours, from noon to 5 pm, the police battled the people in all areas of the capital, desperate to thwart the amalgamation of multitudes in Tahrir Square. A climactic battle erupted on Qasr al-Nil bridge, as surging crowds from the west sought to cross the river to join their brethren converging on Tahrir from the east. Qasr al-Nil has rightly been memorialized in word and video.[33] But there was another climactic Cairo fight in the east, where at least fifteeen citizens died (the youngest of them aged fourteen) and ten troop carriers parked in a row burned. The battle of Matariyya Square, to the east of the suburb of Heliopolis, raged as police sought to stop residents from merging with crowds in the adjacent, densely populated 'Ayn Shams neighborhood. The people's insistent anthem, as outside Parliament on January 25, was "Silmiyya! Silmiyya!" and "No stones! No stones!" When police used overwhelming force, including live rounds, the people switched tactics, forming a barricade with overturned dumpsters, seizing the shields of riot police, and burning the vehicles and the police station. The mother of 'Imad al-Sa'idi, twenty-four, killed by a bullet to the heart and one to the side, wondered: "If there was no way out for a policeman but to fire, then fire on his hand or his foot. But to shoot him in the heart and end his life—why?"[34]

The Egyptian uprising telescoped the daily encounters between people and police that had played out for more than ten years. Al-'Adli's police force did not melt away in the face of a popular onslaught. They fought for four straight days on nearly every street corner in every major city, before finally being rendered inefficient by the dynamism and stamina of exceptionally diverse crowds, each with their own know-how in the art of interfacing with gendarmes. At 5 pm on the afternoon of January 28, when reports started rolling in of police stations burning down, one after another, al-'Adli capitulated and ordered the removal of his forces from the streets. It was a sight unseen in modern Egyptian police rule—the one and only time

---

32   The report was obtained by *al-Masry al-Youm*, March 16, 2011.

33   *New York Times*, January 28, 2011.

34   *Al-Masry al-Youm*, February 15, 2011.

that Egypt's three protest subcultures were able to jointly defeat the coercive apparatus that had existed to keep them apart.

By the end of the street fighting, preliminary estimates were that 365 citizens had died and some 5,000 had been hurt. On the police side, there were thirty-two deaths and 1,079 injuries, while ninety-nine police stations and 3,000 vehicles had burned. Al-'Adli stayed bunkered inside the Ministry of Interior until January 31, when he was transported out sitting huddled in an army tank. In a six-hour interrogation by the prosecution, on charges of responsibility for the deaths and injuries, al-'Adli shunted the blame upward and downward. He accused his four top assistants of providing him with false intelligence, and demanded that Husni Mubarak be held accountable for the decision to fire on demonstrators, in his capacity as head of the Supreme Police Council. But he did concede defeat.

> The situation was beyond imagination. The faces of the demonstrators showed how clear they were in challenging the regime and how much they hated it, how willing they were to resist with their bodies all attempts to divide them with truncheons and water cannons and all other tools. They outnumbered security forces by a million or more, a fact that shocked the Interior Ministry leaders and the president. Those government officials all sat at home watching the demonstrations on TV. Not one of them devised a political solution to what policemen were facing—confrontations with angry people and indescribable hatred of the government. All of us were astonished.[35]

The prosecutor-general referred al-'Adli and his four lieutenants to Cairo criminal court, on charges of murder and endangerment of public property.[36]

THE PEOPLE'S CHOICE

When Husni Mubarak appeared shortly after midnight on January 28 to announce his appointment of a new government, it was the first time in his tenure that he had been summoned to the podium by popular fiat. But he was enacting a familiar script written by autocratic rulers past, offering concessions to a population that had beaten the police and gained control of a country's streets. An offering which, if made only four days earlier, would have been considered shrewd—a cabinet reshuffle—was now foolhardy. It simply sharpened the population's apprehension of imminent

---

35 *Al-Shurouq*, March 19, 2011.
36 *Al-Shurouq*, March 23, 2011.

victory, spurring them to stay outdoors and demand nothing less than the ouster of the president. Since Mubarak had made it impossible to remove him from office through elections, Egyptians resorted to the streets to relay the people's choice.

The liberation of the streets from the occupation forces of the Mubarak regime was only the opening act. Next was the symbolic public acquisition of Parliament, filling the avenue outside with peaceful protesters and plastering the building's gates with the people's insignia. Then came the branding of public goods; "our money," read a scrawl of graffiti on an army tank. With remarkable focus, citizens targeted the structures of rule that had disenfranchised and dispossessed them for decades. The police stations and NDP headquarters were the first targets, but the nascent revolutionaries did not stop there, hitting municipal councils, governors' offices, state security buildings, police checkpoints, traffic departments, toll booths, utility buildings, and other institutions that had taken their resources without giving in return. In Fayyoum, residents stormed the public utility company and destroyed the water bills that charged them exorbitant rates. In Ismailiyya, among the government institutions stormed was the Electricity Administration. In Alexandria, youthful demonstrators grabbed files from the main provincial building that they said showed evidence of corruption. In Isna, a town in Upper Egypt, 1,000 demonstrators stormed a brand-new administrative building that had yet to be formally opened, paid for with their monies.

The genius of the Egyptian revolution is its methodical restoration of the public weal. The uprising restored the meaning of politics, if by that term is understood the making of collective claims on government. It revalued the people, revealing them in all their complexity—neither heroes nor saints, but citizens. It repaired the republican edifice of the state, Mubarak's hereditary succession project being the revolution's very first casualty. It compelled the police to bring back their old motto, erasing al-'Adli's sinister "Police and people in service to the nation" and returning "The police at the service of the people." The countless public institutions branded with the names of Mubarak and his wife are now being rechristened in the names of regular people who died for the revolution. The referendum, a procedure disfigured beyond recognition by authoritarianism, on March 19 regained meaning as a matter for adjudication by the people. The revolution will have realized its emancipatory promise if it achieves one great task: constructing institutional checks against the rule over the many by the few.

Egypt's revolution is still in full swing. It must be expected, however, that the revolution will undergo phases of setback, real or apparent. The apparatus of coercion, indeed, has been quickly rehabilitated and is gingerly reinserting itself into civilian life. But on what terms? For Egypt's revolutionary situation to lead to a revolutionary outcome, existing structures of rule must be transformed. Citizens must be free to choose their presidents, governors, parliamentarians, faculty deans, and village mayors, their trade union, student, and professional association leaders. They must have a binding say in the economic decisions that affect their lives. The coming years will reveal how much of that will happen and how. Just as it provided an archetype of durable authoritarian rule, perhaps Egypt is now making a model of revolution.

CHAPTER 3

The Eighteen Days of Tahrir

Ahmad Shokr

On January 26, 2011, Tahrir Square was under occupation. Hundreds of riot police bearing shields and batons formed cordons along the perimeter to prevent anyone suspected of being a demonstrator from approaching. Traffic was light, an unusual scene for one of Cairo's busiest intersections. On the sidewalks, queues of young, scruffily dressed thugs received instructions from police to attack any crowd that dared assemble. The large, boisterous protest that had filled the square the previous night—January 25—had been violently dispersed by security forces, as the interior minister, Habib al-'Adli, warned that no further demonstrations would be tolerated. His command was enforced harshly. Nary a whisper of dissent could be heard in the square, and the sparse clusters of defiance outside it were quickly chased into the side streets and alleyways of downtown, where many protesters were roughed up and detained. Tahrir Square, usually a palimpsest of Egyptian society, was the uncontested dominion of President Husni Mubarak's police.

Asserting physical control of Cairo's urban space is an old tactic of the state's security apparatus. Tahrir Square, beginning sometime in 2005, has been particularly notable for its police presence, most palpably the armored vans stationed along the edges. The bustling city center, built in the nineteenth century under Khedive Isma'il as a symbol of modernity, has long been a favorite site for popular gatherings. Egyptians have poured into Tahrir to celebrate soccer victories, to mourn the passing of national icons, and to protest injustice. After the Free Officers coup in July 1952, Egyptians flooded the square to hail the birth of a new republic. In 1977, the bread riots that swept Egypt found their locus in the square, and in 2003, Tahrir was home to huge rallies against the Iraq war. But in the years that followed, protesters were rapidly encircled by impenetrable rows of riot police. Inside the plaza, open spaces were fenced off into smaller and smaller plots, significantly impeding even pedestrian traffic. These restrictions were Mubarak's antidote to bottom-up democracy on Cairo's streets.

But everything changed on the evening of January 28, when all-day protests claimed the square as the epicenter of Egypt's revolution. Riot police fought bitterly to protect the territory, deploying their full arsenal of crowd dispersal weapons, but they failed. That night, the streets of Cairo were littered with police vehicles that had been overturned and set ablaze by the raging multitudes. Anti-regime graffiti covered the walls of buildings— not in acts of vandalism, but in release of the thrill of self-empowerment that erupts when fear is overcome. Cheers of triumph echoed throughout the night even as the suffocating smell of tear gas hung in the air. An army curfew was ignored.

When protesters arrived at Tahrir on January 29, they did not come with the intention of creating a radical utopia. Despite the square's name, "liberation" in Arabic, Egyptians did not think of it as a place with emancipatory potential before the 2011 uprising. In many ways, Tahrir had come to represent the overall decline of public space—people could barely congregate or mingle, let alone protest—under Mubarak's thirty-year rule. The commune that Tahrir was to become was wholly improvised through the lived experience of sharing the area and protecting it from regime encroachment. As the revolution unfolded, Tahrir was elevated from a rally site to a model for an alternative society.

In the days that followed, the excitement of entering the plaza never subsided. Crossing the popular checkpoints, one was greeted, like a hero, by a chorale of young men chanting, "Welcome, revolutionaries!" It was shocking enough to see no cars or police, and more so to merge into a roaring, colorful sea of Egyptians. "The People Demand the Removal of the Regime," read one of the largest banners, hoisted above the grassy island in the center of the square. And indeed, the dwellers of Tahrir had proudly declared themselves to be a people. Everyone had a place: rebels young and old, professionals, factory workers, friends, families, performers, lovers, street vendors. Resources were the sole property of no one; a spirit of mutual aid prevailed. Canteens offered free food to anyone in need, makeshift clinics provided first aid to the wounded and volunteers stepped up to ensure communal comfort and security—distributing woolen blankets on cold nights and organizing guards at the entrances. Evenings gave way to music and poetry, which people from all walks of life were free to enjoy. From homemade banners to cartoons mocking Mubarak to photo displays and live concerts, every inch of Tahrir offered something novel to see. The atmosphere evoked an endless carnival, where visitors were enticed by every stall.

To anyone acquainted with Tahrir, the place was unrecognizable. Before January 25, regular visitors would enter a din of pollution and congestion, a zone outside the writ of proper urban planning. In the past decade, downtown Cairo began to attract the attention of state technocrats and private investors, who proposed to revive its imagined glory under the khedives through the restoration of old buildings and the redesign of major squares. Geared largely toward elite desires and consumption patterns, these efforts at gentrification threatened to drive out the poor and impose additional limits on access to the city. By moving into the square en masse, the people of Tahrir defied the exclusionary logic that had governed their urban space for years. What they created was an anti-city of sorts. The pervasive sense of impatience and never having enough time that characterizes everyday life in a metropolis suddenly vanished. Social codes that customarily define appropriate interactions between people collapsed. In Tahrir, there were no strangers; everywhere people talked to each other with a newfound ease.

One night, a man I had seen many times before approached me for a box of matches. In ordinary times, he would have been an alien face among millions, but during those eighteen days there was no such thing as anonymity. Salih introduced himself and showed me a packet of candles, explaining that he wanted to create a piece of impromptu street art spelling out the word "*Irhal*" (Leave)—the simplest, most unambiguous slogan of the revolution. I searched my pockets as he struggled to place the first few candles upright on the ground. Meanwhile, a few dozen people gathered to help without questioning the wisdom of something as impermanent as lighted candles on a windy evening. Some knelt down to light the candles, others directed our motions from above, while still others ferried over additional lighters and matches from nearby vendors as candles went out. An even larger crowd surrounded us, capturing the event on their cellular phones and video cameras. In a matter of moments, one man's eccentric wish turned into an improvised collective endeavor, gracefully unfolding like a well-choreographed composition.

But Tahrir was not all fun and festivity. The space was also infused with serious politics: fierce battles were waged against government thugs trying to break in, fiery speeches were delivered denouncing the regime, and animated discussions about Egypt's political future resounded in the night air. During the day, marches and mourning processions circled the square, commemorating those killed during the uprising and vowing to fight on. The center of Tahrir became a tent city where people of every political stripe and social class gathered to exchange views about everything from religion to television to politics to soccer. "This is the kind of society I want to live in. Tahrir brings out the best in every Egyptian," was a commonly heard refrain.

Over the course of eighteen days, the plaza had turned into a veritable polis, where people were bound together by more than a common political demand. Together, the people of Tahrir forged a society, marked by interdependence and collective decision-making—at times even hierarchies. They were preoccupied with everything necessary for the smooth functioning of a social order, from basic necessities—food, shelter, security—to questions of political strategy. Even the most mundane acts—sweeping the streets, preparing food, pitching tents—became moments of inspiration that proved the people's ability to sustain themselves, despite the regime's attempts at sabotage. Daily struggles to hold the space and feed its inhabitants, without the disciplined mechanisms of an organized state, were exercises in democratic process. It was through these everyday practices that Tahrir became a truly radical space.

On February 2, ruling-party officials sent ruffians to attack the people of Tahrir, culminating in what has become known as the "Battle of the Camel," an allusion to a seventh-century clash between forces allied with the prophet Muhammad's cousin and those allied with his widow. The charge on camelback was intended to stir up chaos in the square and turn popular opinion against the revolution. For the people in the square, however, it was an experiment in self-defense, the outcome of which was hardly predetermined.

Pro-regime thugs descended upon the square around noon, and for two straight days the assault did not stop. Taken by surprise, the people of Tahrir fought back with whatever they could find. Within hours, the scraps of Tahrir's built environment were fashioned into instruments of fortification. Steel barriers erected years before to cut up the square were taken down and used as barricades. Burned-out police vehicles were flattened and positioned to block the main entrances. Groups of men crowded along the sidewalks, breaking the stone tiles into rocks to repulse the attackers. The street clinics mushroomed. Tahrir turned into a mass cooperative where everyone was involved in some form of labor to protect the square. In the end, the people of Tahrir won.

The experience was transformational. "The moment we were able to keep Tahrir was the happiest moment of my life," said one young film-maker who took part in the battle. "The Mubarak regime had always forced us to be losers. For the first time in my life, I feel like I belong to the winning side. Now I cannot leave this place." The battle gave the denizens of the square a sense of ownership of the space, and a boldness mixed with resolve: it became imperative to hold on to Tahrir until their key demands were met.

In this spontaneous effort lay the secret to Tahrir's success. The more tactics people tried to keep the square, the more their hope was cemented that their struggle to build a better political order would prevail. The square represented more than the unity of a people seeking to overthrow a tyrant. It exemplified the finest in popular politics: a space where people worked things out, issue by issue and step by step, not where preconceived dreams came to realization.

Liberation was a word with several meanings in the square. People arrived demanding free elections, regime change, an end to police brutality, improvements in their economic lot, or all of the above. As the days passed, the discourse was slowly taken over by expressions of patriotism. The people's art in every corner of the square became less and less visible in a staggering mass of Egyptians flags. The consensus against Mubarak developed into a jubilee of national pride. Following Mubarak's resignation on February 11, Tahrir erupted in joy. "Hold your head high," chanted hundreds of thousands. "You are an Egyptian!" Smaller groups demanding "civilian, not military rule" were drowned out.

The next morning, Egyptians once again flooded Tahrir Square. Moved by a new sense of solidarity, they packed up the tents, dismantled the barricades, swept the streets, and repainted the pavement. Some, in the rush to return to normalcy, began scrubbing away graffiti. The impressive clean-up effort embodied the spirit that sustained Tahrir over the eighteen days of revolt. But in the haste to move on, many memories inscribed on the walls were erased, and with them testimony to the kaleidoscope of possibilities created in the square. And so a thousand energies were harnessed in the service of one: national consensus.

Since Mubarak's resignation, the Supreme Council of the Armed Forces has tried to clamp down on protest inside the square and out. Labor actions are denounced by the military as "factional" and damaging to the economy. Young women who rallied on International Women's Day were violently attacked by organized thugs. Figures from the old regime are looking to reinvent themselves in an effort to restore their political influence. The post-Tahrir developments are a sharp reminder that what happened in the square over eighteen days does not efface the totality of Egyptian history—sectarianism, class divides, sexual harassment, opportunism, and other ills persist and must be confronted within the new political order.

Tahrir did not deliver a complete revolution, but it did awaken an exhilarating sense of possibility that had been absent for far too long. Its impact has been felt in Cairo's political and intellectual scene, where conversations are no longer colored by hopeless cynicism about the future. The urgency of Tahrir has passed, but its place in history has yet to be determined. The square remains a contested symbol, not yet in the full possession of this or that metanarrative. The people of Tahrir may soon be cast as protagonists in larger dramas of democratization, national renaissance, and class struggle, rather than as human beings who strove to forge their own future. As the memory of Tahrir Square enters the canon and the official story is written, the lived experiences that offer some of those eighteen days' most inspiring moments must not be lost.

CHAPTER 4

The Poetry of Revolt

Elliott Colla

It is truly inspiring to see the bravery of Egyptians as they rise up to end the criminal rule of Husni Mubarak. It is especially inspiring to remember that what is happening is the culmination of years of work by activists from a spectrum of pro-democracy movements, human rights groups, labor unions, and civil society organizations. In 2004, when Kifaya began their first public demonstrations, the protesters were usually outnumbered thirty to one by Central Security Forces. Now the number has reversed—and multiplied.

No less astonishing is the poetry of this moment. I don't mean "poetry" as a metaphor, but the actual poetry that has played a prominent role from the outset of the events. The slogans the protesters are chanting are rhyming couplets—and they are as loud as they are sharp. The diwan of this revolt began to be written as soon as Ben Ali fled Tunis, in pithy lines like "*Ya Mubarak! Ya Mubarak! Al-Sa'udiyya fi intizarak!*" (Mubarak, O Mubarak, Saudi Arabia awaits!). In the streets themselves, there are scores of other verses, ranging from the caustic "*Shurtat Masr, ya shurtat Masr, intu ba'aytu kilab al-'asr*" (Egypt's police, Egypt's police, you've become nothing but palace dogs), to the defiant "*Idrab, idrab ya Habib, mahma tidrab mish hansib!*" (Hit us, beat us, O Habib [al-'Adli, the now former minister of interior], hit all you want—we're not going to leave!). This last couplet is particularly clever, since it plays on the old Egyptian colloquial saying, "*Darb al-habib zayy akl al-zabib*" (The beloved's fist is as sweet as raisins). This poetry is not an ornament to the uprising—it is its soundtrack, and also composes a significant part of the action itself.

A HISTORY OF REVOLUTIONS, A HISTORY OF POETS

There is nothing unusual about poetry playing a galvanizing role in a revolutionary moment. And in this context, we might remind ourselves that making revolution is not something new for Egyptians, who have had no less than three "official" revolutions in the modern era: the 1881 'Urabi revolution which overthrew a corrupt and comprador royalty; the

1919 revolution, which nearly brought down British military rule; and the 1952 revolution, which inaugurated sixty years of military dictatorship under Nasser, Sadat, and Mubarak. The first revolution succeeded in establishing the second parliamentary government on the African continent, before it was crushed by foreign military intervention. In the aftermath of 'Urabi's defeat, the British established a rapacious colonial rule over Egypt for more than seventy years. The second revolution was a sustained, popular uprising led by pro-democracy activists from a range of civil institutions. Though savagely repressed, it did force the British to grant some concessions. The third revolution officially celebrated in Egypt stands apart from the first two, in that it was a *coup d'état* that went out of its way to circumscribe popular participation. In any case, it was accepted at the time, since it finally ended the rule of the royal family first overthrown in 1881, and initiated a process of British withdrawal from Egypt.

Besides these three state-commemorated events, Egyptians have revolted against the corruption, greed, and cruelty of their rulers many more times in the last sixty years. On January 26, 1952, Egyptians emerged onto the streets to protest an array of issues—including the corruption of the monarchy; the decadence, power, and privilege of foreign business elites; and the open-ended British occupation. The revolt was quickly suppressed, though the damage to property was massive, and it set in motion an exodus of foreign elites—and the military coup months later. In 1968, Egyptian students launched huge and daring protests against the repressive policies of Nasser's police state. In the early 1970s, Egyptian students engaged in sustained mass protests against the radical political reorientations of the new Sadat regime, eventually forcing the state to re-engage in military confrontation with Israel. On January 18–19, 1977, Egyptians rose up en masse to protest against IMF austerity measures imposed on the country by the corrupt, inept, and ruthless regime of Anwar al-Sadat. The Egyptian president was already on his jet ride into exile before the Central Security Forces (or riot police) and army finally gained the upper hand. In Egypt, it is the Central Security troops rather than the military that deal with civil unrest and popular protest. Yet, even this "solution" to the problem of recurring popular revolt has proven at times uncertain. Like the military itself, the riot police has seen mutinies, one of which, in late February 1986, involved 20,000 low-paid conscripts and was put down only when the army entered the fray. During the early 1990s, Islamist protests against the authoritarian rule of Mubarak escalated into armed conflict, both in the slums of the cities and in Upper Egypt. Hundreds of militants, soldiers, and innocent civilians were killed before the revolt was finally suppressed. This list leaves out other significant moments of mass civil protest and contestation—like the huge demonstrations against the 1991 Gulf war, the US invasion of Iraq, and Israel's attacks on Lebanon and Gaza—but even so, the tally is impressive: no less than ten major revolts and revolutions in 130 years. In other words, despite what commentators might say, modern Egyptians have never passively accepted the failed colonial or post-colonial states that fate has dealt them.

Many of these revolts have had their own poets. 1881 spawned the neo-classical *qasidas* of Mahmoud Sami al-Baroudi; 1919, the colloquial *zajals* of Bayram al-Tunsi. Salah Jahin became one of the leading colloquial poets of the 1952 revolution, and his patriotic verse became core material for 'Abd al-Halim Hafiz, who pinned his career to Nasser. From the same period, Fu'ad Haddad's *mawwals* also stand out—and are still sung today. Since the 1970s, it has been Ahmad Fu'ad Nagm who has played the leading role as lyricist of militant opposition to the regimes of Egypt. For forty years, Nagm's colloquial poems—many set to music by Sheikh Imam—have electrified student, labor, and dissident movements from the Egyptian underclass. Nagm's poetry ranges from praise (*madh*) for the courage of ordinary Egyptians to invective (*hija'*) directed at Egypt's overlords—and it is no accident that you could hear his songs being sung by the leftist activists who spearheaded the first day of revolt on January 25. Besides these poets, we could mention many others—Naguib Surur, 'Abd al-Rahman al-Abnoudi, Tamim Barghouti—who have added to this literary-political tradition in their own ways.

And beyond these recognized names are thousands of other poets—activists all—who would never dare to protest publicly without an arsenal of clever couplet-slogans. The end result is a unique literary tradition whose power is now on full display across Egypt. Chroniclers of the current Egyptian revolt have already compiled long lists of these couplets—and hundreds more are sure to come. For the most part, these poems are composed in a colloquial, not classical, register and they are extremely catchy and easy to sing. The genre also has real potential for humor and play, reminding us of the fact that revolution is also a time for celebration and laughter.

HOW TO DO THINGS WITH POETRY

The poetry of this revolt is not reducible to a text that can be read and translated in words, for it is also an act in and of itself. That is, the couplet-slogans being sung and chanted by protesters do more than reiterate complaints and aspirations which have been communicated in other media. This poetry has the power to express messages that could not be articulated in other forms, as well as to sharpen demands with ever keener edges.

Consider the most prominent slogan being chanted today by thousands of people in Tahrir Square: "*Al-sha'b/yurid/isqat/al-nizam.*" Rendered into English, it might read: "The people want the regime to fall"—but that would not begin to translate the power this simple and yet complex couplet-slogan has in its context. There are real poetic reasons why this has emerged as a central slogan. For instance, unlike the more ironic—humorous or bitter—slogans, this one is sincere and states it all perfectly clearly. Furthermore, the register of this couplet straddles colloquial Egyptian and standard media Arabic, and it is thus readily understandable to the massive Arab audiences who are watching and listening. Like all the other couplet-slogans being shouted, this has a regular metrical and stress pattern (in this case: short-LONG, short-LONG, short-LONG, short-SHORT-LONG). But, more importantly, the cadence of these lines is borrowed from a pre-existing slogan that begins "*Bil-ruh, bil-damm, nafdik ya . . .*" and whose rhythm is a familiar part of the soundtrack of Arabic-language activist public culture. While unlike most others, this particular couplet is not rhymed, it can be sung and shouted by thousands of people in a unified, clear, and preordained cadence—and that seems to be a key factor in why it has worked so well.

The prosody of the revolt suggests that there is more at stake in these couplet-slogans than the creation and distillation of a purely semantic meaning. For one thing, the act of singing and shouting with large groups of fellow citizens has created a certain and palpable sense of community that had not existed before. And the knowledge that one belongs to a movement bound by a positive collective ethos is powerful in its own right—especially in the face of a regime that has always sought to morally denigrate all political opposition. Likewise, the act of singing invective that satirizes feared public figures has an immediate impact that cannot be explained in terms of language, for learning to laugh at one's oppressor is a key part of unlearning fear. Indeed, witnesses to the revolt have consistently commented that in the early hours of the revolt—when invective was most ascendant—protesters began to lose their fear.

And having lost that fear, Egyptians are showing no signs of wanting to go back. As the Mubarak regime has continued to unleash more violence, and as it steps up its campaign to sow chaos and confusion, the recitation of these couplet-slogans has continued, as if the act of repeating them helps the protesters concentrate on their core principles and demands. Only hours ago, as jets and helicopters attempted to intimidate protesters in Tahrir Square, it seemed as if the crowd understood something of this—for with each sortie, their singing grew louder and more focused. It was difficult to determine whether the crowd sustained the words, or the words the crowd.

POETRY AND CONTINGENCY

Anyone who has ever chanted slogans in a public demonstration has also probably asked herself at some point: Why am I doing this? What does shouting accomplish? The question provokes a feeling of embarrassment, the suspicion that the gesture might be rote and thus empty and powerless. Arguably, this nervousness is a form of performance anxiety that, if taken seriously, might remind us that the ritual of singing slogans was invented precisely because it has the power to accomplish things. When philosophers speak of "doing things with words," they also remind us that the success of the locutionary act is tied to the conditions in which it is performed. This is another way to say that any speech act is highly contingent—its success only occurs in particular circumstances, and even then, its success is never a given. Success, if it is to occur, happens only in the performance of it.

Since January 25, Egyptians have been leaping into the uncertainty of this revolutionary performance. They have now crossed multiple thresholds—and each time, they have acted with no guarantee of success. This is, I think, the core of their astonishing courage: at each point it has been impossible to say that victory is assured. Even now, six days into the revolt, we still cannot say how things will eventually turn out. Nor are there rules of history or previous examples that can definitively tell us. Certainly, revolutions follow patterns—and those who rise up tend to be the most diligent students of past uprisings. Activists in Cairo ask comrades in Tunis about tactics, while others try to glean lessons from Iran's Green Movement that might be applied here. Yet, in the end, each revolution is its own moment.

Those who decide to make their own history are not only required to write their own script and build their own stage, they are also compelled to then play the new roles with enough force and conviction to make the work cohere, even in the face of overwhelming violence. We have already seen examples of rescripting in Egypt—from the extraordinary, original pamphlet entitled, *How to Revolt Intelligently*, to the emergence of a new graffiti culture in the urban centers. The poetry of the streets is another form of writing, of redrafting the script of history in the here and now—with no assurances of victory, and everything in the balance.

January 31, 2011

CHAPTER 5

Revolution and Counterrevolution in the Egyptian Media

Ursula Lindsey

It took eighteen days of mass mobilization, the deaths of hundreds and the wounding of thousands, the crippling of Egypt's tourism industry, and the crash of its stock market, to bring an end to the thirty-year presidency of Husni Mubarak. And almost every minute of the revolution was televised.

Although protesters faced violence from police and—infamously— regime-enlisted thugs, for the most part the revolution was peaceful. After tens of thousands occupied central Cairo on January 28, and millions more came out in their support across the country, what the cameras captured was mostly a prolonged stand-off between demonstrators and Mubarak's regime, including his newly appointed military leadership, former intelligence chief 'Umar Sulayman and former air force head Ahmad Shafiq.

In the tense and unpredictable days between January 28 and February 11, when Mubarak stepped down, the mood of the TV-watching Egyptian public veered from support for the protesters' demands, to a desire to return to normalcy, to sympathy with the beleaguered president, and back again. To a large extent, the contest of wills between a spontaneous, grassroots movement and an entrenched authoritarian regime became a battle of words and images, in which issues of national authenticity were paramount and modes of communication vital. Who could legitimately claim to speak for Egypt? Who could not? The protesters and the government debated these questions through very different means—the former using freewheeling, peer-to-peer, mostly digital networks, the latter with top-down announcements through channels over which they retain exclusive control.

Access to and use of communication and information networks— cellular phone services, the Internet and new social media, TV and newspapers—was pivotal as events unfolded. While the regime used the state information apparatus to unleash propaganda against the protesters and the journalists covering them, the protesters disseminated their message in ways that were at once disciplined, creative, and subversive. The triumph of the revolution—at least in its primary demand, Mubarak's resignation—was accompanied by a discrediting of government-controlled news, a flourishing of "homemade" media of all sorts, and a validation of outlets such as Al Jazeera and other pugnacious satellite channels, some privately owned.

As the post-Mubarak era dawns, and the country seems to be moving toward historic legal and political change, the question is whether the transformation will include a new media landscape that is more diversified, uncensored, and truly representative of the Egyptian people's concerns and views.

THE "FACEBOOK KIDS"

Social media, while they did not cause the Egyptian uprising, played a huge role in connecting many of the people who would eventually join the protests. Facebook groups like "We Are All Khalid Sa'id," created in late 2010 to honor a young Alexandrian man beaten to death by police and boasting a half-million members on January 25, 2011, were instrumental, so much so that a new expression has entered the Egyptian lexicon. The politicized, Internet-savvy generation that organized the initial events is known as the "Facebook kids."

Over 80,000 people pledged on the Internet to attend the "day of rage" scheduled for January 25. Yet previous attempts to mobilize the masses online had fallen flat, including the April 6, 2008 general strike, for which one of the key organizer movements is named. Both the protesters and the riot police sent to contain them therefore seemed caught off guard when the day ended with joyful crowds milling freely through Tahrir Square and adjacent parts of the city center.

The regime's decision to interfere with telecommunications seems to have been made almost immediately. Already on January 25, cell-phone coverage was unavailable to the protesters who had streamed into Tahrir Square. The next day, telecom operators received instructions from the authorities to lower data-rate limits—a way to reduce the speed of the Internet. By the night of January 27, the Internet was down. Text messaging was disabled. The following morning, all cell-phone coverage in Egypt was gone. Officials of Vodafone, one of the major telecom operators in the country, have said they were obligated to obey government shutdown orders by Egyptian law, which gives the authorities broad emergency powers.

The protesters knew to expect the outage. They had already been organizing through face-to-face meetings and, as the January 28 "day of rage" neared, they started exchanging landline numbers and identifying safe houses where they could meet early that morning.

Organizers were concerned by the prospect that security and intelligence agents would infiltrate social-media networks. A set of instructions for the January 28 protests was introduced with the following warning: "Please distribute by e-mail or by hand (printouts and photocopies). Facebook or Twitter are under surveillance. Please make sure this information does not fall into the hands of police or state security personnel." The document gave detailed guidance about what to wear and bring to the protests; how best to gather and converge on a location; what slogans to shout; and how to mount effective self-defense in case of clashes with the riot police. It also designated the state-owned radio and TV building, known as Maspero, as the highest-value target in downtown Cairo. "The building should be surrounded from all sides," the document read, "and then entered so as to take control of the live-broadcast facilities and announce the people's takeover of state TV and radio and its liberation from the tyrannical dictator." (The protesters tried several times, but never made it all the way to Maspero, which was heavily guarded.)

While the phone service returned on January 29, SMS and the Internet remained disabled for a full five days, plunging the country into an unprecedented telecommunications black hole. It is unclear what the Internet shutdown achieved, besides contributing to a general sense of predicament. The absence of connectivity did not knock out the broadcasts of the foreign media, nor did it significantly impede the protests' momentum. One group of young people said they had originally read about the demonstrations online, but once the protests began, they continued: "We just headed to Tahrir every day."

And while social media and online communities did much of the spadework for the success of the protests—fashioning a new political consensus among hundreds of thousands of middle-class Egyptians and functioning as organizing tools—the revolution included many, many people, maybe a majority, who did not have Internet access at home, let alone Facebook accounts.

THE TWILIGHT ZONE

Even as satellite and private TV channels began to penetrate the Egyptian market in the 1990s, the government kept tight control over terrestrial broadcasting, which depended directly upon the Ministry of Information for its content. State TV was compelled to update its programming to be more relevant and engaging, by focusing on local news and playing to viewers' feelings of patriotism. As the regime knew very well, the eight state TV channels were the only source of visual information for the many poor Egyptians who do not have satellite channels or Internet connections at home. Meanwhile, Egyptian private channels, which must be licensed by the government, repeatedly encountered pressure from state security agents to cancel the appearances of certain guests or entire shows.

At first, state TV barely acknowledged the protests that were to bloom into popular revolt. The official *al-Ahram* newspaper did not deign to mention them, either. Then, after January 28, when demonstrators seized control of Tahrir Square for good, state-sponsored broadcasts not surprisingly began to mirror the government's rhetoric, presenting the peaceful rallies across the country as a national security emergency. Under the tagline "Protect Egypt," the government channels' focus turned to the chaos and looting that was supposedly sweeping the country, and the heroic efforts of Egyptian citizens to defend their homes and property. Of course, no suggestion was made that this security vacuum might be orchestrated by the state itself. The coverage seemed designed to scare Egyptians into staying at home.

State TV also focused on the government's promises of reform, repeating that President Mubarak had in fact granted all the protesters' demands by promising to resign upon the expiration of his term in September. It highlighted the economic hardships that many Egyptians were enduring, due, it was claimed, to the protesters' intransigence.

Mubarak's speech on February 1, in which he emphasized his years of service to the country in the air force and political office and spoke of his desire to end his life in Egypt, genuinely moved many Egyptians. After the speech, the state channels ran footage from Mubarak's years as president with a soundtrack of patriotic music. They also devoted extensive coverage to the "pro-Mubarak demonstrations" staged by the regime. Crowds of middle-aged men kissed the president's portrait, danced, and pantomimed their general enthusiasm before state cameras that filmed them in tight close-ups. Meanwhile, the throngs in Tahrir Square were filmed only from a distance. None of the many people who called in to talk shows to chat about Egypt's crisis were from the ranks of the revolutionaries.

The next day's violent attacks on the protesters were also entirely elided. State TV spoke only of "clashes," and showed none of the widely circulating pictures of young men charging the crowds on horses and camels or throwing chunks of masonry from rooftops.

The coverage was so disingenuous and disconnected from reality that it prompted defections. Shahira Amin, the deputy head of Nile TV, resigned on February 3, saying that she had been given instructions to air only footage of the pro-Mubarak gatherings. Significantly, she announced her resignation to Al Jazeera, from Tahrir Square. Another well-known anchor, Suha al-Naqqash, followed suit.

As the protests continued throughout the week, government and some private media began a campaign of xenophobic incitement and disinformation. They broadcast interviews with "demonstrators" who had their faces and voices disguised and claimed they had been trained in Israel. At least one of these impersonators was later identified, as a female journalist working for the *24 Hours* newspaper run by Samir Ragab. Hints at foreign infiltration multiplied. Presenters took calls from people who reported, again and again, that they had seen people in the protesters' ranks who looked foreign, spoke foreign languages, or spoke Arabic in non-Egyptian dialects. References were made to Iran and Hamas; to the Muslim Brothers and al-Qaeda; to international NGOs like the International Crisis Group and Freedom House; and to Israel and the United States.

In an interview on February 4, the *al-Ahram* journalist Yahya al-Ghani remonstrated with a Nile TV presenter who had zeroed in on the alleged foreign elements in the demonstrations. "Your questions imply a lack of trust. There are many political and popular groups [in the protests]. We shouldn't demonize anyone in Egypt. Why are you acting in a way that destroys the trust between the government media and the public?" But the presenter went on immediately to take a call from someone who claimed that Arabs with non-Egyptian accents were preventing Egyptians from leaving the protests. There was so much food in Tahrir Square, the caller continued, that protesters were throwing it away. One of the wilder rumors spread on state TV was that the US-backed demonstrators' meals were catered by the fried-chicken chain KFC. The light-hearted, quick-witted crowds in Tahrir Square began referring to all food as "Kentucky."

The protesters were, of course, completely ready for the incitement against them. An Egyptian blogger called Nasry wrote a long post entitled: "How to Betray Your People in Four Steps: Guide for a Clever Government to Deceive the Media." The steps include: "Call them traitors," "Keep them worried day and night," "Denial and postponement are always useful," and "Repeat your lies."

FOREIGN REPORTERS, FOREIGN AGENTS

As the government attacked the protesters, and tried to bamboozle Egyptians sitting at home, it carried out a simultaneous and concerted campaign of intimidation against the press. Dozens of local and foreign journalists were physically threatened, assaulted, and detained, in some cases at secret state security facilities, where they could hear the sounds of Egyptians being beaten nearby. Reporters' accounts suggest that police or intelligence officers were often close at hand during attacks by government supporters, directing the mob and then stepping in to detain journalists "for their protection." Journalists at hotels overlooking Tahrir Square had their cameras confiscated by hotel management. The manager at one such establishment claimed to be following orders from the army, which had said that otherwise it would be obligated to "storm the hotel."

The local opposition press was also singled out for rough treatment. The offices of the independent daily *al-Shurouq* were attacked, and writers with the privately owned *al-Masry al-Youm* newspaper reported threats.

But the most heavily targeted media outlet was Al Jazeera. The Qatar-based satellite channel had been the *bête noire* of the Mubarak regime for some time. Mubarak was the Arab leader who, upon visiting the channel's Doha offices, exclaimed, "All that noise from this little matchbox?" His regime, like others in the Arab world, reacted to the channel's critical coverage by accusing it time and again of plotting against Egypt. For its part, Al Jazeera made no secret of its sympathy with the protesters and its skepticism toward the statements of government officials. It featured the most extensive coverage of any TV channel, reporting not only from Cairo but also from Alexandria and Suez.

The government removed Al Jazeera's feed from the state-owned NileSat satellite and ordered the channel to close its offices, which were subsequently torched and looted. Nine of the station's reporters were arrested. The regime-backed thugs that attacked demonstrators in downtown Cairo were reportedly on the lookout for the satellite channel's personnel, aggressively asking all journalists: "Are you Al Jazeera?" Al Jazeera reporters removed the well-known circular golden logo from their microphones; several correspondents of Egyptian (as opposed to dual or non-Egyptian Arab) nationality were forced into hiding for a week, not to emerge until the night of the president's resignation.

Egypt came back online on February 2. Almost immediately, protesters and their sympathizers began uploading a stream of visual and aural
material: YouTube clips showing unarmed citizens being shot, updated
lists of what supplies the protesters might need, music videos and online
slide shows celebrating the scope of the demonstrations and popular solidarity with them, and cartoons mocking the president's speeches. Huge
banners were hung around Tahrir Square outlining the protesters' shared
demands: the removal of Mubarak; the dissolution of Parliament, elected
fraudulently in December 2010; the trial of former Interior Minister
Habib al-'Adli and other government officials; the lifting of emergency
law; the writing of a new constitution; and the holding of free and fair
elections.

The protesters—almost all of whom were eager to be interviewed by
journalists—displayed a consistent, articulate vision of their movement.
They emphasized their peaceful intentions and their commitment to a broad
set of democratic demands, rather than to any single ideology. Persistently
if not always patiently, they told reporters: "We are Egyptians. We aren't
criminals. We aren't thieves. We aren't foreigners." Waving Egyptian flags
and eschewing any divisive religious or political symbolism, the protesters
stuck to simple and positive slogans: "Non-violence!" "Long live Egypt!"
"Down with Mubarak!" And then there was the ubiquitous, rhythmic
chant, "The people . . . want . . . the fall . . . of the regime!" Their posters,
meanwhile, ranged from the witty ("Control + Alt + Delete Mubarak") to
the straightforward ("Take a hike," "Get out," "Leave and let live") to the
poignant ("I'm sorry I was silent"). The humor, the use of English phrases
and technological jargon (one poster was a clever flow chart) were all ways
to send other messages: We are educated, non-threatening, part of the
world community, these posters said. We deserve democracy.

One of the more interesting developments in the media wars that
surrounded the protests was the changing role of local private TV channels such as Dream TV (owned by industrialist Ahmad Bahgat) and O TV
(owned by businessman Naguib Sawiris). Less open to charges of foreign
manipulation, both of these channels seem to have been pushed into open
sympathy with the protest movement by the propaganda on state TV, the
pressure from the security services to tone down their own coverage, and
the dawning realization that the regime was tottering. Muna al-Shazli,
the charismatic host of a popular evening talk show, who had choked up
with emotion while commenting on Mubarak's second speech, a few days
later revealed on the air that she had been instructed how to cover the

demonstrations. "They told us to say 'dozens' of demonstrators," she said. Al-Shazli started to question government officials aggressively and was the first to interview activist Wael Ghonim, the administrator of the "We Are All Khalid Sa'id" Facebook group, who was kidnapped and detained for twelve days. The station had campaigned for Ghonim's release. His emotional response—he broke down crying when shown photographs of people killed during the protests—was a galvanizing moment that contributed to a huge turnout in the square the following day.

But the demonstrators' best way of getting their message out was arguably their very perseverance. As days went by, and hundreds of thousands of Egyptians visited Tahrir Square or participated in protests across the country, it became increasingly difficult to portray the gatherings as marginal or alien. More and more Egyptians had direct experience to the contrary, and the protest organizers made a point of asking visitors to spread the word about what they had seen.

As the protests not only continued but also increased in size, the state-run channels found it impossible to sustain the crude tenor of their propaganda. They began adjusting the official line, abandoning some of their more outrageous claims, showing footage of Tahrir Square and even suggesting that the early protests had been genuinely nationalist and legitimate. It was only later, the state's anchors now said, that Islamists and foreign interlopers had hijacked the demonstrations.

Finally, on the afternoon of February 11—mere hours before Mubarak's resignation was announced—pro-democracy crowds gathered outside government buildings across Cairo, including Maspero. A presenter from the official al-Akhbar news channel stepped outside the building and began interviewing protesters. Acknowledging that state media had made "mistakes," he asked them how they would like to see it change. "I don't want to have to rely on foreign media to get the truth," a protester told him. "I want the Egyptian media to be free and neutral. I want it to be the voice of the people, not of the regime." Another protester was less polite: "How can you ask us to forgive you?" he asked the presenter. "How can we forgive you for spreading lies and bad news? You should be judged by the people!" The next day, the state-owned *al-Ahram* ran the headline, "The People Brought Down the Mubarak Regime," echoing the chant that had reverberated in Tahrir Square for the last two weeks.

THE ARMY'S MEDIA STRATEGY

When Mubarak stepped down, he handed over power to the Supreme Council of the Armed Forces (SCAF), which said it wanted to install a new civilian government as soon as possible and was committed to safeguarding the "gains of the revolution." During the revolution, the army did not take action against the protesters, but it did not side with them, either. Its position was one of cultivated, convenient ambiguity.

During the first five days of the protests, even as it was impossible to send text messages, all Egyptians received several from the army. Telecom operators, again, say they were obliged to relay these brief missives under the country's Emergency Law. The first, sent on February 1, read: "The armed forces implore the loyal men of Egypt to confront traitors and criminals and to protect our people, our land, and our precious Egypt." Another, dated February 4, said: "To every father, mother, sister, and brother, to every honorable citizen, watch over this country, for the nation is forever." On the same day, another message informed Egyptians that "the armed forces are guarding your safety and will not resort to using force against this great people." Yet another warned: "Young people of Egypt, beware of rumors and be reasonable. Egypt is above all else, so watch over her."

For months after it convened on February 11, the SCAF addressed the public only through a series of terse communiqués. Even as it abruptly notified the public of momentous changes—the dissolution of Parliament and the suspension of the constitution—the army provided little information about how it intended to midwife a transition to democracy. Plainly, it is an institution that is not accustomed to explaining itself in public. In a February 14 meeting between young protest leaders and army representatives, the "Facebook kids" gently suggested that the army should "change its media discourse and explain its points of view in a clearer manner." Indeed.

The young protest leaders did commend the army, however, for speaking with them "without paternalism." In many ways, the uprising in Egypt was the product of a yawning generation gap—a gap in expectations, attitudes toward authority, and ways of communicating. One of the reasons the uprising succeeded in its immediate goal may be the regime's inability to hear, understand, and respond to a new discourse. And one thing the revolution made clear is Egyptians' determination to speak to their government, and be spoken to, very differently than in the past. While Mubarak's second speech was greeted with some sympathy, his third TV appearance, in which he pointedly did not resign, infuriated protesters with its utter tone-deafness. In Tahrir Square that night, the thousands who were crouched over portable TVs erupted in sarcastic disgust when the president said that he had once been young himself and would never be above listening to the youth of the country. Young Egyptians will no longer stand for such condescension, for father figures who presume to tell them what to do simply on the strength of their age and power. The great daily gatherings in central Cairo changed many Egyptians' sense of who can speak, who can answer, and who can decide.

WANTED: AN ACCOUNTING

After the revolution, some top state media officials were dismissed. Former Minister of Information Anas al-Fiqqi faces charges of corruption, but as of the late summer of 2011 he had yet to be investigated for his role in the government's disinformation campaign. An unofficial accounting, meanwhile, has taken place—mainly online—with comedians and enthusiastic amateurs collecting and editing the most egregious YouTube clips from the revolution, and creating "blacklists" of lying celebrities and TV presenters.

The Egyptian media is notably freer today, with journalists and presenters trying to reassert their professionalism and get real scoops. This opening has led to some memorable exchanges, particularly on the country's evening TV talk shows—most notably the impromptu debate between novelist Alaa Al Aswany and then Prime Minister Ahmad Shafiq on O TV, an exchange in which the writer so bested the unprepared politician that Shafiq resigned the next day.

Egyptian state TV—rocked by months of internal employee protests and calls for reform, as well as widespread criticism from society at large—is also attempting to regain credibility. But neither the exemplary punishment of a few high-ranking officials (if that indeed happens as promised), nor the state media's collective *mea culpa* and late adoption of the revolution, are guarantees that the state information apparatus will not again be used against the interests of the Egyptian people.

It is not encouraging that the state-run media has adopted the same uncritical (if not fawning) attitude toward the country's current military commanders as it held toward the Mubarak regime. The army, for its part, has aggressively asserted its privilege to draw "a red line" around itself and its activities—threatening with military trial those few journalists and guest speakers who, in the independent media, have been daring enough to criticize its actions.

Whatever additional concessions the protesters and their leadership are able to extract, somewhere near the top of the list should be a full accounting for the disinformation campaign and the coordinated attacks on journalists. They should demand the appointment of a trustworthy reformist to head the Ministry of Information, or even the gradual dismantling of that ministry altogether; the curtailment of the government's arbitrary power to shut down Egyptians' means of communication; and an end to state control over all terrestrial TV transmissions. They should also strongly assert the media's right to freely question, investigate, and report on the actions and words of the military commanders. Egypt cannot move toward democracy without guarantees that its citizens will have access to free, accurate information.

CHAPTER 6

Taking Out the Trash:
Youth Clean Up Egypt After Mubarak

Jessica Winegar

On February 12, 2011, thousands of Egyptians flooded into Tahrir Square to celebrate the previous night's ouster of Husni Mubarak, their country's dictator of thirty years. It was an unusually bright and clear-skied Cairo Saturday, full of promise of a new Egypt. From atop the October 6 bridge that spans the 'Abd al-Mun'im Riyad portion of Tahrir, where just nine days earlier government-paid attackers had rained down ammunition upon pro-democracy demonstrators in the most brutal battle of the revolution, one could see dozens of crews of young people cleaning the square.

Many of the middle-class youth wore surgical masks and gloves as they swept the streets of their thick layer of dust and pushed into piles the chunks of pavement that had broken under the weight of army tanks as well as the hammering of protesters making projectiles for self-defense. With large black plastic bags brought from home or purchased by largely youth-led NGOs, they collected food and drink containers, old newspapers, empty cigarette packages, and other remnants of the tent city sit-in. Other volunteers washed off or painted over the spontaneous graffiti that protesters had written on buildings, sidewalks, and bridges. Toward the end of the afternoon, human chains formed to protect the curbs that were receiving a fresh coat of paint. Hundreds of young people had turned out for what was called "Tahrir Beautification Day." And in the coming weeks, one would regularly see youthful cleaning brigades all around Cairo picking up trash, painting curbs, and adorning light posts and tree trunks with the colors of the Egyptian flag.

What does it mean that the day after Egyptians accomplished one of the most amazing feats in modern history, the most prominent activity at the epicenter of the struggle was one of earnest, vigorous cleaning? Of course, Tahrir had been strewn with debris during the eighteen days of protest,

Author's note: Thanks to Farha Ghannam, Sherine Hafez, Sherine Hamdy and Julie Peteet for their thoughtful suggestions during the writing of this chapter.

despite the protesters' valiant and well-documented efforts to tidy up as they went. But there was something more to this diligent scrubbing and sweeping.

CLEANING URBAN SPACE

During the Mubarak years, the amount of litter on the streets of Cairo increased exponentially, a development lamented not only by tourists and in the Western press, but also by citizens who had to live amidst the mounds of trash. There were several reasons for this pile-up, most having to do with the intensification of neoliberal policies, especially in the areas of urban development and waste management. The implementation of structural adjustment programs in the 1980s and 1990s on the heels of President Anwar al-Sadat's shift toward a free-market economy sucked capital out of rural areas and concentrated it in the hands of city elites. Massive labor migration accompanied the economic opening, contributing to a population surge in Cairo such that the greater metropolitan area was home to approximately 17 million by the end of Mubarak's tenure. Densely populated informal settlements sprung up all over Cairo. By and large, the government managed the urban development and housing needs of low-income migrants poorly—in many cases ignoring them entirely. The government was slow to provide these new communities with adequate public services, whether clean water or trash collection.

The Sadat and Mubarak governments' economic policies were at the root of the garbage problem in another way. The number and variety of mass-produced consumer goods grew at astonishing rates after the neoliberal economic "reforms" announced in 1990 and 1996, and especially after the National Democratic Party's intense liberalization push of 2004. Soon Egyptians were eating elaborately packaged snacks and fast-food meals made by big companies, instead of food cooked in the home or at corner eateries whose takeout meals were usually wrapped in newsprint or other reused paper.

The problem was compounded when, starting in 2000, the government privatized its sectors responsible for waste collection and staged an "industrial takeover" of the *zabbalin*, the independent workers who had gathered garbage from many doorsteps in Cairo (as well as Alexandria, Egypt's second-largest city) since the 1940s. Several European companies were given contracts worth hundreds of millions of dollars, and substantial tax breaks, to come in and replace these systems. The process was encouraged by USAID, which supplied technical assistance and billed privatization as necessary to sustain urban hygiene and attract investment. The garbage workers complained about these companies' meager pay, lack of health insurance, illegal dumping near residential areas, and low recycling rates (the *zabbalin* had traditionally recycled 80 percent of trash).

What most Cairenes began to notice, with their noses as well as their eyes, was the build-up of trash in the streets. By 2004, and especially by the end of the Mubarak era, it became clear that this new system was less an improvement than a step backward in dealing with the 10,000 tons of rubbish produced every day in the city. Citizens, especially but not exclusively in lower- and middle-income areas, complained of extremely erratic service as they now faced a new garbage tax that the government tacked onto skyrocketing electricity bills (regardless of income or property value). Much of the equipment imported by the foreign companies would not fit down the narrow streets of the informal settlements, so trash bins were placed in central areas of the neighborhood. Company executives and government elites complained that Cairenes were too "lazy" to take their trash to the dumpsters, without considering the expectations of customers who had enjoyed the convenient door-to-door service of the *zabbalin*, or that local mores might make people feel unrespectable carrying trash down the street in front of their neighbors.

Disgruntled Cairenes argued that these companies, like the government system that preceded it, did not provide an adequate number of containers in the public areas. It did not help that customs sat on some of the necessary equipment for months, or that urban redistricting resulted in fights between governorates over who would pay the garbage bill. Some governorates delayed payment, or paid less than the contracted amount, to penalize the companies for their poor service. The companies, in turn, shifted the burden to their employees and withheld their pay. As workers struck, garbage piled up more and more.[1] And then, in a colossal mistake, the government culled the *zabbalins'* swill-eating pigs in response to the swine flu scare of 2009. The Christian *zabbalin* understood this move as a sectarian attack on their livelihood (given the institutionalized discrimination against Christians during the Mubarak years), and refused to pick up organic waste. All of these developments added a singular stench and a multitude of flies to the summers of the 2000s, the hottest on record in Egypt.

---

1   For an excellent overview of the waste management issue, see Rachel Leven, "The Pharaoh's Garbage: Growth and Change in Egypt's Waste Management System," *NIMEP Insights* 2 (2006).

When the battalions of youth cleaned up Tahrir Square and other neighborhoods, they were expressing their desire for a city cleared of refuse. The physical cleanup was highly symbolic of the larger drive to "purify" the Egyptian government, ridding it of the kind of mismanagement, discrimination, and corruption that characterized the sanitation crisis. Indeed, the Tahrir demonstration of April 8, 2011, not quite three months after Mubarak's resignation, was called "the Friday of purification" (*gum'at al-tathir*).

RECLAIMING PUBLIC SPACE

As Egyptians cleaned, they were also reclaiming their public space from decades of neglect by the Mubarak regime. As the 1990s and 2000s wore on, Cairenes griped not only about the trash, but also about the filth and disrepair of public spaces such as squares, parks, bus stops, government offices, and schools. As state welfare policy shifted its focus from the poor to the rich, urban space became extremely segregated and militarized. Many with the means moved out of what they viewed as the "chaos" of mixed- or lower-class areas of Cairo into gated communities or other secluded areas with private security systems. They shopped in exclusive malls and stores, and attended private schools, all of which restricted entry on the basis of class. Meanwhile, the rest of the city's residents were left with a public transportation system bursting at the seams, crowded and dilapidated government hospitals and schools, and decrepit parks thirsty for the water that was siphoned off for the new golf courses and lawns of the rich. And when they went out in public, they were always in danger of arbitrary harassment, arrest, detention, and torture by the corrupt police forces or state security, sometimes at the behest of upper-class Egyptians threatened by any transgression of the social hierarchy, real or perceived. In the Mubarak years, most Cairenes had little to no urban space that was well maintained and that they could enjoy unthreatened.

Thus when the youth came out in groups to paint curbs, bridges, murals, signposts, and tree trunks, they were reclaiming that public space as their own. Even though the thirty-year-old Emergency Law preventing gatherings was still in effect, the revolution enabled them to break it without fear of the security forces. Perhaps for the first time in their lives, they could work, laugh, and play together in public space without an overwhelming sense of state surveillance or upper-class disgust. They were trying to reverse, and reject, the neglect of the Mubarak government by taking the repair and beautification of the city into their own hands. Many cleaners whom I interviewed spoke of treating plazas and avenues as they would their "own home," even stating that these places are "our home"—meaning the home of Egyptians.

And while the ruling elite and their cronies had sneered that Egyptians were by nature indolent and disorganized, and thus not ready for democracy, the ranks of young cleaners were showing, through their very painting and polishing, that they were energetic and efficient. They were thus demonstrating that they deserved, and were capable of, democracy—that they, contrary to the claims of the government and many upper-class Egyptians, had the wherewithal to build a society through grassroots, democratic means. They presented themselves as clean, well-behaved citizens, not dirty threats to the social order. On February 12, many members of the cleaning crews wore photocopied Arabic-English signs on their backs that captured the mannered civic pride: "Sorry for disturbance. We build Egypt."

WINDOW DRESSING?

It is clear that the burst of beautification immediately following the removal of Mubarak was both literal and metaphorical. It was an attempt to reverse decades of neglect, corruption, and failure in waste management, and in urban public space generally, that revealed itself not only in the form of piles of trash, crumbling buildings, and peeling paint, but also in the threatening and policed segregation of urban space.

At the same time, however, the intense focus on cleaning could reproduce the logics of power that led to the revolution in the first place. The Mubarak government had long relied on window dressing, building major public works such as fancy libraries and museums with spectacular opening ceremonies that were partly intended to give the appearance of a state that cared for its citizens. They often fell into disrepair, because the underlying problems of malfeasance and mismanagement were not solved.

Will all of the cleaning of Tahrir have been for naught if the roots of the problem—the concentration of capital in Cairo, the political economy of commodity production and waste management, the channeling of public funds into corporate welfare—go unaddressed? Will the beautification have served as a cover for economic problems, much as the Mubarak regime's famous projects did? Furthermore, did the youths' concentration on neatness and order—while wearing surgical masks and gloves—represent a middle-class disdain for dirt, a ranking of appearances above substance, thereby entrenching the biases of the elites who reigned in the Mubarak era? There is no doubt that poor people like cleanliness and beauty, and that some of the middle-class cleaners in Tahrir that day went on to work to establish a decent minimum wage or reform the legal system. But the question remains as to whether the priority placed on cleaning the streets will remove the garbage of the Mubarak era, or merely recycle it.

Workers from the Suez Canal Company for Ports and Large Projects demonstrate during a sit-in, Ismailiyya, September 9, 2008. © Hossam el-Hamalawy

Part II

PROTEST UNDER AUTHORITARIAN RULE

CHAPTER 7

The "Arab Street"

Asef Bayat

In the tense weeks between the September 11 attacks and the first US bombing raids over Afghanistan, and continuing until the fall of the Taliban, commentators raised serious concerns over what the *Wall Street Journal* later called the "irrational Arab street."[1] If the US attacked a Muslim country, the pundits worried, would the "Arab street" rally behind Osama bin Laden and other radical Islamists, endangering US interests in the region and rendering George W. Bush's "war on terrorism" a troublesome, if not doomed, venture from the outset? As US troops prepared to deploy in Afghanistan, some officials in Washington implored Israeli Prime Minister Ariel Sharon to exercise restraint in his campaign to crush the Palestinian uprising by force. Should Israeli incursions into Palestinian territory continue during the US assault on the Taliban, they feared, the simmering rage of the Arab masses might "boil over," leaving the local gendarmes powerless to prevent the furious crowds from attacking Americans, trashing US property, and threatening the stability of friendly Arab regimes. Senator Joseph Biden broached the possibility that "every US embassy in the Middle East [would be] burned to the ground."[2]

Beginning with the war in Afghanistan, and continuing through the major Israeli offensives in the West Bank and the build-up to Bush's war on Iraq, the "Arab street" became a minor household word in the West, bandied about in the media as a subject of profound anxiety and an object of withering condescension. The "Arab street," and by extension, the "Muslim street," became code words that immediately invoked a reified and essentially "abnormal" mindset, as well as a strange place filled with angry people who, whether because they hate us or just don't understand us, must shout imprecations against us. Arab or other Muslim actions were described almost exclusively in terms of "mobs, riots, revolts,"[3] leading to the logical conclusion that "Western standards for measuring public opin-

---

1   Robert Bartley, "Resolution, Not Compromise, Builds Coalition," *Wall Street Journal*, November 12, 2001.
2   Cited in Robert Satloff, "The Arab 'Street' Poses No Real Threat to US," *Newsday*, September 27, 2002.
3   Ibid.

ion simply don't apply" in the Arab world. At any time, American readers were reminded, protesting Arab masses might shed their unassuming appearance and "suddenly turn into a mob, powerful enough to sweep away governments"—notably the "moderate" Arab governments who remained loyal allies of the US.[4]

Worries about the Arab street notwithstanding, US forces did move into Afghanistan, US bombs did kill Afghan civilians in their thousands, the Israeli–Palestinian conflict cooled off only briefly, and Bush moved full speed ahead with plans to attack Iraq. But, though numerous protests in the Muslim and Arab worlds did occur, no US embassy was burned to the ground. Nor did the Arab and Muslim masses rally behind bin Laden. Only when Israel invaded the West Bank in the spring of 2002 did ordinary people in the Arab world collectively explode with outrage. The millions of Arab citizens who poured into the streets of Cairo, Amman, Rabat, and many other cities to express sympathy with the Palestinians stirred memories of how Arab anti-colonial movements in the postwar period were driven from below. But because the "Arab street" had not erupted at the possible US bombing in Afghanistan during Ramadan, this very real example of latent popular anger in the Arab world was airily dismissed. Abruptly, the image of the "Arab street" shifted from an unpredictable powder keg to a "myth" and a "bluff," somehow kept alive despite the fact that Arab countries were filled with "brainwashed" people trapped in "apathy."[5] The implication for US policymaking was clear: Arabs do not have the guts to stop an attack on Iraq or any other unpopular US initiative, and therefore the US should express "not sensitivity, but resolution" in the face of remonstrations from Arab allies.[6] Neither the slogans of the actual demonstrators nor the insistence of Arab governments that they faced unbearable pressure from their populations needed to be taken at face value. The *Economist* declared the "death" of the Arab street, once and for all. It was not long before National Security Adviser Condoleezza Rice concluded that because the Arab peoples were too weak to demand democracy, the US should intervene to liberate the Arab world from its tyrants.[7]

---

4   John Kifner, "Street Brawl," *New York Times*, November 11, 2001.

5   See, for example, Reuel Marc Gerecht, "Better to Be Feared than Loved," *Weekly Standard*, April 29, 2002; and "The Myth of the Arab Street," *Jerusalem Post*, April 11, 2002. Authors sympathetic to Arab protest can have similar takes. See, for example, Ashraf Khalil, "The Arab Couch," *Cairo Times*, December 26, 2002; and Robert Fisk, "A Million March in London, but Faced with Disaster, the Arabs Are Like Mice," *Independent*, February 18, 2003.

6   *Wall Street Journal*, November 12, 2001.

7   *Al-Hayat*, November 6, 2002.

STREET POLITICS AND THE POLITICAL STREET

In the narratives of the Western media, the Arab street is damned if it does and damned if it doesn't—it is either "irrational" and "aggressive" or it is "apathetic" and "dead." There is little chance of its salvation as something Western societies might recognize as familiar. The Arab street thus becomes an extension of another infamous concept, the "Arab mind," which likewise reifies the culture and collective conduct of an entire people in a violent abstraction.[8] It is another subject of Orientalist imagination, reminiscent of colonial representation of the "other," which sadly has been internalized by some Arab selves. By no simple oversight, the Arab street is seldom regarded as an expression of public opinion and collective sentiment—as its Western counterpart often is—but is perceived primarily as a physical entity, a brute force expressed in riots and mob violence. The Arab street matters only in its violent imaginary, when it is poised to imperil interests or disrupt grand strategies. The street that conveys the collective sentiment is a nonissue, because the US can and often does safely ignore it. Such perceptions of the "Arab street" have informed Washington's approach to the Middle East—flouting Arab public opinion with its increasingly unequivocal support for Israel as it proceeded to dismantle the Palestinian Authority, and simultaneously with the determination to wage war on Iraq.

But street politics in general and the Arab street in particular are more complex. Neither is the street a mere physicality or brute force, nor is the Arab street simply inert. The Arab street is an expression not simply of street politics in general, but primarily of what I like to call the "political street." Street politics represents the modern urban theater of contention par excellence. We need only to remember the role the "street" has played in such monumental political upheavals as the French Revolution, nineteenth-century labor movements, anti-colonial struggles, the anti–Vietnam War movement in the US, the Velvet Revolutions in Eastern Europe, and, perhaps, the global anti-war movement of the early 2000s. The street, in this sense, is the chief locus of politics for ordinary people, those who are structurally absent from the institutional positions of power—the unemployed, casual workers, migrants, people of the underworld, and housewives. It serves as a key medium wherein sentiments and outlooks are formed, spread, and expressed in unique fashion.

But "street politics" enjoys another dimension. That is, it is about more than just conflict between the authorities and the de-institutionalized or

---

8   Raphael Patai, *The Arab Mind* (London: Macmillan, 1983).

informal population over the active use of public space and the control of public order. Streets as spaces of flow and movement are not only where people protest, but also where they extend their protest beyond their immediate circles to include also the unknown, the "strangers" who might espouse similar grievances, real or imagined. That is why not only the de-institutionalized groups such as the unemployed, but also actors with some institutional power, like workers or students, find the street to be a useful arena for the extension of collective sentiments. It is this pandemic potential that threatens the authorities, who as a result exert a pervasive power over public spaces with police patrols, traffic regulation, and spatial division. Students at Cairo University, for example, often staged protest marches inside the campus in the Mubarak era. The moment they came out into the street, however, riot police were immediately and massively deployed to encircle the demonstrators, push them into a corner away from public view, and keep the protest a local event. Indeed, this heavily guarded actual street pointed to the fact that the metaphorical street was not deserted so much as it was controlled.

Beyond serving as the physical place for "street politics," urban streets also signify a different but crucial symbolic utterance, one that transcends the physicality of the street, to convey the collective sentiments of a nation or community. This I call the political street—a notion that is distinct from "street politics." The political street signifies the collective sensibilities, shared feelings, and public judgments of ordinary people in their day-to-day utterances and practices, which are expressed broadly in the public square—in taxis and buses, in shops and on sidewalks, or more audibly in mass street demonstrations. The Arab street (and by extension the "Muslim street") should be seen in such terms as the expression of collective sentiments in the Arab public sphere.

THE SHIFTING ARAB STREET

How does the Arab world fare in terms of its "political street"? Arab anti-colonial struggles attest to the active history of the Arab street. Popular movements arose in Syria, Iraq, Jordan, and Lebanon during the late 1950s after Gamal Abdel Nasser nationalized the Suez Canal. The unsuccessful tripartite aggression by Britain, France, and Israel in October 1956 to reclaim control of the canal caused an outpouring of popular protest in Arab countries in support of Egypt. Although 1956 was probably the last major pan-Arab solidarity movement until the pro-Palestinian wave of 2002, social protests by workers, artisans, women, and students calling for domestic social development, citizens' rights, and political participation have been documented.[9] Labor movements in Lebanon, Syria, Egypt, Yemen, and Morocco have carried out strikes or street protests over both bread-and-butter and political issues. Since the 1980s, when the era of IMF-recommended structural adjustment programs began in earnest, Arab labor unions have tried to resist cancellation of consumer commodity subsidies, price rises, pay cuts, and layoffs. Despite no-strike deals and repression of activists, wildcat stoppages have occurred. Fear of popular resistance has often forced governments, as in Egypt, Jordan, and Morocco, to delay structural adjustment programs and retain certain social policies.[10]

When traditional social contracts are violated, Arab populations have reacted swiftly. The 1980s saw numerous urban protests over the spiraling cost of living. In August 1983, the Moroccan government reduced consumer subsidies by 20 percent, triggering urban unrest in the north and elsewhere. Similar protests took place in Tunis in 1984 and in Khartoum in 1982 and 1985. In the summer of 1987, the rival factions in the Lebanese civil war joined hands to stage an extensive street protest against a drop in the value of the Lebanese currency. Algeria was struck by cost-of-living riots in the fall of 1988, and Jordanians staged nationwide protests in 1989, over the plight of the Palestinians and economic hardship, forcing the late King Hussein to introduce cautious measures of political liberalization. Lifting subsidies in 1996 provoked a new wave of street protests, leading the king to restrict freedom of expression and assembly.[11] In Egypt in 1986, low-ranking army officers took to the streets to protest the Mubarak regime's decision to extend military service. The unrest quickly spread to other sectors of society.

While the lower and middle classes formed the core of urban protests, college students often joined in. But student movements have had their own contentious agendas. In Egypt, the 1970s marked the heyday of a student activism dominated by leftist trends. Outraged opposition to the Camp David peace treaty and economic austerity brought thousands of students out into urban streets. Earlier years had seen students organizing conferences, strikes, sit-ins, and marches, and producing newspapers for the walls,

---

9   See Edmund Burke and Ira Lapidus, eds. *Islam, Politics, and Social Movements* (Berkeley: University of California Press, 1990); and Zachary Lockman, ed., *Workers and Working Classes in the Middle East: Struggles, Histories, Historiographies* (Albany, NY: State University of New York Press, 1994).

10   On labor struggles, see Alan Richards and John Waterbury, *A Political Economy of the Middle East* (Boulder, CO: Westview Press, 1990) and Marsha Pripstein Posusney, *Labor and the State in Egypt* (New York: Columbia University Press, 1997).

11   Lamis Andoni and Jillian Schwedler, "Bread Riots in Jordan," *Middle East Report* 201 (Fall 1996).

the "freest of publications."[12] In 1991, students in Egypt, Algeria, Morocco, Jordan, Yemen, and Sudan demonstrated to express anger against both the Iraqi invasion of Kuwait and the US-led war to drive Iraq out of Kuwait. Starting in 1986, Palestinian students were among the most frequent participants in actions of the first *intifada*, often undeterred by the Israeli army's policies of arresting or shooting students and closing down Palestinian universities.

Things changed drastically for the Arab street during the 1990s. The pace of cost-of-living protests slowed, as governments enacted structural adjustment programs more slowly and cautiously, deployed safety nets such as social funds (Egypt and Jordan), and allowed Islamic NGOs and charities to help out the poor. Indeed, the Arab world showed the lowest incidence of extreme poverty in the world's developing regions.[13] Meanwhile, the discontent of the impoverished middle classes was channeled into the Islamist movements in general, and the politicization of professional syndicates in particular.

During this period, the more traditional class-based movements— notably, peasant organizations, cooperative movements, and trade unions—seemed to be in relative decline. As peasants moved to the city from the countryside, or lost their land to become rural day laborers, the social basis of peasant and cooperative movements eroded. The weakening of economic populism, closely linked to structural adjustment, led to the decline of public-sector employment, which constituted the core of state-sanctioned trade unionism. Through reform, downsizing, privatization, and relocation, structural adjustment undermined the unionized public sector. New private enterprises linked to international capital were largely union-free. Although the state bureaucracy remains weighty to this day, its underpaid employees are unorganized, and a large proportion of them survive by taking second or third jobs in the informal sector. Currently, much of the Arab workforce is self-employed. Many wage earners work in small enterprises where paternalistic relations prevail. On average, between one third and one half of the urban workforce is involved in the unregulated, unorganized informal sector.

Although the explosive growth of NGOs since the 1980s heralded autonomous civic activism, NGOs are premised on the politics of fragmentation. NGOs divide the potential beneficiaries of their activism into small

---

12   Ahmed Abdalla, *The Student Movement and National Politics in Egypt* (London: Saqi Books, 1985).

13   UN Development Program, *Arab Human Development Report 2002* (New York, 2002), p. 90.

groups, substitute charity for principles of rights and accountability, and foster insider lobbying rather than street politics. It was largely the advocacy of NGOs, involved in human rights, women's rights, and democratization—not wealth and income gaps—which offered different and new spaces for social mobilization during the 1990s in the Arab world.

As people relied more on informal activities and their loyalties were fragmented, struggles for wages and conditions lost ground to concerns over jobs, informal work conditions, and affordable cost of living, while rapid urbanization increased demands for urban services, shelter, decent housing, health, and education. Under such conditions, the Arab grass-roots resorted not to politics of collective protest but to the individualistic strategy of "quiet encroachment." Individuals and families strove to acquire basic necessities (land for shelter, urban collective consumption, informal jobs, and business opportunities) in a prolonged and unassuming, though illegal, fashion. Instead of organizing a march to demand electricity, for example, the disenfranchised simply tapped into the municipal power grid without authorization.

Thus, in the Arab world, the political class par excellence remained the educated middle class—state employees, students, professionals, and the intelligentsia—who mobilized the "street" in the 1950s and 1960s with overarching ideologies of nationalism, Ba'athism, socialism, and social justice. Islamism has been the latest of these grand worldviews. With its core support coming from the worse-off middle layers, the Islamist movements succeeded for two decades in activating large numbers of the disenchanted population with cheap Islamization—moral and cultural purity, affordable charity work, and identity politics. By the mid-1990s, however, it became clear that the Islamists could not go very far with more costly Islamization—establishing an Islamic polity and economy and conducting international relations compatible with the modern national and global citizenry. Islamist rule faced crisis where it was put into practice (as in Iran and Sudan). Elsewhere, violent strategies failed (as in Egypt and Algeria), and thus new visions about the Islamic project developed. The Islamist movements were either repressed or became resigned to a revision of their earlier outlooks.

Anti-Islamic sentiment in the West following the September 11, 2001 events, and the subsequent "war on terrorism," have undoubtedly reinforced a feeling that Islam is under global attack, strengthening the languages of religiosity and nativism. Several Islamist parties that, among other things, expressed opposition to US policies scored considerable successes in national elections. The Justice and Development Party in Morocco doubled its share to forty-two seats in the September 2002 elections. In

October 2002, the Islamist movement came in third in Algerian local elections, and the alliance of religious parties in Pakistan won fifty-three out of 150 parliamentary seats. In November, Islamists won nineteen out of the total forty parliamentary seats in Bahrain, and the Turkish Justice and Development Party captured 66 percent of the legislature. These electoral victories, however, pointed less to a "revival of Islamism"[14] than to a shift of Islamism—from a political project with national concerns, into a more fragmented language concerned with personal piety and the global menace of antipathy toward Islam. If anything, we are on the threshold of a post-Islamist turn.[15]

Whatever its merit, a major legacy of Islamism has been to change the Arab states. It rendered the Arab states more religious (as they moved to rob Islamism of its moral authority), more nativist or nationalist (as they moved to assert their Arab authenticity and to disown democracy as a Western construct), and more repressive, since the liquidation of radical Islamists offered states the opportunity to control other forms of dissent. This legacy of the Islamist movements has further complicated the politics of dissent in today's Arab world.

A RENEWAL

The revival of the "Arab street" in 2002 in solidarity with the Palestinians was truly spectacular. For a short while, states lost their tight control, and publicly vocal opposition groups proliferated, even within the "Westernized" and "apolitical" student body at the American University in Cairo. The Palestinian solidarity movement showed that there is more to Arab street politics than Islamism, and spurred the renewal of a political tradition.

In January 2003, as the US moved closer to attacking Iraq, one million Yemenis marched in Sana'a, chanting, "The declaration of war is terrorism." Over 10,000 protested in Khartoum, thousands in Damascus and Rabat, and hundreds in the Bahraini capital of Manama.[16] Twenty thousand Christians in Jordan staged a prayer for the people of Iraq, condemning Bush's war.[17] One thousand Yemeni women demonstrated in the streets to protest the arrest of a Yemeni citizen mistaken for an al-Qaeda member in

---

14   See Reda Hilal, "Blowback: Islamization from Below," *al-Ahram Weekly*, November 21–27, 2002. See also 'Ali Abu al-Khayr, "Al-Islam al-Siyasi wa al-Dimuqratiyya," *al-Wafd*, February 15, 2003.

15   See Asef Bayat, *Making Islam Democratic: Social Movements and the Post-Islamist Turn* (Stanford, CA: Stanford University Press, 2007).

16   *Al-Hayat*, January 28, 2003.

17   *Al-Hayat*, February 15, 2003.

Germany.[18] Large and small protest actions against war on Iraq continued in Egypt and other Arab countries, amid massive deployments of police. And with the US–British invasion of Iraq, street protests throughout the Arab world assumed a new momentum.

At least with regard to Palestine, the tremendous rise of the Arab street occurred with the tacit approval of the Arab states. The extremity of Israel's violence during the 2002 invasions and the later invasion of Iraq by US forces brought the politicians and the people together in common nationalist sentiments. In addition, street dissent was directed largely against an outside adversary, and protesters' slogans against their own governments were voiced primarily by ideological leaders rather than ordinary participants.[19] Only in the later Cairo rallies of 2005 and 2006 did crowds demand the repeal of the thirty-year-old Emergency Law that continued to hamper public assembly, as well as an end to Husni Mubarak's presidency. These rallies then evolved into an explicitly pro-democracy movement led by Kifaya and other political groupings.

These movements came up against the state's intolerance of independent dissent. Since 2000 the authorities had ignored demands for collective protests against the US and Israel, while unofficial street actions faced intimidation and assault, with activists being harassed and detained.[20] On February 15, 2003, the day that over ten million people throughout the world demonstrated against the US war on Iraq, thousands of Egyptian riot police squeezed some 500 demonstrators into a corner, separating them from the public.

Faced with formidable challenges to expression in the street, Arab activists developed new means of articulating dissent, mostly in the form of civic campaigns encompassing boycotts, cyber-activism, and protest art. As the Arab states exercised surveillance over the streets, activism was pushed inside the confines of civil institutions—college campuses, schools, mosques, professional associations, and NGOs. Given the lack of a free political climate, professional associations offered venues for political campaigns, to the extent that they often assumed the role of political parties where intense competition for leadership prevailed. Their headquarters served as sites for political rallies, meetings, charity work, and international solidarity campaigns. Other civil associations, chiefly the new advocacy NGOs, began to promote public debates on human rights, democratization,

---

18   *Al-Hayat*, January 20, 2002.

19   In Arab countries other than Egypt, there was little evidence of demonstrators targeting their own governments' policies.

20   As reported by Human Rights Watch, in Egypt some eleven activists were detained by security agents in February 2003. *Cairo Times*, February 6–19, 2003.

women's and children's rights, and labor rights. In the early 2000s, some ninety to a hundred human rights organizations operated in the Arab world, along with hundreds of social service centers, and many more social service organizations that began to employ the language of rights in their work.[21]

Innovations in mobilization, styles of communication, and organizational flexibility brought a breath of fresh air to stagnant nationalist politics in the early 2000s. The Egyptian Popular Committee for Solidarity with the Palestinian Intifada represented one such trend. Set up in October 2000, the Committee brought together representatives from Egypt's various political trends—leftists, nationalists, Islamists, women's rights groups, and others. It set up a website, developed a mailing list, initiated charity collections, organized boycotts of American and Israeli products, revived street actions, and collected 200,000 signatures on petitions to close down the Israeli embassy in Cairo. The Egyptian Anti-Globalization Group and the National Campaign Against the War on Iraq, as well as the Committee for the Defense of Workers' Rights and some human rights NGOs, adopted similar styles of activism.[22] These organizations and their brand of mobilization served as the precursor for the emergence of a new kind of politics in Egypt, later galvanized by Kifaya and other pro-democracy movements.[23]

Grassroots charity, boycotts, and product campaigns became new mediums of political mobilization. Collecting food and medicine for Palestinians involved thousands of young volunteers and hundreds of companies and organizations. In April 2002, students at the American University in Cairo gathered thirty 250-ton truckloads of charitable products from factories, companies, and homes in the space of four days and nights, bringing them to Palestinians in Gaza. Millions of Arabs and Muslims joined in boycotting American and Israeli products, including McDonald's, KFC, Starbucks, Nike, and Coca-Cola. The remarkable success of local products caused Coca-Cola to lose some 20 to 40 percent of its market share in some countries, while fast-food companies also lost sales.[24] The Iranian Zamzam Cola captured a sizable Middle Eastern market; within four months, the company exported 10 million cans to Saudi Arabia and Persian Gulf states. Alongside Zamzam, Mecca Cola appeared in Paris to cater to European Arabs and Muslims who boycotted the US beverages. It sold 2.2 million

---

21   Interview with Fateh Azzam, coordinator of human rights program, Ford Foundation, Cairo, February 2003.
22   Hossam el-Hamalawy, "Closer to the Street," *Cairo Times*, February 6–19, 2003.
23   For an analysis of Kifaya and new democracy movements in Egypt, see Bayat, *Making Islam Democratic*, pp. 181–6.
24   *Payvan Iran News*, October 14, 2002; *Asia Times*, January 24, 2003; *al-Qahira*, January 7, 2003.

bottles in France within two months. Mecca Cola allocated 10 percent of its revenue to Palestinian children.

Information technology was also increasingly employed to mobilize political campaigns. "Small media" has a long history in the Middle East. The sermons of Islamic preachers like Sheikh Kishk, Yusuf al-Qaradawi, Sheikh Fadlallah, and the popular Egyptian televangelist 'Amr Khalid had been disseminated on a massive scale through audio and videocassettes. Followers of 'Amr Khalid, banned from preaching in late 2002, gathered over 10,000 signatures in his support via websites. Later, activists used emails to publicize claims and mobilize for rallies and demonstrations. These mediums proved instrumental in disseminating news, calling for rallies and street mobilization. In February 2003, the Egyptian Coalition in Solidarity with Palestine and Iraq planned to send 1 million petitions to the UN and the US and British embassies in Cairo, via the Internet.

Alternative news websites, social networking tools, and satellite television emerged as the most important means of forming networks of critical and informed constituencies. The increasing use of Facebook allowed Egyptian youth in 2008 to build what came to be known as the April 6 Movement. The "movement" mobilized some 70,000 mostly educated youths who called for free speech, economic welfare, and an end to corruption. Activists succeeded in organizing street protests and rallies and, more spectacularly, in initiating a general strike on April 6, 2008 in support of striking textile workers. Social networking has gained considerable ground in most Arab countries, where Facebook is among the ten most visited sites on the Internet.[25] In addition, satellite TV has been rapidly spreading in the Arab world, bringing alternative information to break the hold of the barren domestic news channels. The skyline of Damascus, bristling with satellite dishes, helps to explain the desolation of the street newsstands where the ruling party's dailies are displayed.

While cyber-campaigns still remain limited to the elite (despite increasing Internet use), the politics of the arts reaches a mass audience. The Israeli reoccupation of the West Bank in 2002 revived the political legacy of Egypt's Umm Kulthoum, Lebanon's Fairouz, and Morocco's Ahmad Sanoussi. Arab artists, movie stars, painters, and especially singers became oracles of public outrage. In Egypt, major pop stars such as 'Amr Diab, Muhammad Munir, and Mustafa Qamar produced best-selling albums that featured exclusively religious and nationalist lyrics. Muhammad Munir's high-priced single, "Land and Peace, O Prophet of God," sold 100,000 copies in a short period.

---

25   See Samantha Shapiro, "Revolution, Facebook-Style," *New York Times*, January 29, 2009.

Other singers, including 'Ali al-Hajjar, Muhammad Tharwat, and Hani Shakir, joined together to produce the religio-nationalistic album "Al-Aqsa, O God," which cornered Arab marketplaces.

The scope and efficacy of these new spaces of contention initially seemed modest. Yet attempts by most Arab governments to control them—closing NGOs, banning publications or songs, arresting web designers—offered a hint of their potential to overcome impediments facing the Arab street. The street remains the most vital locus for the audible expression of collective sentiments, so long as the local regimes or the global powers ignore popularly held views. As the revolutions of 2011 demonstrated, the Arab street was neither "irrational" nor "dead" in the preceding decade. Instead, it underwent a major transformation, caused both by old constraints and the new opportunities brought about by global restructuring. As a means and mode of expression, the Arab street shifted, becoming once more a powerful vehicle for the expression of collective grievances.

CHAPTER 8

Activist Dissent and Anti-War Protests in Egypt

Paul Schemm

Eight years before the momentous events of January 25, 2011, Egyptians occupied Tahrir Square in a protest that began over the US invasion of Iraq and soon turned into one against President Husni Mubarak and his regime. Like today's Tahrir protests, it featured a broad cross section of the opposition, from leftists to Islamists to young Western-educated liberals. In the end it failed, but many of those who protested in 2011 remembered occupying the square in 2003 and had learned the lessons. This time they didn't leave the square, so that they could not be picked off one by one in a campaign of arrests. Activists also had eight more years of sparring with the police. In 2011 they were helped by soaring food prices and rage over corruption that helped bring the rest of the country to their side after they made their stand in the square. The protests of 2003 were a beginning. One year later, Kifaya was formed, then came the brief political opening of the 2005 election year, followed by a renewed crackdown in 2006. In the dark years for street politics that followed, there was always the memory of the taking of the square in 2003.

For the second consecutive Friday, on March 28, 2003, thousands of Egyptians gathered at Cairo's al-Azhar mosque to voice their opposition to the US-led invasion and bombing of Iraq. But it was immediately apparent upon arrival at al-Azhar that the March 28 demonstration would be very different from the dramatic protests of the previous week. Riot police lined the streets leading to the thousand-year-old mosque, but the state deployed only token forces around the building itself, in contrast to the massive presence on the previous Friday. Instead of clubs and riot shields, anti-war cartoons drawn by some of Egypt's most famous caricaturists were arrayed in front of the mosque. Instead of police commanders, Muslim Brothers wearing badges issued by the "order committee" bustled around the street. Following noon prayers, a very orderly crowd of 10,000 marched out of the mosque away from downtown Cairo and dispersed peacefully within an hour. Three effigies with Halloween masks for heads bore the requisite Israeli, British, and American flags, but the protest leaders refrained from shouting slogans against the regime of President Husni Mubarak.

The previous weekend, Cairo had witnessed two days of protests like nothing seen since the 1970s, complete with a day-long occupation of the central Tahrir Square on Thursday and running battles between riot police and demonstrators trying to reach the square again on Friday. At times, security forces were overwhelmed; at times, they reacted savagely, beating protesters with their batons. The regime cracked down. By nightfall, Tahrir Square was like an armed camp. According to human rights groups, a massive campaign of arrests picked up 800 to 1,500 people—including two members of Parliament. Though some detainees were quickly released, Human Rights Watch verified that several were severely beaten while in custody, to the extent that many suffered broken arms. Even those protesters who got out of jail faced the prospect that their cases would be referred to Egypt's notoriously opaque State Security Courts.

But Mubarak's regime responded to anti-war sentiment in Egypt with more than repressive security measures and large-scale detentions. As the March 28 demonstration showed, the regime recognized the need to provide a state-sanctioned outlet for the growing rage over the US-led assault upon Iraq. Crowd control and specially printed placards were supplied by the Muslim Brothers, the officially outlawed party that was widely regarded as the strongest organized opposition to the nominally secular government. Brother cadres sporting black bandanas dotted the demonstrators' ranks, and yellow-sashed marshals periodically ordered sections of marchers to slow down. "Whenever the government is threatened by the street, it goes to the Brothers," commented veteran activist Muhammad Wakid.

TAKEOVER

The regime's twin strategies of repression and co-optation aimed to reduce the likelihood that the March 20 popular takeover of Tahrir Square in downtown Cairo would be repeated. Normally a snarl of honking traffic which pedestrians cross at the peril of death, the square belonged to the demonstrators on that day. For about twelve hours, they wandered almost bemused across its suddenly car-less expanse. "This is the first time we've made it out of the cage," said one jubilant activist. Riot police were present in vast numbers, but only on the edges of the square. They had surrendered the center, which was filled with some 3,000 people listening to speeches and chanting slogans.

The protest had originally been scheduled for 1 pm on "the day after America begins bombing," according to the e-mail and text messages circulated in advance. Events began early when a few hundred students from the tony American University in Cairo (AUC) made their way to the 'Umar Makram mosque on the far edge of the square, about as close to the US Embassy as anyone was allowed to go that day. The students were soon joined by a small contingent of Muslim Brothers who conducted a symbolic prayer overseen by their Supreme Guide Ma'moun al-Hudaybi. Security forces closely hemmed in what looked set to become the usual symbolic demonstration.

But the crowd managed to burst through the cordons toward the main square, where they met other groups of leftist and Nasserist activists. The result was a surprisingly ecumenical demonstration that featured the stylish AUC students, hardened activists, Islamists, and passersby. Aside from a few scuffles on the edges, the protest remained peaceful, as anti-regime slogans filled the air. "Mubarak! Leave! Leave!" chanted protesters. "'Alaa [Mubarak's son], tell your dad that millions hate him!" Other chants accused the Egyptian government of failing to take the long-term implications of the war in Iraq seriously. "Mubarak, wake up! Tomorrow the bombing will be in Bab al-Louq," demonstrators shouted, referring to a nearby neighborhood.

State security officers watching from the sidelines affirmed that they were allowing the anti-regime tenor of the demonstration, and that the seeming takeover of the square was in fact part of their plan to gather small, disparate demonstrations under their supervision. "Our policy is to collect them in one place and control them," one of them said. But several times throughout the day, hundreds of demonstrators broke off from the main group and marched down the streets toward the US embassy. When they encountered the cordons of riot police, they began tearing up pieces of pavement and throwing rocks, while chanting "Close down the embassy, take down the flag!" and "There is no god but God, and Bush is the enemy of God!" In the small side streets about a block from the embassy, the march was met with additional riot police and a water cannon. Eventually, the marchers were dispersed and allowed to rejoin the main demonstration, which continued to occupy the square until almost midnight.

RUNNING BATTLES

These confrontations were harbingers of the next day's events, when security forces locked down Tahrir Square with massive numbers of troops to prevent it from being occupied again. Instead, smaller roving groups of demonstrators ran through downtown, neither "collected" nor "controlled," and periodically clashed with police. The demonstration on March 21 began in Islamic Cairo at the al-Azhar mosque. Following a quick sermon by the state's leading cleric, Muhammad al-Sayyid Tantawi, in which he spoke vaguely about solidarity with the Iraqi people in the face of their hardships, the chants and slogans began immediately. Riot police immediately blocked the main doors and refused to allow worshippers to leave, trapping them in the small vestibule. Worshippers responded by breaking up furniture to trade blows with the batons of police and throw their shoes, all the while chanting, "With our blood and soul, we will sacrifice ourselves for Islam." In Egypt, that particular chant usually references Palestine or Baghdad.

While the melee at the mosque doors continued, however, bystanders gathered in clumps of vocal protest in the streets around the mosque. Soon, up to three distinct crowds waving banners and loudly denouncing the US invasion of Iraq—as well as the Egyptian regime—confronted police. The small groups were ruthlessly broken up with attack dogs and water cannons, sending individual demonstrators fleeing into the narrow alleys of the nearby market. Modifying a well-known chant at soccer games, onlookers chorused, "Stop! Look! Egyptian is beating Egyptian!" Eventually, one large group of several thousand protesters remained about 100 meters up the street from al-Azhar. After burning makeshift American and Israeli flags, they turned away from the security forces and headed toward downtown, approximately an hour away at a normal walking pace.

All the while, groups of police clashed with the marchers and herded them toward the wide European-style boulevards and squares that lead to Tahrir Square, close to the Nile River. The way to the square, however, was blocked and soon masses of angry youth were surging through downtown, crashing into one wall of riot troops after another. Several different groups converged on the Nile from different directions, and some 10,000 protesters spilled out of the downtown streets into the area just north of Tahrir Square between the Ramsis Hilton and the Egyptian Museum. There, the demonstrators overwhelmed units of riot police and set fire to a water truck busy reloading one of the water cannons. Marching along the Corniche, they stopped to torch the poster of Mubarak outside the ruling party headquarters and burn all the foreign flags outside the Nile Hilton. They even attempted to march on to the US Embassy, before being scattered by a massed phalanx of riot police. "Today wasn't like yesterday at all," said one activist, surveying the smoldering remnants of the water truck and the squads of police rounding up the remaining demonstrators. "Security was definitely not in control of the situation, because people were not willing to give up."

CRITICAL PERIOD PAST

Though the Mubarak regime was wary of all types of organized protest, it intervened most forcibly to channel popular anger over the Iraq war and other regional issues away from the government. Mubarak's own statement upon the outbreak of war on March 19 focused on Saddam Hussein's role in bringing Washington's wrath down upon his country. His statement provoked a response almost as rare as rioting in the capital, when twenty-six intellectuals signed a counter-statement in the Nasserist weekly *al-'Arabi*, blaming the war on US "colonialist aggression." Most of the signatories were sufficiently prominent not to fear reprisals, but nonetheless it was an unusual step for Egyptian intellectuals to contradict Mubarak directly in a major publication. Intellectuals, however, were not the ones to lead street demonstrations and already, a week after March 20–21, there was a sense that momentum was being lost.

"There is no continuity, there is no enlargement," said 'Abd al-Mun'im Sa'id, director of the al-Ahram Center for Political and Strategic Studies. "Obviously there is no core organization working with the demonstrations." If there had been, the authorities moved quickly to neutralize it, first by surrounding the Lawyers' Syndicate on March 21 and arresting activists inside, and then by going after well-known activists in their homes over the next few days. According to those involved in the protests, the opportunity to build on the spontaneous explosions of anger was squandered. Whether helped along by State Security intimidation or internal disarray or both, the critical period passed. "By being a little bit disillusioned and confused and not knowing what to do, the leadership decided to resort to conferences and seminars to figure out what to do," said one activist who preferred to remain anonymous.

MATURING STREET POLITICS

Still, the takeover of Tahrir Square and even the government-approved demonstration on March 28 were part of a slow expansion of the purview of Egyptian street politics—which had been moribund for most of the Mubarak era. Since the beginning of the second Palestinian *intifada* in September 2000, demonstrations (though often small and encircled by large security presences) had become an almost weekly feature of Egyptian life. Under Egypt's 1981 Emergency Law, repeatedly renewed under Mubarak, public assembly of any kind was prohibited. Occasional demonstrations were penned inside mosque or university premises. There was talk, however, at the Interior Ministry of allowing organizers to obtain permits for demonstrations, a measure never before discussed. Emad Shahin, professor of political science at AUC, considered the regularity of street protest itself a significant development. "The continuity of demonstrations will teach people," he says. "People are maturing politically."

Two weeks before the March 20–21 protests, while the government was holding its own rally to hail national unity, a little-noticed knot of 150 people protested the renewal of the Emergency Law half a block from the Parliament building. Traditionally, protests in Egypt have concerned regional politics, whether Israeli incursions into the Occupied Territories or sanctions and war upon Iraq. During Israel's major invasion of the West Bank in the spring of 2002, crowds in Cairo and Alexandria swelled the wave of pro-Palestinian protests across the Arab world. But the protesters on March 5 represented a public mobilization over a domestic political issue. The 150 activists were surrounded by twice as many riot police, with plainclothes officers on hand to prevent bystanders from joining in. Their numbers seemed insignificant compared to the hundreds of thousands bussed in by the ruling party to applaud the government, as well as to say a few words against the war in Iraq. But the explicitly anti-government message expressed outside Parliament—its fire directed at Mubarak and also at his son Gamal—probably could not have been heard in public a year previous.

The state was determined to stop nascent anti-government dissent in its tracks, as shown by the arbitrary campaign of arrests and the decision to co-opt protests emanating from al-Azhar by bringing in the Muslim Brothers. For their part, the Brothers were only too happy to raise their profile in society and do something to slow the relentless campaign of oppression against them. On February 27, the Brothers, together with a few other opposition parties, staged a rally of 140,000 at Cairo's main stadium that was markedly devoid of anti-government slogans, as was the procession starting at al-Azhar on March 28. Mubarak himself went out of his way in speeches to affirm that Egypt was not aiding George W. Bush's "coalition of the willing" in its war effort—something that crowds in the region, especially Syria, did not believe. Anti-war demonstrations were back within the relatively safe confines of university campuses, or were carefully orchestrated with the government's blessing. But as the war in Iraq dragged on—exactly what the Egyptian regime feared would happen—and anger grew at images of Iraqi casualties, street politics threatened to take over Cairo on subsequent occasions.

CHAPTER 9

The Working Class and the Popular Movement in Egypt

Joel Beinin

In the last decade of Husni Mubarak's rule, the longest and strongest wave of worker protest since the late 1940s rolled through Egypt. Beginning to swell in 1998, it spiked following the installation of the "government of businessmen" in July 2004 and that government's accelerated implementation of the neoliberal project. Some 3 million workers participated in 3,500–4,000 strikes, sit-ins, demonstrations, and other collective actions from 1998 to 2010, reaching over 600 per year in 2007 and 2008 (see Figure 9.1). Worker militancy remained high up to and through the 2011 revolutionary upsurge.

From their center of gravity in the textile sector, the strikes and protests spread to the makers of building materials, Cairo subway workers, bus drivers, garbage collectors, bakers, food processing workers, tax collectors, and many other blue-collar and white-collar workers, as well as doctors and other professionals. Like almost all strikes in Egypt since the 1950s, these work stoppages were "illegal"—unauthorized by the state-sponsored Egyptian Trade Union Federation (ETUF) and its national and local affiliates. But unlike strike waves in the mid-1980s and early 1990s, which were largely confined to state-owned industries, during the 2000s as many as 40 percent of protesting workers were employed in the private sector, where there were very few local trade union committees. This development was unprecedented in post-1952 Egyptian labor history.

Wildcat strikes and protests were frequently successful in bread-and-butter terms, winning higher wages and better working conditions or stopping proposed cutbacks. The government was eventually forced to raise the basic monthly minimum wage to £E 400 (about $70): wholly inadequate, but nearly four times the previous rate. However, the most important gains by workers in the period leading up to the revolution were political, with the establishment of four independent trade unions. These included the Independent General Union of Real Estate Tax Authority Workers in 2008, the largest of the four, followed by the General Union for Health Technicians, the Independent Teachers

Year	Strikes, Sit-ins, and Other Collective Actions			Number of Workers Involved
1998	114			
1999	164			
2000	135			
2001	115			
2002	96			
2003	86			
2004	266			386,346
2005	202			141,175
2006	222		222**	198,088
2007	614	(756+)*	692**	474,838
2008	609		447**	541,423
2009	432	(700+)*	478**	
2010	371	(484+)*		
TOTAL	3,426	(3,949+)		

Figure 9.1 Collective Labor Actions and Number of Workers Involved, 1998–2010

*LCHR considers a series of actions over a dispute in a workplace (a petition, a demonstration, then a strike) as one action. The larger figures in parenthesis (when available) count each individual action.

** Figures according to Khalid 'Ali 'Umar, 'Adil Wilyam, and Mahmud al-Munsi, 'Ummal misr, 2009 (Cairo, 2010), 17.

Source: Markaz al-Ard li-Huquq al-Insan (Land Center for Human Rights), Silsilat al-huquq al-iqtisadiyya wa'l-ijtima'iyya, no. 5 (December 1998); no. 14 (April 2000); no. 18 (May 2001); no. 22 (March 2002); no. 28 (March 2003); no. 31 (January 2004); no. 34 (July 2004); no. 35 (February 2005); no. 39 (August 2005); no. 42 (January 2006); no. 49 (July 2006); no. 54 (February 2007); no. 56 (July 2007); no. 58 (February 2008); no. 65 (March 2009); no. 75 (March 2010) no. 76 (May 2010); no. 79 (July 2010); no. 81 (August 2010); no. 84 (January 2011). Available at lchr-eg.org. These statistics should be considered approximations. For a more detailed version of the table see Joel Beinin, "A Workers' Social Movement on the Margin of the Global Neoliberal Order, Egypt 2004–2009," in Social Movements, Mobilization, and Contestation in the Middle East and North Africa, ed. Joel Beinin and Frédéric Vairel (Stanford, CA: Stamford University Press, 2011).

Union, and the Retired Workers Union in 2010. On January 30, 2011, with the historic Tahrir Square sit-in underway, these autonomous unions and representatives of workers from a dozen factory towns declared their intention to form a new trade union federation, independent of the ETUF, which had functioned as an arm of the state since it was established in 1957. This was the first attempt to establish a new institution based on the popular movement—itself a revolutionary act in a place like Mubarak's Egypt.

Throughout the long strike wave, many more workers became engaged in building democratic networks and practices in their workplaces, challenging the ETUF's monopoly on trade union organization by electing strike committees and other informal bodies to fill the vacuum created by ETUF functionaries' absence. These activities involving millions of workers and their families were the largest arena for democratic practices in Egypt, until the occupation of Tahrir Square. The workers' movement did not consciously aspire to topple Mubarak, though many despised him and especially his son Gamal (known derisively as "Jimmy"), the symbol of Egypt's neoliberal project. But as Khaled El-Khamissi, author of the best-selling novel *Taxi*, said: "There is continuity between those strikes and the 2011 revolution."

A DISTINCTION ERODES

On February 13, 2005, some twelve miles north of Cairo, 400 textile workers at the Qalyoub Spinning Company, a branch of the ESCO conglomerate, sat down on the job. They were protesting the government's sale of their mill to a private investor, because they believed private-sector management would not maintain the levels of wages and benefits they had achieved since ESCO, like most other significant Egyptian manufacturing firms, was nationalized in the early 1960s. The strike began because the government and company management failed to deliver on promises to provide an adequate early retirement package, won in response to a shorter ten-day strike in October 2004.

Washington, as well as Egypt's creditors at the International Monetary Fund and the World Bank, pushed for privatization of the public sector beginning with Mubarak's predecessor Anwar al-Sadat. Like Sadat, Mubarak feared social unrest, and delayed the recommended privatization measures for years before moving with relative vigor to sell off state-owned enterprises after 1991. Despite several bitter wildcat strikes, the state transferred over 100 factories into private hands between 1993 and 1999. In May 1999, IMF observers declared themselves satisfied that Egypt was finally heeding their advice. Sell-offs stalled in the early 2000s due to a recession, but regained momentum when "friends of Jimmy" assumed control of the government in July 2004. The sale of the ESCO Qalyoub Spinning Company exemplified the renewed push for privatization. Textiles, one of the largest and perhaps the most storied of Egyptian industries, were targeted. The state-owned textile sector had been in crisis since the 1970s, due to competition from East and Southeast Asia.

The first step in preparing firms for privatization is reduction of the labor force. The six ESCO mills employed some 24,000 workers in 1980; the rolls were subsequently reduced to 3,500 through a combination of attrition, hiring freezes, and early retirement packages. At ESCO's Bahtim facility, the administrative offices, garage, and spinning mill were sold to a private investor without any obligation on his part to employ the existing workers. The striking ESCO workers believed their seniority—many had spent twenty to thirty years in the mills—entitled them to keep their jobs rather than be replaced by new workers who would undoubtedly receive lower wages and benefits.

The strikers also believed the state was divesting itself of valuable assets at bargain-basement prices. Muhammad Gabr 'Abdallah, a night supervisor with twenty-eight years' seniority, explained that in 1999 the company was valued at £E 60 million. In 2003 the government invested £E 7 million in capital improvements, including computerized spindles. It then concluded a three-year lease agreement for £E 2.5 million per year with a businessman named Hashim al-Daghri, expecting that he would buy the mill. Before the lease expired, al-Daghri bought the mill for the steeply discounted price of £E 4 million.

The ESCO workers were highly conscious that their strike questioned the fundamental direction of the Mubarak regime's economic strategy. Not only were Gamal Mubarak and his entourage of US-educated economists and business tycoons intent on introducing more free-market policies, but in December 2004 Egypt also concluded a highly unpopular trade agreement with the US creating Qualifying Industrial Zones (QIZs). Any commodity produced in a QIZ whose assessed value includes 10.5 percent Israeli content receives duty-free and quota-free access to the US. Rashid Muhammad Rashid, the former minister of industry, attempted to parry nationalist criticisms of the agreement by claiming that QIZs would revitalize the struggling textile sector. Previously, various Special Economic Zones were created to attract investors with concessionary conditions of all sorts, including few or no unions.

Because of the political importance of the Qalyoub strike, activists from the Center for Trade Union and Workers' Services (CTUWS) in Helwan supported the workers. Journalists from *al-Ahali*, the weekly of the "legal left" Tagammu' Party, and the then left-leaning English-language *al-Ahram Weekly* wrote sympathetic accounts. In contrast, Ibrahim Nafie, chief editor of *al-Ahram*, made it known that he was not enthusiastic about covering the strike in the quasi-official Arabic-language daily. The workers received no backing whatsoever from the state-sponsored Federation of Spinning and Weaving Unions. Failing to stop the privatization of ESCO, they settled for a much larger early retirement package than they had initially been offered, though less than what others had received in the late 1990s.

The ESCO Qalyoub Spinning Company strike was emblematic of the mid-2000s wave in several respects: the workers' grievances were economic and specific to ESCO, but by no means parochial. Not only did workers in other textile mills and other industries across the country echo their grievances, but throughout Egypt workers, especially in recently privatized public enterprises, came to oppose the ravages of neoliberal policies even when they did not identify them as such. The ETUF bureaucracy, which in the 1980s and 1990s had sometimes foiled privatization and other neoliberal schemes through foot-dragging and passive resistance,[1] was now completely in the regime's pocket. Workers with grievances were thus forced to organize themselves for struggle. Even if they rarely targeted the regime itself, their self-organization and demands constituted a practical challenge to neoliberalism that began to efface the distinction between the "economic" and the "political."

AN AMBIVALENT OPPOSITION

This erosion occurred from the bottom up, through the experiences of workers themselves, rather than the interventions of the organized oppositional intelligentsia. That intelligentsia lacked the credibility and grassroots support to provide political leadership.

In the 1970s and 1980s, the "legal left" Tagammu' party was closely connected to workers, publicizing and offering material support to their struggles. It issued a workers' magazine and covered labor affairs regularly in the pages of its weekly *al-Ahali*. In addition, several independent workers' newspapers based on industrial regions or sectors were established.[2] During the 1990s the party lost most of its popular base, amidst a general retreat of leftist politics, because of the party's strategic decision to support the Mubarak regime in its battle against the Islamist insurgency based in southern Egypt and the urban slums of Cairo and Alexandria, and

---

1   See Marsha Pripstein Posusney, *Labor and State in Egypt* (New York: Columbia University Press, 1996).

2   Joel Beinin, "Will the Real Egyptian Working Class Please Stand Up?" in Zachary Lockman, ed., *Workers and Working Classes in the Middle East: Struggles, Histories, Historiographies* (Albany, NY: State University of New York Press, 1993), pp. 262–6.

eventually against the non-violent Muslim Brothers as well. This strategy was the brainchild of Tagammu' chief and former Communist Party leader Rif'at al-Sa'id. It was embraced by the underground Communist Party, some remnants of which work actively inside Tagammu'.

The rest of the Egyptian left embraced a more or less Nasserist perspective that effectively separated the "national question" and the "social question," even as they paid lip service to the organic link between the two. The result was the subjugation of the demands of labor and other social justice movements to the nationalist agenda of opposition to Western imperialism and Israel's dispossession of the Palestinians. There was a link, of course, between the strike wave and US domination of the Middle East in alliance with Israel, as the neoliberal program that sparked the strikes was heavily promoted by the Mubarak regime's US ally. But few opposition intellectuals were able to translate their slogans against Zionism and imperialism into concrete support for labor—the one social movement in Egypt with a mass base and a record of measurable victories.

The largest and best organized political opposition movement of the late Mubarak era, the illegal but semi-tolerated Muslim Brothers, adopted a two-faced policy toward labor. The Brothers have never had a strong base in the industrial working class. Indeed, they have a long history of breaking strikes and opposing militant trade union activity going back to the 1940s, when they clashed with communists in the textile center of Shubra al-Khayma, north of Cairo. In the 1980s and 1990s, the Brothers were allied with the so-called Labor Party in which 'Adil Husayn, a former communist who became an Islamist, was prominent. During this period, some Islamists spoke more frequently about the importance of "social justice." After Husayn's death in 2001, the Brothers reverted to their traditionally pro-business stance. Some Brothers verbally supported the mid-2000s spate of worker activism. There have long been differences between the affluent businessmen who dominate the leadership and rank-and-file members from the middle classes and working poor. Following the ouster of Mubarak, leading Brothers have repeated the imprecations of the SCAF and the state-run media against the "special-interest protests" (*ihtijajat fi'awiyya*) of discontented blue- and white-collar workers.[3]

The pro-business attitude of the Brothers is exemplified by Ahmad 'Abd al-'Azim Luqma, the former owner of the Egyptian–Spanish Asbestos Products Company (Ora Misr) in Tenth of Ramadan City, one of six satellite communities built by the state to ease population pressure in greater Cairo,

---

3   See Hesham Sallam, "Striking Back at Egyptian Workers," *Middle East Report* 259 (Summer 2011).

hosting a Special Economic Zone and a QIZ. In November 2004 Luqma, who was known as a member of the Brothers, closed the factory and fired all his workers after the Ministry of Manpower and Migration fined him for health code violations. Luqma absconded without paying the legally required severance pay. The workers won some of their severance pay after a ten-month campout at the factory and in front of ETUF headquarters.

The historical record did not deter the Mubarak regime from trying to discredit militant workers by tying them to the Brothers. In March 2007, and again in April, nearly half of the 12,000 workers at Arab Polvara Spinning and Weaving in the coastal city of Alexandria went on strike. It had been a fairly successful enterprise privatized in the first tranche of the public-sector sell-off during the mid-1990s. When it became less profitable, workers struck to protest discrimination between workers and managers in the allocation of shares when the company was privatized; failure to pay workers dividends on their shares; and the elimination of paid sick leave and a paid weekend. The demands of the Arab Polvara workers indicated that public-sector workers were correct to suspect that, even if privatized firms initially offered pay and benefits similar to those in the public sector (in some cases, the pay is higher), the requirements of competing in the international market would eventually drive down wages and worsen working conditions. Moreover, private-sector workers lacked even the weak institutional mechanism of the ETUF to contest the unilateral actions of private capital.

The government charged the Muslim Brothers with inciting the Arab Polvara strike, but there was no evidence that they played any role in this or any other labor action of the period. The Brothers' occasional pro-labor interventions appeared to be rooted in political expediency rather than conviction. In February 2007, Muslim Brother MP 'Abd al-'Aziz al-Husayni announced his backing for the walkout of Misr Spinning and Weaving workers in Kafr al-Dawwar, south of Alexandria. His parliamentary colleague Sabir Abu al-Futouh, from Alexandria, followed up by issuing several statements on a Brother-sponsored website supporting the Arab Polvara strike. Earlier, Abu al-Futouh had coordinated the Brothers' campaign to run candidates in the fall 2006 trade union elections. The government disqualified thousands of Muslim Brothers, leftists, and independents from running in those elections—consequently judged "undemocratic and non-transparent" by independent observers. Abu al-Futouh had declared that if the elections were rigged, the Muslim Brothers would establish a trade union independent of the regime, similar to the independent student unions they founded in cooperation with the Trotskyist Revolutionary Socialist group at several universities.

Yet in November 2006, after the first rounds of voting were over and their undemocratic character was apparent, the Brothers' Deputy General Guide Muhammad Habib (who has since resigned from the organization) sounded more reserved. In an interview at the American University of Cairo, Habib said: "Establishing an independent labor union requires a long period of consistent organizing. Workers are different than students because they have family responsibilities and will not lightly risk their livelihoods."

The Alexandrian Brothers are generally considered more militant, more confrontational toward the regime, and closer to the popular classes than the organization's other branches. Even if Abu al-Futouh was serious in his initiative, however, it was spurned by the Nasserists and the Tagammu', who rejected an alliance with the Islamists.[4] Nowhere were Muslim Brothers involved in setting up trade union structures on the ground.

THE MILITANCY OF MAHALLA AL-KUBRA

The more political dimension of the workers' movement—the demands for trade union independence and a national minimum wage—grew out of two large strikes by the 24,000 workers of the Misr Spinning and Weaving Company in Mahalla al-Kubra. In the final week of September 2007, for the second time in less than a year, they went on strike—and won. As they had the first time, in December 2006, the workers occupied their mammoth textile mill and rebuffed the initial mediation efforts of the ruling National Democratic Party (NDP). Yet this strike was even more militant than in 2006. Workers established a security force to protect the factory premises, and threatened to occupy the company's administrative headquarters as well. Most important, the Mahalla workers scored a huge victory that reverberated throughout the Egyptian textile industry and beyond. After halting production for less than a week, they won a bonus equivalent to ninety days' pay, payable immediately. In addition, a committee was formed in the Ministry of Investment to negotiate increases in extra compensation for the hazardous nature of their work, and clothing allowances. Incentive pay was linked to basic pay and subject to a 7 percent annual increase. The executive board of the company was dissolved, and the hated CEO, Mahmoud al-Gibali, was sacked. The days of the strike were considered a paid vacation.

The strike in Mahalla al-Kubra was impelled by unfulfilled promises made at the conclusion of its December 2006 antecedent. At that time, workers said they would accept annual bonuses equal to forty-five days'

---

4   *Al-Masry al-Youm*, November 12, 2006.

pay, rather than the two months' pay they had been promised the previous March. In exchange, Minister of Investment Mahmoud Muhi al-Din agreed that if the firm earned more than £E 60 million in profit in the fiscal year that ended in June, then 10 percent of that profit would be distributed among the employees. Egyptian statistics being malleable, it is possible to say only that Misr Spinning and Weaving reaped somewhere between £E 170 and 217 million of profit in the 2006 fiscal year. Consequently, workers claimed that they were due bonuses equal to about 150 days' pay. But they had received only the equivalent of twenty. They also demanded increases in their clothing allowances and production incentives. Finally, the workers contended that al-Gibali took extravagant trips abroad, a manifestation of the corruption and mismanagement that squandered the company's resources. The workers were acutely aware that this was their money, since Misr Spinning and Weaving is the flagship public-sector firm in Egypt. "Save us! These thieves robbed us blind! (*Ilhaquna! Al-haramiyya saraquna!*)" read one placard held aloft before the cameras.

The underlying economic grievance of the strike was that the standard of living of most workers, along with civil servants and others (to say nothing of the unemployed and marginally employed), was deteriorating sharply because of punishing inflation. The formerly "Arab socialist" government still subsidized bread and gasoline, whose prices were therefore subject to a measure of central control. But even with "the market" determining most of the cost of living, prices tended to rise on a predictable timetable. Modest upticks in the summer were conventional and generally uncontroversial, because the millions working in the public sector received their annual raises in July. But the 2007 round of price increases came after a period of annual inflation rates as high as 12 percent (according to government sources; unofficial estimates are typically considerably higher). In September, the Central Agency for Public Mobilization and Statistics announced that the price of food had risen 12.4 percent on an annual basis. Fresh vegetables, which are cultivated in abundance throughout the country, led the list with an astounding 37.6 percent increase. The impact of these price hikes was exacerbated because Muslims were then celebrating the holy month of Ramadan.

As in the past, government mouthpieces claimed that the Mahalla workers were "incited" to action by the Muslim Brothers and other opposition political parties. This charge was baseless. When representatives of the regime-sponsored National Council for Human Rights visited Mahalla to investigate, several workers displayed their NDP membership cards. Strike leaders repeatedly said that theirs was a workers' movement and that the opposition parties had nothing to do with it. Opposition to the regime primarily took the form of opposition to the ETUF. The Mahalla workers renewed their call for impeaching the local union committee, which reported to the ETUF and sided with the regime and company management throughout 2006 and 2007. ETUF representatives were less than useless in the September strike. The head of the local factory committee resigned after he was beaten by workers and taken to the hospital. ETUF Secretary-General Husayn Mugawir announced that he would not visit Mahalla until the crisis was resolved.

As with many of the work stoppages of the 2000s wave, the immediate causes of the Misr Spinning and Weaving workers' discontent were local and economic: unpaid bonuses and charges of venality on the part of management. But the Mahalla workers' leadership understood the national and political implications of their struggle, although they usually refrained from saying this publicly. By challenging the economic policies of the Mubarak regime, they undermined its political legitimacy. In this challenge, they received the support of not only the bulk of the population of Mahalla, but also workers from the textile mills of Delta towns Kafr al-Dawwar and Shibin al-Kom, railway workers, and urban intellectuals.

One group of urban sympathizers was the Kifaya movement, the loose coalition of liberals, leftists, and human rights activists, most of them middle-class, which had sprung onto Egypt's political scene in 2004 and 2005. Kifaya activists had marched in the streets of Cairo chanting "Enough!" to Egypt's draconian Emergency Law, rampant corruption, and—most daringly—the increasingly arbitrary reign of the Mubarak clan. Creative and courageous in rhetoric and tactics, Kifaya had attracted considerable sympathy in Egypt and a great deal of positive media coverage in the West. Its core demand for "change" spawned a host of imitators, from Physicians for Change to Teachers for Change. But the group proved largely unable to mobilize effectively after the end of the Lebanon war in August 2006—and part of the reason was its lack of a wide social base. Its labor connections were slim, for instance: the few candidates from its labor affiliate Workers for Change who were not banned by the security forces from running in the fall 2006 union elections performed poorly.

In early September 2007, the Kifaya movement was proclaimed "clinically dead" in the pages of the independent daily *al-Badil* (now shuttered). But the events in the Delta mills brought Kifaya activists back into the streets, as they demonstrated in solidarity with the Mahalla workers on the evening of September 27. Some 150 activists were jammed against the front doors of the Journalists' Syndicate by uniformed riot police and the plainclothes thugs of State Security. They were not permitted to leave until late in the night, a new tactic in the regime's creative efforts to intimidate opposition of any sort. Several thousand security personnel of various stripes were deployed throughout downtown Cairo for the occasion, one of several indications that the State Security apparatus, the ultimate authority in Egypt, had lost all sense of proportion.

Back in Mahalla al-Kubra, the workers remained barricaded in the hulking mill. Eight strike leaders were arrested on the third day of the action. The sympathetic local police released them two days later to thunderous chants of approval from their colleagues. But the compromise proposal of an immediate payment of a forty-day bonus they presented to the strikers was derisively rejected. The leaders, who may have been compelled to make this offer as a condition of their release, then announced that the strike would continue indefinitely. There was broad support for a long and militant struggle, the threat of which brought ETUF head Mugawir (breaking his earlier pledge) and company officials to the negotiating table in Mahalla, according to a statement released by the Workers' Coordination Committee. Such high-level negotiations could not have occurred except at the behest of State Security.

No doubt the political implications of the strike worried the state as much as the millions of dollars which company managers claimed to be losing every day it ground on. Muhammad al-'Attar, an arrested strike leader who was in contact with the Cairo-based CTUWS, was also a key organizer of the March petition drive to impeach the local union committee, which the ETUF ignored. On September 27, after he had been released from jail, al-'Attar told the *Daily News Egypt*:"We want a change in the structure and hierarchy of the union system in this country . . . The way unions in this country are organized is completely wrong, from top to bottom. It is organized to make it look like our representatives have been elected, when really they are appointed by the government."

MOMENTUM BUILDS

Scorned by the ETUF, more workers had begun to raise the demand for independent trade unions. In early February 2007, strikers at the Shibin al-Kum Spinning and Weaving Company echoed the Mahalla workers' call for mass resignations from the ETUF.[5] Workers in Kafr al-Dawwar and other localities also adopted the idea of independent trade unions.

A landmark day was April 15, 2007, when a delegation of one hundred workers from Misr Spinning and Weaving in Mahalla al-Kubra

---

5   Mohamed El-Sayed Said, "Silent No More," *al-Ahram Weekly*, February 8–14, 2007.

planned a trip to Cairo to submit the resignation of 13,000 of their colleagues at ETUF headquarters and announce their intention to establish an independent union. Security forces aborted the trip: police first confiscated the license of the driver of the bus the workers had hired, and then physically blocked the workers from boarding a Cairo-bound train. Some of the Mahalla leaders contacted leftist activists in Cairo to ask for their support that day. While the demand for a representative and independent trade union appears modest and "apolitical," it struck at one of the most important repressive institutions of the regime—the ETUF. The regime understood the implications, and refused to budge. The Mahalla workers have still not been able to establish an independent union. Because of the enormous economic and symbolic significance of their enterprise, they remain heavily supervised by security officials, even after the ouster of Mubarak. Their April 15, 2007 action, however, moved the question of independent unions to the top of the agenda for militant workers and their supporters.

This idea had circulated among trade unionists for over a decade, and was supported in principle by many progressives. Among them were the CTUWS and its general director, Kamal 'Abbas; veteran trade union organizers like Sabir Barakat; labor lawyer Khalid 'Ali 'Umar, now director of the Egyptian Center for Economic and Social Rights; the prominent independent socialist 'Abd al-Ghaffar Shukr; and others. The seeds of independence had been planted, among white-collar employees as well as among blue-collar workers. Ultimately, it was not abstract ideas about the virtues of self-organization that persuaded workers to take this dramatic step, but the experience of victory through protracted solidarity against a hostile regime.

In December 2007, 3,000 municipal real estate tax collectors occupied the street in front of the Ministry of Finance building in Cairo for eleven days. They won a 325 percent salary increase; and their action led, one year later, to creating the first independent trade union since the government-controlled ETUF was established in 1957. "Our union was born in the womb of our strike," said the tax collectors' union president, Kamal Abu Eita.[6] It proved difficult to replicate the tax collectors' success among industrial workers. But activist elements in the labor movement were encouraged to think big. Amidst the revolutionary fervor of early 2011, dozens of new independent unions were established, and many have affiliated with the Egyptian Federation of Independent Trade Unions. By the day of Mubarak's resignation, there were banners in Tahrir Square proclaiming: "The Federation

---

6   Lauren Geiser, "Egyptian Labor Activists Assess Their Achievements," *Middle East Report* 256 (Fall 2010).

of Independent Trade Unions Demands an End to the Regime."

The appearance of these banners showed that the strike wave had opened an important channel of communications between several groups of workers and radical activists in Cairo. Left-wing labor journalists had courageously covered strikes and protests, sleeping in factories or workers' homes. By 2008 there were solidarity trips, especially to Mahalla al-Kubra in the central Nile Delta, and mobilizations of material aid for strikes. But, until the heady days of 2011, only a few dozen workers ever participated in events organized by leftist groups in Cairo.

The aspirations and limits of the urban intelligentsia were demonstrated on April 6, 2008, when the workers of Mahalla al-Kubra announced they would strike in support of the demand for a national monthly minimum wage of £E 1,200 (about $205). State Security authorities repressed the Mahalla strike and co-opted some of the worker leaders. A more ambitious plan for a general strike never got off the ground, though it was promoted by many leftists. Overenthusiastic opposition newspapers published headline stories announcing its success. In anticipation of a broad strike, Israa Abdel Fattah established a Facebook group calling on people to stay home on April 6. She received 65,000 "likes," but there is no way to measure how many stayed home. Israa retreated from politics after she was detained for two weeks. But her initiative eventually morphed into the April 6 Youth Movement, a prominent group among those who called for the demonstration of January 25, 2011, which led to the ouster of Mubarak eighteen days later. April 6 members and supporters are largely upper middle class, and most of them initially opposed linking the "national" demand for regime change to the "economic" demands of workers. It was not until June 2011 that April 6 and other liberal revolutionaries began to raise slogans like "the poor first" or "a national minimum and a national maximum wage."

The worker protests had begun to raise the latter demand in the spring of 2010. Supported by NGOs like the CTUWS and the recently established Egyptian Center for Economic and Social Rights, a growing number of workers coalesced around the demand for a national monthly minimum wage of £E 1,200 first advanced by workers at Misr Spinning and Weaving in Mahalla al-Kubra in 2008. The demand was revived when Nagi Rashad, a worker at the South Cairo Grain Mill and a leading figure in the workers' protest movement, sued the government over its 2008 decision not to increase the national minimum wage. The basic monthly minimum wage, equivalent to about $6.35 at the current exchange rate, was established in 1984. With cost of living increases, it reached nearly $25 in 2008. Khalid 'Ali was the lead attorney on Rashad's case. On March 30, 2010, he won an administrative court ruling ordering the president, the prime minister and the National Council for Wages to set a "fair" minimum wage reflecting the current cost of living.

Bonuses and supplements to the basic wage—if they are paid—make it difficult to calculate actual wages precisely. But the wages of most Egyptian workers are inadequate to pay for food, clothing, shelter, and education. Even with two wage earners, the typical monthly wage of textile workers, which ranges from $45–107 per month, is below the World Bank's poverty line of $2 per day for the average Egyptian family of 3.7 people. According to the World Bank, nearly 44 percent of Egyptians are "extremely poor" (unable to meet minimum food needs), "poor" (unable to meet basic food needs), or "near-poor" (able to meet basic food needs, but not much more).

On April 3, 2010, workers rallied in Cairo while a delegation sought to present to cabinet members a copy of the court ruling ordering the government to implement a minimum wage. After cabinet representatives refused to meet with them, they called another demonstration to support a national monthly minimum wage of £E 1,200 for May 2. Hundreds of workers gathered in downtown Cairo that day, demanding that the government implement the court order. They were confronted by a massive deployment of security forces attempting to intimidate them.

Protesters chanted, "A fair minimum wage, or let this government go home" and "Down with Mubarak and all those who raise prices!" Khalid 'Ali told the press, "The government represents the marriage between authority and money—and this marriage needs to be broken up." Workers brought this understanding of the marriage between authority and money to Tahrir Square in January–February 2011. While many liberal youth opposed this idea then, it became more popular after late June 2011 as more people understood that the ruling SCAF was not a neutral institution.

LESSONS OF STRUGGLE

Workers' collective actions in the 2000s usually targeted bread-and-butter issues—the failure of owners of newly privatized enterprises to abide by the terms of the contracts in force before privatization, as the law requires; failure to pay long-overdue bonuses, incentives, and other wage supplements; failure of public enterprises to pay workers their share of profits; fear of large-scale firings before or after privatization; and low wages. Many observers wondered if or when workers might raise "political" demands. In an autocracy, however, organizing large numbers of people outside state strictures is in itself a political act.

At the appropriate moment, workers did not hesitate to fuse economic and political demands as conventionally understood. On February 9, 2011,

Cairo transport workers went on strike and announced that they would be forming an independent union. According to Hossam el-Hamalawy, a well-informed blogger and labor journalist, their statement also called for abolishing the emergency law in force for decades, removing the NDP from state institutions, dissolving the Parliament fraudulently elected in 2010, drafting a new constitution, forming a national unity government, prosecuting corrupt officials, and establishing a basic national minimum wage of £E 1,200 a month. As Mubarak's time in office ran out, similar strikes mushroomed all over Egypt, in the populous mill towns of the Nile Delta, the oil and fertilizer facilities of Suez, the sugar refineries of the southern provinces, and numerous other industrial plants, not to mention the workplaces of white-collar employees. Although there is not yet a credible insider account of Mubarak's last days, it seems plausible that the renewed militancy of the working class was a key factor convincing the army to push the octogenarian dictator to the exit.

In the 2000s, unlike in the 1980s and 1990s, the government did not routinely repress workers' protests by massive violence, including shooting strikers dead. The cumulative effect of the workers' movement taught millions of Egyptians that it was possible to win something through collective, action and that the regime, perhaps because it feared scaring away foreign capital, would likely respond with only limited repression.

In March 2011, the SCAF banned demonstrations and strikes that "disrupted production" and called for calm. Nonetheless, thousands of workers, including ambulance drivers, airport and public transport workers, and even police, took to the streets, demanding higher pay, three days after Mubarak's resignation. Since their unions do not represent them adequately, and they are not a party to the negotiations with the generals over Egypt's political future, street protest is the only vehicle workers have for asserting their demands. The extent to which workers and others remain mobilized and willing to take to the streets may determine the extent to which popular aspirations for democracy and social justice are realized.

CHAPTER 10

The Wall Mubarak Built

Ursula Lindsey

In late December 2009, Arab TV channels aired footage of throngs of demonstrators, surrounded by the usual rows of riot police, on the streets of downtown Cairo and in front of foreign embassies. Street protests in Egypt had been sharply curtailed in the preceding few years, but the scene was familiar to anyone who had been in the country in 2005, when protests against President Husni Mubarak's regime and in favor of judicial independence were a semi-regular occurrence. Yet there was something unusual about these protesters: they were all foreigners.

The demonstrators were Palestine solidarity activists from forty-three countries, and they had come to Egypt planning to cross the Egyptian-controlled Rafah gate into Gaza and participate in the Gaza Freedom March, a peaceful procession to the border of the tiny coastal strip with Israel. The march was scheduled to commemorate the anniversary of Operation Cast Lead—the winter 2008–09 Israeli military assault that, according to Amnesty International, killed some 1,400 Palestinians in Gaza—and to protest the ongoing international blockade of the territory.

But the international activists, who started arriving in Cairo on December 27, found that the Egyptian authorities had no intention of letting them into Gaza. Bus companies that had been hired to transport the would-be marchers to Rafah were told by State Security to cancel their agreements; activists who made their way to the Sinai Peninsula on their own were turned back or detained.

Hence, the protests. Several hundred French activists headed to the French Embassy, where they briefly blocked traffic, and then staged a five-day sit-in on the sidewalk. Americans tried to reach the US Embassy, but were held up by Egyptian security forces and eventually allowed to enter in small groups to confer—fruitlessly—with State Department personnel. The activists also took more creative tacks. Giant Palestinian flags and banners were unfurled on three separate occasions on the steps of the Pyramids. About thirty people undertook a hunger strike, led by an eighty-five-year-old Holocaust survivor, Hedy Epstein.

The Egyptian authorities finally offered to let one hundred of the 1,400 internationals into Gaza. On the morning of December 31, after bitterly contentious meetings and a fair amount of soul-searching, eight-five activists departed; the rest rejected the offer, seeing it as a shallow public relations maneuver antithetical to the march's fundamental demand: free access to Gaza.

Those still in Cairo held a vigorous, day-long rally in Tahrir Square—where the revolutionary sit-ins of 2011 were to take place—and, later, a candlelit New Year's Eve vigil. The demonstrators held signs that read "Free Gaza" in English; they alternated chants of "Resistance," "Viva Palestina," "We are not afraid," and—in a reproach to the Egyptian police—"Shame on you!" They were hemmed in by large contingents of State Security forces, who shooed away curious passersby and aggressively discouraged media coverage.

Then, a few days after the Gaza Freedom Marchers left Egypt, another convoy of internationals going by the name Viva Palestina—made up of hundreds of volunteers and vehicles delivering medical aid—reached the Sinai port of al-'Arish. They entered Gaza on January 6, after clashes with police left fifty activists injured.[1] A Palestinian protest at the border in support of the convoy also turned violent, leaving one Egyptian border guard dead and several Palestinians wounded.

The rallies and aid delegations took place a few weeks after the discovery that the Egyptian authorities had commenced building a subterranean steel wall along the border with Gaza, in order to block the tunnels that Gazans were using to undercut the international embargo upon their territory. Quickly dubbed "the wall of death" by Hamas officials and "the wall of shame" by Egyptian critics, this latest measure to enforce the blockade of Gaza sparked a heated round of recriminations in Egypt and the Arab world. The debate over the barrier, the foreign protesters in Cairo, the clashes near the Gaza border—all this hubbub focused renewed, intense, and, as far as the Mubarak regime was concerned, unwelcome attention on Egypt's policies toward the besieged Palestinian enclave.

THE SIEGE

Gaza has been under one degree or another of "closure" since the outbreak of the second *intifada* in the fall of 2000, but Israel and its allies imposed an import embargo after Hamas won the Palestinian parliamentary elections in 2006. The blockade was tightened considerably in June 2007, after Hamas fighters seized the Palestinian Authority (PA) security and administrative apparatus in Gaza from loyalists of the rival Fatah faction. Israel

---

1   See an activist's diary republished by the *Palestine Telegraph*, January 19, 2010, available online at: paltelegraph.com/opinions/diaries.

permits only a very restricted list of items to pass through the crossings it controls; most construction materials, much needed to repair the damage of Cast Lead's bombardments, are not allowed. In 2010, UN agencies estimated that at least half of all Gazans were suffering from "food insecurity."

The blockade of Gaza as it existed in the late 2000s would not have been possible without Egyptian cooperation. After Israeli soldiers left Gaza in 2005, the Bush administration sponsored a deal whereby the Rafah crossing—the only gateway to Gaza not on the Israeli border, and hence no longer physically controlled by Israel—would be jointly monitored by Egypt and the Presidential Guard of the PA. In practice, Egypt and the PA continued to accept Israeli remote control of the crossing via closed-circuit television. When Hamas ousted the Presidential Guard in 2007, Egypt closed Rafah, claiming that it could not enforce an agreement one of whose parties was absent.[2] Palestinian people and goods were allowed to cross Rafah only sporadically from that time until May 2011, when Egypt's post-revolution government announced a "permanent" reopening.

In January 2008, Hamas militants blew up part of the long-standing wall aboveground along the Egypt–Gaza boundary, and hundreds of thousands of Palestinians streamed into the Egyptian town of Rafah. For eleven days, until the Egyptians were able to seal the border again, the inhabitants of Gaza went on a joyful shopping spree, leaving the shelves of Rafah stores bare. Otherwise, Gaza weathered the blockade thanks to the tunnels, through which Palestinians smuggled food, cigarettes, fuel, and—allegedly—drugs, cash, and weapons. According to the director of the UN Relief Works Agency, in 2009 60 percent of Gaza's economy depended on the tunnels.[3]

THE "ENGINEERING INSTALLATIONS"

The new wall whose construction the Mubarak regime authorized was intended to cut off these underground lifelines. Construction was first reported by the highbrow Israeli daily *Haaretz*, in an article stating that the wall would be more than five miles long, driving steel panels down to 100 feet below the surface.[4] Some claimed the barrier would be connected to pipes that would saturate the ground along the border with pumped-in seawater, thus rendering the tunnels liable to collapse. It was also widely reported

---

2   See Gisha/Physicians for Human Rights–Israel, *Rafah Crossing: Who Holds the Keys?* (Tel Aviv, March 2009), pp. 23–38.

3   *Islam Online*, December 17, 2009.

4   *Haaretz*, December 9, 2009.

that the wall was being built with American assistance; US Embassy officials said that while the US Army Corps of Engineers provides Egypt with continuous assistance in securing its border, they were not directly involved in the construction of the barrier.

Egyptian officials justified the construction of what they preferred to call "engineering installations" or "reinforcements" with a national security argument: Egypt as a sovereign state has a right and a duty to protect its borders. The tunnels were a threat—the terrorists who carried out the attacks in the Sinai resorts Taba and Sharm el-Sheikh were believed to have come through them. And the drugs, cash, and weapons that purportedly flowed into Gaza might have been leaking into Egypt as well. Appearing on national TV on January 24, 2010, Minister of Interior Habib al-'Adli gave an analogy "for the simple citizen," asking: "Should I leave the door of my house open all night when the kids and the wife are inside? Where's my sense of patriotism, my sense of loyalty to my house?"[5]

Furthermore, Egyptian officials continuously pointed out, Israel and Hamas were the ones truly responsible for the situation. Gaza remained under Israeli occupation in the eyes of international law and Israel could lift the siege immediately; Hamas made the plight of Gazans worse by removing the Presidential Guard, firing rockets into Israel, hence provoking further tightening of the siege, and resisting Egypt's attempts to broker a reconciliation with the office of Mahmoud Abbas, who lays continued claim to the PA presidency despite the expiration of his term in 2009.

On the other hand, the Egyptian government's critics maintained that even genuine security concerns and treaty constraints could not justify its participation in a blockade that contravened international human rights law. Mohammed ElBaradei, the former head of the International Atomic Energy Agency and a possible candidate in post-Mubarak presidential elections, told a *Foreign Policy* interviewer that at the same time as they fought to prevent smuggling, Egyptian authorities could have established a "free trade zone" in the town of Rafah, noting that "there is a difference between protecting national security, which no one questions, and providing humanitarian assistance." Others doubted the sincerity of the Mubarak-era Foreign Ministry's efforts to achieve Hamas–Fatah reconciliation, a feeling that seems well-founded given the speed with which Egyptian diplomats secured a deal (albeit a tentative one) after Mubarak fell.

---

5   *Daily News Egypt*, January 26, 2010.

In the Egyptian and pan-Arab press, the Mubarak regime was accused of being a tool of the Israelis and the Americans, enforcing the blockade on their behalf. Certainly, Israel and the US pressured Egypt for years to "crack down" on smuggling, and, in 2008, Congress threatened to withhold $100 million in aid over this issue. And certainly Egypt's cooperation in maintaining the siege was part of what made the Mubarak regime a valuable US strategic partner. Perhaps not coincidentally, criticism from Washington of Egypt's human rights record and its illiberal political system was remarkably muted after the 2007 closure of Rafah. And in 2010 Egypt won two important concessions from the United States: part of its aid package was to be put into an endowment (which makes it harder for Congress to make the aid conditional on particular reforms); and on December 30, it was announced that Egypt would acquire at least twenty new F-16 fighter jets from US manufacturers.

Yet one should not discount the Mubarak regime's internal reasons for backing the blockade. The regime mistrusted Hamas, an armed militant Islamist group that it considered both an Iranian proxy and an ally of the Egyptian Muslim Brothers, its largest and best-organized opposition.

And the Egyptian government feared becoming Gaza's main opening to the outside world, and being further embroiled in the management of the troublesome, impoverished, and crowded enclave. Such involvement might have facilitated Israeli plans to separate the West Bank from Gaza, or Hamas's supposed ambitions to establish an independent "Islamic emirate," wrote one pro-regime intellectual.[6] These concerns were perhaps not unjustified. Egypt controlled the Gaza Strip from 1948 to 1967, and there are still some in Israeli and American policy circles who would like to hand the area back; meanwhile, the ongoing rift between the Western-recognized PA in the West Bank and Hamas in Gaza was leading to talk of a "three-state solution."

The Egyptian authorities viewed Hamas-ruled Gaza as a serious security threat, a potential destabilizer of the entire Sinai Peninsula. The construction of the subterranean wall was the culmination of a decades-long process of Egyptian disengagement from the Palestinian cause and growing security cooperation with Israel—a process that was given one last dramatic push by Hamas's election. The official line that Egypt sacrificed enough for Palestine from 1948 to the 1979 Camp David agreement struck a chord with some

---

6 Abdel-Moneim Said, "Défendre l'Egypte contre toute menace," *al-Ahram Hebdo*, January 6-12, 2010.

Egyptians. Yet many, across the political spectrum, were deeply uncomfortable with the shift in policy that had turned the Palestinians from historical "brothers" into something like enemies. "Egyptian security doctrine has come—incomprehensibly—to consider Gaza and not Israel the main threat to Egypt," wrote Ahmad Yusuf Ahmad.[7] Similarly, the columnist Fahmi Huwaydi remarked that Egypt's "strategic vision has changed, and Egypt has come to reckon the Palestinians and not the Israelis a danger. And if this sad conclusion is correct, then I cannot avoid describing the steel wall . . . as a wall of shame."[8]

FROM HIGH DAM TO LOW WALL

Within days of the announcement of the construction of the underground wall, people across the Arab world ventured unfavorable comparisons between Mubarak's "engineering installations" and President Gamal Abdel Nasser's landmark project—the High Dam north of Aswan—playing on the double meaning of the words for "high" and "low" in Arabic. Wags suggested adding a comment upon Mubarak to Nasser's epitaph: "The highly esteemed one (al-ʿali) built the High Dam (al-sadd al-ʿali); the low-down one (al-wati) built the Low Wall (al-sadd al-wati)."

Egypt's standing in the Arab and Islamic world has long been partly linked to its role as a patron of the Palestinian cause in the era of Nasser. In the late Mubarak era, due to its participation in the Gaza blockade, its leadership and legitimacy in the region came under considerable fire, recalling the outrage when President Anwar al-Sadat concluded a separate peace with Israel at Camp David. There were demonstrations at Egyptian embassies in Turkey, Malaysia, Jordan, and Lebanon—where a newly formed Campaign to Stop the Wall of Shame targeted the Egyptian construction company Arab Contractors, which was reportedly building the wall.[9] Writing in *al-Ahram Hebdo* magazine, Egyptian journalist Hassan Abou-Taleb lamented, "Criticizing Egypt and its policies has become common in the Arab world . . . These bitter critiques . . . have developed to the point that they disfigure the image of Egypt."[10]

By highlighting its role in the Gaza siege, the Gaza Freedom Marchers put the Egyptian government in a distressing position, particularly since

---

7   Ahmad Yusuf Ahmad, "Stories of Walls," *al-Shurouq*, January 7, 2010.
8   Fahmi Huwaydi, "The Wall of Shame," *al-Masry al-Youm*, December 14, 2009.
9   Ahmed Moor, "Lebanon Activists Launch Campaign Targeting Egypt's 'Wall of Shame,'" January 21, 2010.
10   Hassan Abou-Taleb, "La Palestine en 2010 et le rôle Egyptien," *al-Ahram Hebdo*, January 27–February 2, 2010.

the authorities could not crack down on the international demonstrators as harshly as they would have on locals without causing a diplomatic incident. Several internationals were beaten and thrown to the ground in scuffles with the police. But by and large their demonstrations were met with an unusual (by local standards) degree of tolerance. In fact, the Egyptian government machinery seemed initially discomfited by the bad publicity attending the foreign convoys to Gaza. Some suggested that the reluctant, defensive, and disorganized response of the government to the criticism and questioning of its policies toward Gaza was indicative of "the degree of embarrassment felt by a government that—it has become clear—is helpless."[11] The defensiveness came out as a combination of bluster and conspiracy theory. Officials in the Foreign Ministry referred to the international activists as "conspirators" and "troublemakers." Foreign Minister Ahmad Abu al-Ghayt said the members of the Viva Palestina convoy "committed hostile acts, even criminal ones, on Egyptian territory."[12] British MP George Galloway, who led the delegation, was declared persona non grata in Egypt.[13]

Others insinuated that opposition to the wall and the blockade was part of a plot to humiliate Egypt. Minister of Parliamentary Affairs Mufid Shihab suggested that the Gaza Freedom Marchers were mostly "Algerian women with French nationality . . . carrying a message from the Algerian media into the heart of Cairo."[14] The accusation, innocuous as it may sound, was venomous in view of the rift between Egypt and Algeria following Algeria's victory over Egypt in a World Cup qualifying match, and the ensuing violence in both countries (as well as in Sudan, site of the match) targeting the other country's nationals. Shihab also blamed the coverage on the Al Jazeera network—"the Qatari channel of discord," he called it—for fomenting anti-Egyptian feeling. In the end, the Egyptian official political establishment more or less declared the subject of its policies toward Gaza verboten. President Mubarak, in a speech on January 24, 2010, announced flatly: "We do not accept debate on this issue with anyone."

The authorities also resorted to religious authority to try to quash dissent. The Islamic Research Council, headed by the Sheikh of al-Azhar (Egypt's highest, semi-official Muslim institution), on the preceding December 31 issued a legal ruling in support of the wall. The council released a statement saying: "It is one of Egypt's Islamically legitimate rights to place barriers that prevent the damage inflicted by the tunnels built under Egyptian land

---

11   Yusri Fawda, "What's Good About the Gaza Wall," *al-Masry al-Youm*, December 27, 2009.

12   *Haaretz*, January 19, 2010.

13   *Daily Mail*, January 9, 2010.

14   *Al-Ahram*, January 2, 2010.

at Rafah, which are used to smuggle drugs and other products, threatening and upsetting the security and stability of Egypt and its interests." "Those who oppose the construction of this wall violate the *shari'a*," the council concluded. Other Islamic scholars immediately and indignantly contradicted this fatwa, and al-Azhar was condemned by many for seeming to put religion at the service of unpopular government policies.

ACTIVISM AND ITS LIMITS

International activists chose to come through Egypt to get to Gaza because this route was the only one available; entering through Israel, they felt, would have been impossible. They hoped that Egypt would be sympathetic to their mission, and at first they did their best to avoid confrontation with the regime. When Egypt announced in advance of their arrival that the way into Gaza would be closed, the activists were undeterred. Egypt had vowed to obstruct numerous delegations in the past, a December 21 press release from the Gaza Freedom March steering committee allowed. "But after public and political pressure, the Egyptian government changed its position and let them pass."

At the demonstration on New Year's Eve in downtown Cairo, participant Ali Abunimah, the Palestinian-American cofounder of the *Electronic Intifada* web magazine, said: "People did not come to Cairo with the goal of protesting Egypt or making trouble in Egypt. They came here to go to Gaza and show solidarity with people in Gaza and break the siege. And what has inevitably refocused attention on the Egyptian role is that it is Egypt that has prevented people from traveling to Gaza … and so it's really Egypt that's highlighting its own role in maintaining the siege in Gaza."

The Gaza Freedom March did not coordinate with local activists; in fact, it did not allow them to join. A statement on the march's website read: "Unfortunately, the Egyptian government decides who can and cannot cross into the Gaza Strip from Egypt. In our experience, it has been difficult for Egyptian citizens and people with Palestinian Authority passports to enter the Gaza Strip. We have tried to overcome this unfair restriction on previous trips, but without success. So, unfortunately, we cannot take people with Egyptian or Palestinian passports." Muhammad Wakid, an activist and member of the Socialist Studies Center in Cairo, said locals understood that the choice to exclude them was necessary, "so as not to alienate the regime, so as to maximize access to Gaza." Wakid noted that "our presence would have been a liability; it would have changed their focus."

Once the internationals were stuck in Cairo—and their focus was changed for them—they reached out to local pro-Palestinian groups. But there remained significant differences. The Gaza Freedom Marchers, for example, asked Egyptians not to chant pro-Hamas, pro-Hizballah, or anti-Mubarak slogans at their joint demonstration on December 29 on the steps of the Journalists' Syndicate. The Egyptians refused. And then there was a pricklier problem. "We couldn't possibly consult or coordinate with [the Gaza Freedom Marchers] given the presence of Israeli activists," said Wakid. This position was shared by Egyptian activists of all political persuasions—even the goal of breaking the siege could not trump their opposition to normalization of relations with Israel through direct contact with Israelis.

Despite these differences, and despite deploring the internationals' naiveté in thinking they would be allowed to enter Gaza, for the most part Egyptian activists were supportive. "We wished them well from afar," said Wakid. "They had an important effect," said Diya' al-Sawi, a founder of the Egyptian Committee to Break the Siege of Gaza. "They changed world public opinion toward the Egyptian regime." Critics of the march in the Western activist community were skeptical of the idea, on the grounds that it was impractical and wrongly focused: Egypt's certain denial of access would shine the spotlight on Egypt, instead of Israel (and the US), the real forces behind the blockade. For Egyptian activists, however, opposition to the Gaza blockade and opposition to the Mubarak regime were one and the same. They were pleased that the international media attention attracted by the Gaza Freedom Marchers and Viva Palestina convoy helped to cement the connection. In fact, the mobilization against Mubarak's never-ending rule and his son's planned inheritance of power—a mobilization that started in 2005 with the Kifaya movement—in many cases had sprung from the same activist circles that formed popular committees of support for the Palestinians during the second *intifada*. Foreign and domestic causes—opposition to Israeli violence, to the US invasion of Iraq, and to torture and repression under the Mubarak regime—were part of a continuum that alimented Egyptian activism in the 2000s.

Furthermore, Arab public intellectuals used the foreign activists to chide Arab governments and populations for insufficient solidarity with the Palestinians. Salama Ahmad Salama, writing in *al-Shurouq* newspaper, noted: "These marches, of course, may not solve the problem. But at least they ring an alarm bell from time to time, and do something to grab the attention of world opinion, whereas the Arab countries and peoples have submitted to the existing situation and are no longer able to resist it, but rather have come to beg for solutions and concessions that the Palestinians themselves refuse."[15]

---

15   Salama Ahmad Salama, "The Culture of Protest," *al-Shurouq*, January 4, 2010.

In fact, despite the severe constraints under which Egyptian pro-Palestinian activists were operating—such as the threat of arrest, police abuse, and the absence of international media coverage—they continued to organize actions on a regular basis. The same week the Gaza Freedom Marchers were in Cairo, Islamist students demonstrated against the construction of Egypt's underground barrier on several university campuses.[16] The "wall of shame" was also the subject of spirited parliamentary debate and court challenges: in early 2010, Egyptian MPs were leading a legal effort calling on the president and the Ministry of Interior to halt construction.[17]

On January 15, about one hundred members and supporters of the Committee to Break the Siege of Gaza tried to convene at the Doctors' Syndicate in downtown Cairo, in preparation for attempts to enter Gaza. They encountered the heavy hand of state security: the nearby subway station was closed, the area was surrounded by riot police, taxi and bus drivers were detained, and the activists themselves were beaten and harassed. They regrouped at an alternate location and decided to break into smaller groups that would travel separately by public transportation. But the groups were all apprehended, eventually, at different checkpoints on the way to Rafah, whereupon they were packed into minivans and driven back to Cairo under police escort. This sortie was the fifth attempt the Committee—whose leader, Magdi Ahmad Husayn, was convicted of "smuggling" in January 2009 after visiting Gaza by tunnel—had made in the previous year to break the blockade.

TO WHAT END?

After the fall of Mubarak, one question for the historians is exactly what his regime intended to achieve with the steel barrier on the border between Sinai and the Gaza Strip. It is difficult to know if the regime truly believed the barrier was impregnable; indeed, it was difficult to know how soon the wall would be completed. Some suspected the Mubarak government was dragging out construction, as part of the endless bargaining and arm-twisting going on among Israel, Egypt, the US, Hamas, and the PA presidential office in Ramallah.

Clearly, however, even semi-constructed, the Egypt–Gaza wall, like other barriers around the world, became a visible and dramatic symbol—an embodiment of the regime's policy, and a lightning rod for opposition.

The wall heralded a hardening of the Egyptian regime's stance on Gaza,

---

16   *Al-Masry al-Youm*, December 30, 2009.
17   *Al-Masry al-Youm*, January 1, 2010.

despite the embarrassment of so openly standing athwart the Palestinian cause, or perhaps because of it. In January 2010, Foreign Minister Abu al-Ghayt announced that "Egypt will no longer allow convoys, regardless of their origin or who is organizing them, to cross through its territory."[18] All foreign aid would have to be handed over to the Red Crescent, which would then deliver it—if and when the Rafah crossing was opened—to Gaza. This stance would only be softened after Mubarak fell.

And the wall also put Egypt, in ways the government found quite awkward, at the center of the international argument over the Gaza blockade. Despite their ideological differences, Egyptian and international activists made contact in 2010, on the sort of unofficial level that was likely to endure, and indeed was strengthened by the revolution of 2011. Through the experience of the Gaza Freedom March, Egypt's role in the blockade—a key preoccupation of local activists—became part of the international pro-Palestinian agenda. It may be that the wall Mubarak built succeeded mostly in drawing global attention to the complicity of Arab governments with Israel and the West in the immiseration of the Palestinians.

18   *Haaretz*, January 9, 2010.

Muslim Brothers deputies to Egypt's People's Assembly oppose
the Mubarak regime's renewal of the Emergency Laws. The deputies wear black sashes reading in Arabic "No to Emergency,"
Cairo, April 30, 2006 © STR/AFP/Getty Images

Part III

POLITICAL PARTICIPATION AND POLITICAL
INSTITUTIONS UNDER MUBARAK

CHAPTER 11

Unsettling the Authorities: Constitutional Reform in Egypt

Mona El-Ghobashy

Nowhere has the belittling designation "the Arab street" been more over-used than in descriptions of Egypt, the most populous and politically central Arab state. Egypt's richly textured history of political opposition, one of the longest in the region, has often been reduced to images of livid young men brandishing copies of the Qur'an and burning American flags. Especially after September 11, portrayals of Egypt, mimicking the Mubarak regime's own rhetoric, propagated the myth of a modernizing, secular regime besieged by the forces of violent Islamism and thus "forced" to resort to repressive measures, such as military trials of civilians and prolonged detention and torture of thousands of Islamist activists. After twenty-two years in power, the regime had mastered the art of impression management, papering over its rampant human rights abuses and routine confiscation of political rights with palliatives such as the appointment of Egypt's first female judge, a war on corruption in high places, and the designation of Coptic Christmas as a national holiday. Yet while the state giveth cosmetic reform, it indiscriminately taketh away the rights of opposition activists and even pro-regime academics, like the American University in Cairo professor Saad Eddin Ibrahim. Convicted twice by a state security court in 2001 and 2002, Ibrahim was finally released from prison after Egypt's Court of Cassation overturned his convictions in 2003.

The reductive tendency to shoehorn all of Egyptian politics into a dead-lock between the regime and the Islamists, on the one hand, and the regime and the unwieldy masses, on the other, kept many Egypt-watchers from noticing all the meaningful and consequential forms of political expression unfolding across the country. At best, Parliament, the courts, and civil society were dutifully noted as sites of well-meaning but ineffective symbolic resistance. Indeed, it was not uncommon for both Egyptian activists and outside observers to announce the death of politics and the triumph of the Egyptian Leviathan in snuffing out all forms of political expression. One writer concluded in 2002, "Little domestic impetus for reform remains."[1]

---

[1] Jason Brownlee, "The Decline of Pluralism in Mubarak's Egypt," *Journal of Democracy* 13/4 (October 2002).

The situation on the ground, however, belied these claims of inaction and political lethargy. True, the Mubarak years witnessed a general impoverishment of political expression and an alarming rise in violations of human rights and civil liberties, but the state's transgressions did not go unchallenged. A hobbled, deeply scarred but still active civil society movement persisted in documenting the regime's abuses and forcing it to answer for its wrongs before international bodies. Egyptian human rights groups regularly publicized the regime's appalling record of torture, and were cited for their persistent work by Amnesty International and the UN Committee Against Torture in their 2002 reports. In response to the challenges posed by domestic human rights groups, the Egyptian government created a human rights desk in the Foreign Ministry in 1992 to represent the regime's line on rights abuses. The administrative courts also became a central arena for limiting the sprawling powers of the executive, prodded into action by the litigation of activist citizens. And the rubber-stamp Parliament received a new lease on life when a landmark July 2000 Supreme Court decision requiring judicial supervision of elections brought in a more representative and more contentious group of deputies, including seventeen Muslim Brothers.

DOMESTIC ROOTS OF INTERNATIONAL SOLIDARITY

Some of the most creative forms of political expression came from the Palestine and Iraq solidarity movements. In the wake of the second *intifada* in September 2000 and Ariel Sharon's subsequent election in February 2001, "popular committees" led by activists of diverse political orientations transformed intense popular support for the Palestinians into tangible political acts. The Egyptian Popular Committee for Solidarity with the Palestinian Intifada (EPCSPI) raised funds, drove food and first aid caravans to the Egyptian–Israeli border (often to have the supplies confiscated by Egyptian border authorities), initiated boycott campaigns of American-made products, and instigated petitions and protest delegations to Egyptian ministries and foreign embassies. The Popular Committee also helped lead demonstrations in April 2002 that were the most intense since the 1991 Gulf war. Dozens of protesters were injured and one Alexandria University student was killed by security forces. Farid Zahran, one of the founders of EPCSPI, was detained by the government in September–October 2001.

Cynics wrote off the Palestine and Iraq solidarity movements as tacitly encouraged and even manipulated by the regime, to let "the street" blow off steam about Israel and the US. However, biting anti-regime slogans—the most pointed since the January 1977 "bread riots"—became part and parcel of every anti-Israel and anti-US demonstration. Especially popular were "Husni Mubarak is like Sharon, same looks, same breed" (*Husni Mubarak zayy Sharon, nafs al-shakl wa nafs al-lawn*) and "Revolution, revolution till victory! Revolution in Palestine and in Egypt" (*thawra, thawra hatta al-nasr, thawra fi Filastin wa fi Masr*). Further, those active in the *intifada* and Iraq solidarity movements are the leading lights of general opposition to the government; the solidarity movements were in fact an outgrowth of a long Egyptian opposition tradition of politically heterogeneous alliances for domestic reform. Leaders of the pro-Palestine and anti-war movements, such as independent Nasserist MP Hamdin Sabahi, reformist Islamist Abu al-'Ila Madi, publisher Farid Zahran, Nasserist activist Amin Iskandar, opposition MP 'Adil 'Id, and veteran journalist Muhammad Ouda are familiar names from their years-long involvement in coalitions for domestic reform.

One of the most important such alliances was an ideologically, generationally, and professionally diverse gathering of Egyptian opposition elements around the issue of domestic political and constitutional reform. The Political and Constitutional Reform Committee (PCRC), launched in September 1999, brought together forty-something Islamist activists, septuagenarian retired judges, octogenarian political party leaders, middle-aged writers and journalists, human rights activists, academics, doctors, lawyers, and opposition MPs. It included Muslim Brothers, staunch Nasserists, self-styled liberals, old-guard Wafdists, committed communists, Arab socialists, and free marketeers. In short, the PCRC was a prism of the nation's political diversity, albeit an elite, virtually all-male prism. Still, it was remarkable for bridging the factional divides that have bedeviled Egyptian politics for years. In its political demands, the PCRC went right to the heart of the matter, demanding a revision of Egypt's basic law, particularly the sensitive sections governing presidential selection and prerogatives.

HETEROGENEOUS ALLIANCES

Appearing on the scene with the referendum on Mubarak's fourth presidential term in October 1999, the PCRC gained additional impetus when the regime arrested twenty prominent Muslim Brother professionals in the same month and referred them to a military tribunal. At an October 1999 meeting, PCRC members affirmed solidarity with the arrested Brothers and reiterated five central demands: lifting of the state of emergency, safeguards for free elections, unrestricted formation of political parties, abolition of restrictions on the establishment and ownership of newspapers and other media, and guarantees of independence for syndicates and civil society groups. The spectacle of leftists and Nasserists protesting the political harassment of Muslim Brothers would have been unimaginable in the 1980s. It took the 1990s era of indiscriminate political persecution at the hands of the state to make them see a common cause. The PCRC transcended past rivalries in pursuit of a higher goal: the transformation of Egypt from a presidential to a parliamentary republic, which meant revising the basic text that privileges the president and subordinates Parliament.

Questioning the foundations of the political system raised the specter of "instability"—the perennial bugaboo of the Mubarak regime. The president once said: "I do not believe in change just for the sake of change. I do not even believe in change every now and then or occasionally." He and other government officials made it only too clear how threatening they found the PCRC. In October 2002, considering proposals for a new electoral law, Mubarak commented, "There is no need to amend the constitution. The constitution should not be considered an obstacle in the way of democratization."[2] Taking their cue from the top, government representatives vociferously attacked calls for constitutional reform as unnecessary and divisive. In 1999, in response to the PCRC's announcement of its project to collect signatures nationwide on a plan of constitutional reform, a government spokesman said, "A constitutional debate would not unify the country. It would have divided the country."[3] Ibrahim Nafie, appointed by Mubarak as editor of the state-owned flagship daily al-Ahram, characterized PCRC members as a dangerous minority faction "who seek to hijack the rights of an entire population in order to further the aims of a handful of political and party activists."[4] A few months after his appointment as head of the Supreme Constitutional Court (SCC), the former Deputy Minister of Justice Fathi Naguib pooh-poohed calls for constitutional reform, stating, "For the moment, constitutional reform is not urgent . . . the constitution is a flexible ensemble capable of evolution."[5] Mubarak's appointment of Naguib in August 2001, the first time the SCC chief justice has come from outside the court's ranks, was widely believed

---

2   Gamal Essam El-Din, "Parliamentary Reform Impending?" *al-Ahram Weekly*, October 3–9, 2002.

3   *Atlanta Journal-Constitution*, September 25, 1999.

4   Ibrahim Nafie, "Slowly but Surely," *al-Ahram Weekly*, September 30–October 6, 1999.

5   Magda Barsoum, "La révision de la Constitution n'est pas urgente," *al-Ahram Hebdo*, November 21, 2001.

to be an attempt to silence the overly independent and hence troublesome institution.[6]

Heterogeneous alliances around common political goals have a long history in Egypt, originating in the massive popular upheaval against British occupation in 1919. "'19" left an indelible memory of action committees, marches, national petition drives, work stoppages, student activism, and women's street politics that profoundly shaped twentieth-century Egyptian political expression. In 1946, the students' and workers' committee organized demonstrations against the British, while coalitions formed in Parliament to resist legislation introduced by the palace curbing press freedom. Joint political action adopting a common-front structure took off in earnest in the wake of the 1967 defeat, impelled by the February 1968 student and worker demonstrations that swept the country. Anwar al-Sadat's sudden trip to Jerusalem in November 1977 and the subsequent separate peace with Israel provided more fodder for joint political action.[7]

Since then, issue-specific alliances have crystallized around various facets of Egypt's repressive legal structure, especially laws and statutes proscribing political liberties and freedom of association, such as the notorious law 100/1993 interfering in professional association elections. Campaigns against the law brought together Muslim Brothers and pro-regime figures such as the former MP and medical association chairman, Hamdi al-Sayyid. After 1995, the government's increasing resort to military trials to ostracize reformist Muslim Brothers fueled attempts to mobilize elite public opinion against the practice, such as protest petitions signed by prominent figures of all political persuasions.[8] A dramatic example came when the prominent Coptic engineer and housing expert, Milad Hanna, testified in court on behalf of fellow engineers—who happened to be Muslim Brothers—being tried before a military tribunal in January 2000.

"A JOKE THAT TURNED SERIOUS"

As in much of the Third World, constitutions in the Arab world have long been instruments of rule, rather than instruments of restraint on arbitrary

---

6   Mona El-Ghobashy, "How Supreme Is the Court?" *Cairo Times*, June 27–July 3, 2002.

7   'Abd al-Ghaffar Shukr, *Political Alliances in Egypt, 1976–1993* (Cairo: al-Ahali, 1994) [Arabic].

8   See, for example, the most recent petitions, published in the *al-Sha'b* newspaper (January 11 and 21, 2000), which was shut down by the government in May 2000.

state power. In Egypt after 1952, constitutions became little more than codexes of presidential powers, reflecting their origin in political struggles between the chief executive and his challengers. The constitution promulgated on September 11, 1971 was no exception. Having barely won an internecine battle with the Nasserist old guard in May 1971, Anwar al-Sadat was keen to fuse as many powers as possible in the person of the president to give himself a leg up in the future. A few years before his assassination in 1981, he acknowledged deliberately packing the document with presidential prerogatives. Sadat told veteran journalist and his onetime speech writer Ahmad Baha' al-Din, "Oh Ahmad, Nasser and I, we are the last pharaohs! You think Nasser needed texts to govern, or that I do? The powers you're talking about I put there for those who would come after us: ordinary presidents, Muhammad, 'Ali, 'Umar. They'll need these clauses to get by."[9] Notwithstanding (or perhaps because of) Sadat's attempt to spin the 1971 document as intended for "ordinary presidents," advocates of constitutional reform call it "Sadat's constitution."[10]

Yet despite Sadat's precautions, the 1971 constitution produced the most unintended of consequences. Though handpicked by the president, the committee of legalists entrusted with drafting the document was a curious amalgam of liberal law professors and presidential legal advisers who each worked to tailor the constitution to their own vision.[11] The former, such as Ibrahim Darwish and Tharwat Badawi, sought to limit presidential prerogatives and terms of office and amplify the purview of the traditionally pliant legislature. For their part, the president's men, such as the influential Gamal al-'Utayfi, stressed the need for a strong presidency to manage tense relations with Israel and the permissibility of the president's re-election for two more consecutive terms of six years each, for a total of eighteen years in power. A year before his death, Sadat amended Article 77 to enable the incumbent president to be elected for an unlimited number of terms. Crucially, the liberal camp that advocated direct popular election of the president lost. Instead, Article 76 stipulates that the president is to be selected by two thirds of the 454-member Parliament and their selection ratified by the people in a plebiscite.

---

9   Ahmad Baha' al-Din, *My Dialogues with Sadat* (Cairo: Dar al-Hilal, 1987), p. 64 [Arabic].

10   Popular Committee for Constitutional Reform, *The Constitution We Are Calling For* (Cairo: Amun Printing House, 1991), pp. 5, 17 [Arabic].

11   For a discussion based on the minutes of the committee that drafted the constitution, see Bruce Rutherford, *The Struggle for Constitutionalism in Egypt: Understanding the Obstacles to Democratic Transition in the Arab World* (Ph.D. dissertation, Yale University, 1999), pp. 221–49.

The final document of September 11, 1971 was thus a fundamentally composite creature. On the one hand, it was overwhelmingly weighted toward the chief executive, granting him the power to appoint and dismiss the prime minister and cabinet ministers, start impeachment proceedings against them, issue decrees with the force of law, hold referenda by which parliament can be bypassed, declare a state of emergency, convene emergency sessions of Parliament, and appoint ten members of that body. The constitution grants the president staggering powers over the two other branches, giving him the right to dissolve Parliament after putting the issue to a referendum and empowering him to chair the Supreme Judicial Council, which oversees affairs of the nation's judges. For good measure, Sadat's legal tailors also inserted the famously indeterminate phrase "the president guards the boundaries between the powers" in Article 73, which ostensibly refers to his respect for the separation of powers. In effect, this deliberately opaque construction has proven very useful to the Mubarak regime's scribes, who have interpreted it to mean the president is "the referee" between the powers, further sanctifying his aura in the contemporary political lexicon.

On the other hand, under pressure from the law professors, the constitution guarantees a whole host of freedoms, and Parts III and IV are entirely dedicated to civil rights and the rule of law. It prohibits torture and degrading treatment of detainees and searches without a warrant, while guaranteeing freedom of religion and expression, freedom of the press, and freedom to conduct research and engage in artistic expression. Citizens have the right to congregate peaceably, form associations, establish unions and syndicates, and vote and run for office. Indeed, Article 62 reminds Egyptians that "participation in public affairs is a national duty," while Article 47 states that "constructive criticism is a guarantee of the soundness of the national edifice." Still, the presidential faction on the committee made sure to stipulate that many of these rights are to be "determined by law," thus enabling the government to curtail those rights as it sees fit. Not content with these ample safeguards, the government of Husni Mubarak has ruled Egypt under a continuous state of emergency since Sadat's assassination on October 6, 1981. Emergency law effectively suspends the constitution by prohibiting public marches and demonstrations (indeed any gathering of more than five people), and gives the state huge powers of "preventive" detention without charge and the military trial of dissidents. Scores of activists in the anti–Iraq war movement were detained, joining thousands of Islamist activists who have been locked up for years on end without trial.

Activists exploited the fundamental ambiguity of the 1971 constitution to maximize its liberal potential, bringing cases before the courts to contest the constitutionality of laws and administrative decrees. In the words of lawyer and activist Nasir Amin, the 1971 constitution was "a joke that turned serious." By taking the liberal but dormant portions of the constitution seriously, litigants pushed the reform-minded judiciary to invalidate bad laws and unjust decrees. This piecemeal strategy of legal contestation significantly limited the regime's room for maneuver, and led to outcomes like the landmark July 2000 ruling of the SCC requiring judicial supervision of parliamentary elections. The plaintiff, a lawyer named Kamal Hamza al-Nasharti, ran in the 1990 elections and lost, due, he claimed, to police interference. Al-Nasharti argued in court against the constitutionality of provisions of the electoral law permitting non-judiciary members to oversee polling stations. It took ten years for his case to be decided by the SCC, and in July 2000, the court handed down a ruling agreeing with al-Nasharti, prompting judicial oversight of that year's parliamentary elections, for the first time in Egyptian history.

Citizens' legal mobilization has not always been liberal, and sometimes has led to terrifying consequences. Maverick lawyers used the courts to push for the banning of allegedly impious films and, in the most absurd instance, for the separation of university professor Nasr Hamid Abu Zayd from his wife. In 1993, the principal plaintiff (and Abu Zayd's faculty peer) 'Abd al-Sabbur Shahin argued that Abu Zayd's academic writings constituted apostasy, and as such he had forfeited his right to remain married to a Muslim woman. A puzzling 1995 Cairo Court of Appeals ruling supported Shahin, and Abu Zayd and his wife Ibtihal Younis were forced to live in exile in the Netherlands.

TOWARD A LIVING DOCUMENT

If one strategy of reformers has been to take the existing constitution seriously, transforming it from a tool of political control to a mechanism of accountability, reformers have simultaneously called for a fundamental overhaul of the constitution, not simply the insertion of amendments. What troubles activists are not the clearly obsolete injunctions, such as "the economic foundation of the Arab Republic of Egypt is democratic socialism" or "the public sector bears the primary responsibility in the development plan." Rather, what has spurred the demand for change is the 1971 document's systematic concession of overwhelming presidential powers and stingy extension of puny parliamentary prerogatives. As law professor Muhammad Hilmi Murad wrote, the goal is to rectify the "illegitimate birth" of the 1971 document and replace it with a more democratic version growing out of a more transparent and participatory process.[12]

The tussle over the constitution between the government and reformists began in earnest in 1991, when the heads of all political parties, the Muslim Brothers, and the Communists signed a joint statement requesting that the president consider a proposal for a new constitution drafted by an all-star team of legalists. They held a press conference on July 8 announcing the initiative, arguing that "the time has come for the Egyptian people to regain their rights to true democracy, to freely select their representatives without pressure, terrorism, or rigging."[13] The drafters included Islamists such as Muhammad Salim al-'Awwa, liberal Wafdists 'Atif al-Banna and Muhammad 'Asfour, retired judges, the entire faculty of the Alexandria University law school, and members of the Egyptian Society of Constitutional Law. Among the drafters was judicial titan Yahya al-Rifa'i, a former head of the Court of Cassation (Egypt's highest appellate court) and survivor of a vindictive judicial purge by the Nasser regime in 1969. In response to the 1991 proposal, the regime moved through its classic three-stage reaction process. First, Mubarak simply ignored the document, along with other projects presented to him at the time, including a comprehensive proposal by al-Rifa'i for judicial autonomy from the overbearing Ministry of Justice. When calls for constitutional reform did not abate, the government moved on to its second tactic: co-optation.

In the summer of 1994, Mubarak presided over a conference of "National Dialogue," whose 274 participants included 237 members of the ruling party. The Islamists were excluded. Wafdists and Nasserists boycotted the event in protest, and conference proceedings predictably substituted socio-economic problems for the core issue of political reform. Meanwhile, al-Rifa'i and others kept the impetus for constitutional reform alive by extending the circle of elites advocating the project, building links with a younger generation of activists in the professional syndicates and human rights groups, and forming ancillary configurations to the Popular Committee for Constitutional Reform, such as the National Concord and the Committee for Coordination between Political Parties and Forces. Starting in 1997, the latter body began holding annual conferences at which a common set of both negative and positive freedoms was articulated. They included lifting the state of continuous emergency

---

12 PCCR, *The Constitution We Are Calling For*, p. 5.
13 Ibid., p. 22.

in effect since October 1981, putting a stop to extrajudicial killings and routine torture in prisons and police stations, setting up an independent commission to monitor elections, and lifting all restrictions on freedom of association and the press. By doing so, activists were simply calling for the realization of rights granted in the 1971 constitution but cramped by the reality of broad executive powers. Trimming these powers is the gateway to putting an end to rights abuses.

When activists of the PCRC, the most recent incarnation of the reformist spirit, began to demand direct election of the president with a choice of candidates, rather than a referendum on a single candidate selected by Parliament, the regime deployed its third tactic and went into attack mode. Mubarak and other regime figures explicitly denounced calls for reform as sinister and destabilizing. On a high-level visit to Washington in 2003, presidential scion Gamal Mubarak, who many believed was being groomed as Egypt's next president, told the *Washington Post* that reform of presidential selection was "not on the agenda."[14] Anticipating petition drives and a public demonstration against the renewal of the Emergency Law scheduled for March 9, 2003 and organized by PCRC leader Husayn 'Abd al-Raziq, the government railroaded a bill through Parliament extending emergency law until 2006 on February 23. In words typical of the regime's Orwellian rhetoric, Prime Minister 'Atif 'Ubayd assured MPs that authorities "will not use this law to undermine freedoms . . . [I]t will be used only to ensure and protect the nation and to abort sabotage attempts."

But the taboo of questioning presidential authority was broken, and models of what an alternative constitution might look like literally emerged out of the woodwork. Enterprising leftist journalist and historian Salah 'Isa, a leading organizer of the PCRC, unearthed a long-lost draft copy of a liberal 1954 constitution, which had been discarded by the Free Officers even though they had commissioned the document. The reason? The 1954 draft constitution was a blueprint for a parliamentary system that placed stringent restrictions on the executive and made it truly accountable before the representatives of the people. Nasser resented its requirement that the president be no younger than forty-five (he was thirty-six in 1954). Miraculously, 'Isa located the twenty-six-page typewritten text buried deep in a box in the basement of a Cairo research center. He dusted it off, reconstructed its history, and got former SCC Chief Justice 'Awad al-Murr to write a foreword. The Cairo Institute for Human Rights Studies published it as *Constitution in the Trash Bin: The Story of the 1954 Draft Constitution.*

---

14   Jackson Diehl, "Gorbachev on the Nile?" *Washington Post*, February 10, 2003.

WHO CARES?

Egypt still awaits a thoroughly reformed constitution, but it has at least two models for such a document—the 1991 proposal and the 1954 draft that never saw the light. More importantly, the opposition has worked out a conception of a parliamentary system as a coherent alternative to the status quo. The PCRC and its predecessors were relatively small gatherings of counter-elites with no popular following, but so were the Federalists in the United States; PCRC members sought to mobilize elite opinion first, before taking the issue to the public. Yet even on this elite level, they did not succeed in convening constitution-drafting roundtables as in post-communist Eastern Europe. Before the January 25 revolution, some doubted that such debates mattered, such as the respected former judge, Tariq al-Bishri. Al-Bishri lauded the PCRC's work but did not have much hope that its members could effect a real transformation in the balance of power between state and society. Still, PCRC members demystified the aura surrounding the office of president and unmasked the regime's feeble invocations of "stability." They wrested the initiative of constitution-making from the government. The Mubarak government's periodic extension of emergency law every three years suggests how imperiled it felt by the mere possibility of activating even as flawed a constitution as the 1971 document. As Hafiz Abu Sa'ada, secretary general of the Egyptian Organization for Human Rights, told the Associated Press: "This law will remain a sword that hangs over freedoms and rights granted by the Egyptian constitution." Emergency "law" remains an all-purpose swatter aimed at anti-war activists and political reformists alike, pushing them to address the root of the problem. The dour legalists and tweedy professors who work for constitutional reform may not be as newsworthy as armed insurgents or angry crowds, but their calls for change have always been equally, if not more, unsettling to the authorities.

CHAPTER 12

The Dynamics of Elections Under Mubarak

Mona El-Ghobashy

No one thought parliamentary elections under Husni Mubarak were democratic or even semi-democratic. The elections did not determine who governed. They were not free and fair. They installed a Parliament with no power to check the president. The government National Democratic Party (NDP) always manufactured a whopping majority, never getting less than 70 percent of the seats. The opposition was kept on a tight leash, restrained by police intimidation, rampant fraud and severe limits on outreach to voters. And citizens knew that elections were rigged, with polling places often blocked off by baton-wielding police, so few of them voted.

And yet, both government and opposition took parliamentary elections very seriously, preparing for them months in advance. Out of eight electoral cycles from 1976 to 2010, the opposition boycotted only once, in 1990. "We've tried the bitterness of boycotting in 1990, and secured only five seats in the 1995 elections," said Wafd leader al-Sayyid al-Badawi, explaining his party's decision to field 250 candidates in 2010.[1] The opposition's choice to participate was not as odd at it might seem, for Egypt's parliamentary elections, despite their serious limitations, were not mere props or stereotypical autocratic rituals of acclamation. They were rare moments of open, if unequal, political competition between government and opposition. Their strategic interaction meant that elections were far from trivial.

The elections of December 2010, concluded a month before the revolution that began on January 25, 2011, defied expectations—not because the ruling NDP again dominated Parliament, but because of the lengths to which it proved willing to go to engineer its monopoly. Official and unofficial ruling-party candidates garnered 93.3 percent of the seats in the national assembly, while marginal opposition parties received 3 percent and the Muslim Brothers got a lone seat to be occupied by a member who would not abide by the Brothers' boycott of the run-off.

Reaction to the lopsided results was severe. Egyptian and international observers with no known sympathies for the opposition condemned

---

1   *Al-Shurouq*, September 18, 2010.

the conduct and outcome of the polls. Moderate political analyst 'Amr al-Shubaki of the establishment al-Ahram Center for Political and Strategic Studies called it "the worst election in Egypt's history."[2] US spokesmen expressed "dismay" and "disappointment" at irregularities, in a collective throwing-up of hands that reportedly went to the very top of the State Department. Prominent NDP member Hamdi al-Sayyid, who was ousted from the seat he had held since 1979 by a regime-sponsored "independent," fumed: "The fraud perpetrated against me was systematic. They deserve a Ph.D. in rigging."[3]

The outcome unsettled a widely held belief about the Mubarak regime: that it tolerated a smidgen of parliamentary opposition to disarm domestic and international critics. Indeed, the longevity of Mubarak's rule was often attributed to an omniscient political manipulation that made clever use of opposition, even creating it at times, but never permitting it to threaten the powers that be. The regime employed the results of the 2005 elections, when the opposition secured an unprecedented 25 percent of parliamentary seats, to signal that continued pressure upon Egypt to democratize would only bring fearsome Islamists to power. The 2010 contest's liquidation of all credible parliamentary opposition, both secular and religious, thus raised the question: Why did the government abandon its previous modus operandi? After the revolution broke out, the question became far more pressing, with even NDP insiders quick to blame the unrest on the ham-handed skullduggery at the previous month's polls.

A common answer has been that Mubarak and his inner circle were consolidating their forces in anticipation of a choreographed transfer of presidential power to the aging president's son, Gamal. But the NDP's total (if fleeting) lock on the 2010 Parliament had less to do with securing the presidential transition and more to do with cordoning off the legislature from bottom-up demands for representation. It was not the first time an Egyptian regime had tried this gambit since multiparty legislative elections were restored in 1976. In 1979, the year of the Camp David peace deal with Israel, Anwar al-Sadat increased repression to return an assembly cleansed of credible critics; in 1995, Mubarak did the same thing. In late 2010, the experiences of the outgoing parliament's session made Egypt's ruling cartel wary of normalizing a legislative opposition at a time of economic restructuring and widespread ferment in society. Rather than expand

---

2 'Amr al-Shubaki, "Why Are These the Worst Elections?" *al-Masry al-Youm*, December 2, 2010 [Arabic].

3 *Al-Masry al-Youm*, December 15, 2010.

representative channels to absorb collective grievances, the regime opted to close off all the outlets. It was not the whim of an unchallenged autocrat that prompted this tactical shift, however, but the persistence and ingenuity of Egyptians in struggling for their rights, both outside formal political institutions and inside them. Indeed, vital as social protest was to weakening Mubarak, his regime was also constrained by the very elections through which it sought to cement its grip on the country.

CURIOUS CONTESTS

As in day-to-day politics, the Mubarak-era elections brought together two wildly mismatched players, one holding all the state's resources and force and the other possessing nothing more than the sympathy the public may have had for the underdog. There was no uncertainty about the overall winner, but winning was not what was at stake. Since the playing field was not level, anything but a government victory was ruled out, and so all parties used elections as means of achieving extra-electoral ends. For the regime, elections were one among several implements of rule used periodically to re-establish its domination. Campaigns were seasons for the renewal of political alliances and redistribution of economic resources to the regime's vast pyramid of minions and their respective lower-level clients.

Opposition groups entered elections not to win a majority, and certainly not to govern, but rather to build political standing. They cultivated new and old constituencies, lambasted the government and advertised their own integrity, but also sought seats in Parliament, for to boycott the legislature would have been tantamount to accepting political invisibility. Official status as MPs gave opposition members access to the state bureaucracy overseeing services in their districts, and the standing to meet with foreign delegations. Most Egyptians avoided elections altogether, either because they could be physically dangerous or because there was nothing in it for them. But citizens' stance toward elections was not fixed, and depended on the nature of their ties to the political contestants in a given cycle: some voters sought basic goods and services they did not get otherwise, while others supported particular candidates for ideological or kinship reasons.

As with many authoritarian projects across time and space, elections in Mubarak's Egypt became a fulcrum of both rhetorical and material contention over the basics of regime legitimacy and control. Elections showed how in the details of authoritarian laws and statutes lurks the devil of anti-authoritarian mobilization. "Form creates content" (*al-shakl yikhlaq madamin*) was the refrain among Egypt's patient anti-authoritarians. These overlapping dynamics were clearest in 2005, Egypt's "year of elections." In May, the regime held a referendum on amending Article 76 of the 1971 constitution to allow for direct, multi-candidate presidential elections. Mubarak of course won these elections on September 7, securing a fifth presidential term. Parliamentary elections followed in November–December and they were momentous indeed. Contesting only a third of Parliament's 444 seats, the Muslim Brothers captured 20 percent, a fivefold increase in their representation. The Brothers' gains upped the total proportion of opposition deputies in Parliament to 25 percent, the highest since the return of multi-party elections to Egypt in 1976. By contrast, the performance of the NDP was unimpressive. Despite the active support of the vast bureaucracy and security forces, only 145 of the 432 candidates officially fielded by the NDP won, securing 33 percent of the assembly's seats. The NDP swiftly incorporated 166 "independents," almost all of whom were party-affiliated but had not received the party's nomination, enabling it to maintain the all-important two-thirds majority required to pass legislation and approve constitutional amendments.

There was no doubt that the regime would maintain control of the 2005 parliament, but it was done at high cost. Coming at the peak of President George W. Bush's democracy promotion rhetoric, Egypt's elections received intense attention from foreign governments, media, and domestic human rights organizations, which zeroed in on the fraud and the violence marring the vote that claimed fourteen lives. Unexpected street battles in hotly contested districts and the final results rang alarm bells for a regime facing a crucial decision: the transfer of presidential power from the incumbent, Husni Mubarak, to a successor yet to be named but presumed to be his son Gamal. Arriving at such a delicate juncture, the election gave off several unwelcome political signals. At the level of political organization, the balloting revealed a well-endowed yet disorganized and unpopular ruling party set against a disciplined and relatively popular Islamist movement. At the level of social mobilization, the election of 121 Islamist and non-Islamist opposition deputies indicated that segments of the population were neither disengaged nor easily bought off, the two postures encouraged by the regime. The Egyptian and international media carefully tracked the trouncing of NDP incumbents by Muslim Brother challengers, district by district, damaging the regime's reputation for producing effortless landslides greased by copious patronage.

And there were also the nitty-gritty election procedures, which in 2005 were as crucial as the electoral outcomes. The year's three balloting exercises were all occasions for organized domestic mobilization on the issue of election management and monitoring, with discreet international backing. Mobilization centered not only on voting-day activities but also encompassed critical pre-election procedures such as compiling the voter rolls and ensuring the availability and quality of indelible ink, as well as the all-important issue of the integrity of the ballot count.[4] Leading the campaign for a cleaner vote were Egypt's judges, represented by their elected leadership in the Judges' Club. Judicial mobilization, abetted by citizen activists, was a key motif of the 2005 electoral year, but it did not begin then. How and why judges orchestrated an uncharacteristically high-profile, media-savvy campaign for full supervision in 2005 is a winding story that begins in the legal documents of Nasserist Egypt.

RULERS, RULES AND RESISTANCE

Judicial supervision of elections has its roots in Law 73/1956, Organizing the Exercise of Political Rights.[5] Law 73 codified the Nasserist ethos of popular participation, and as such is best remembered for extending the franchise to women for the first time, lowering the voting age from twenty-one to eighteen and abolishing a host of pre-1952 restrictions on voting and running for office. The law also codified the Nasser-era ambivalence about elections, stipulating judicial supervision while at the same time blunting its subversive potential. The law falls short of granting judges complete jurisdiction over election management, instead dividing that responsibility between judges and other state officials such as the interior minister, provincial security agents, and members of prosecutorial bodies (Articles 16 and 24). In 1971, the law's provision for judicial supervision of elections attained constitutional status. The September 1971 constitution was the keystone of the fledgling Sadat regime's new rhetoric of democracy and the rule of law, and constitutionalizing judicial supervision of elections bolstered the ostensible commitment to rule of law. Article 88 of the constitution thus mandates that "voting occur under the supervision of members of a judicial body." The terse yet pregnant wording created an opening for activists and litigants to exploit the political potential of legal ambiguity. Struggles over the meaning of "supervision" (*ishraf*) and "judicial body" (*hay'a qada'iyya*) would take center stage in future elections.

---

4   For more details, see the seminar convened by the Egyptian Organization for Human Rights in May 2005 bringing together judges and civil society activists to hammer out specific procedural guidelines for elections. A transcript is available online at en.eohr.org, as "Electral Reform . . . Visions and Tools. EOHR Seminar Convened on the 7th May 2005."

5   The text of the amended law can be found in Lorraine Marulanda, El Obaid A. El Obaid, and Lazhar Aloui, eds., *IFES Arab Law Compendium* (Washington, DC: International Foundation for Election Systems, 2002), pp. 77–84, at pogar.org.

The pivotal, capacious Article 24 of Law 73 granted the interior minister the power to determine the number of principal and auxiliary polling stations. The article also specified that the supervisor of each main polling station be a member of a judicial body, though it did not extend this requirement to auxiliary stations, permitting public-sector clerks and other civil servants to oversee those areas. This detail spawned the only instance of successful opposition coordination in Egyptian elections. On October 20, 1990, all of the major opposition parties, including the Wafd and the Labor Party affiliated with the Muslim Brothers (but not the leftist Tagammuʿ), signed a pact to boycott the parliamentary poll in protest at the absence of complete judicial supervision, including auxiliary polling stations.

A disgruntled and resourceful independent candidate, Kamal Hamza al-Nasharti, took the issue a step further. He filed suit after the elections, arguing that Article 24's assignment of public functionaries to supervise auxiliary polling stations was a violation of the constitution's Article 88 requiring judicial supervision. Al-Nasharti argued that non-judicial civil servants lacked the requisite impartiality to ensure fair polling procedures. The administrative court reviewing the case agreed with him and referred the case to the Supreme Constitutional Court (SCC), which took ten years to hand down its landmark ruling on July 8, 2000—also siding with al-Nasharti.[6] The court ruled that for judicial supervision to be effective, it must extend beyond main stations to include auxiliary ones as well. The government scrambled to amend Article 24, and a decades-long opposition and judicial demand was finally realized: parliamentary elections were conducted in stages over several weeks to enable the comparatively small number of judges (8,000) to supervise thousands of main and auxiliary polling stations.

But the legal wrangling did not end there. The court ruling left a key item unresolved, namely the definition of a "judicial body." Ever since the 1960s, this vague term had been a persistent node of contention among legal scholars and practitioners, resurfacing during every election as independents and the opposition decried the government's manipulative electoral practices, most especially the smuggling of non-judicial legal officers into the definition of a "judicial body." The SCC's 2000 ruling reignited the debate with a vengeance. Between July, when the SCC ruling was issued, and November, when the parliamentary elections began, debates raged in newspapers and political salons over what and who got included in the definition of a judicial body.

---

6   Supreme Constitutional Court ruling on Case 11 in the Thirteenth Judicial Year, published in the official gazette on July 22, 2000.

Legal scholars and practitioners, along with opposition candidates and civil society activists, insisted that a judicial body meant only sitting bench judges. Government officials and their legal experts disagreed vociferously, arguing that legal officers in the administrative prosecution and the State Cases Authority (government attorneys) were also legitimate judicial bodies. At issue was a legitimate academic dispute and a pressing matter of regime survival. As legal officers of the executive branch, who answer to the justice minister in ordinary times and to the interior minister at election time, non-judicial legal personnel lacked the potential for autonomous action that bench judges enjoyed and repeatedly demonstrated. By law, they were professionally and organizationally dependent on executive dictates, perfect accessories to lend elections a patina of legality without compromising certainty of outcome. Hence, a seemingly prissy legal definition had obvious political ramifications.

Naturally, the government insisted on its own definition of the term and deployed thousands of its legal officers to supervise polling stations. Still, the 2000 poll was cleaner than previous elections, returning a parliament with a marginal decrease in ruling-party dominance (87.8 percent, down from 90.4 percent in the 1995 parliament) and a relative increase in the representation of Muslim Brothers running as independents (seventeen seats, up from one in the 1995 parliament). A combination of fierce competition between NDP members and more effective electoral supervision led candidates officially nominated by the NDP to secure only 38 percent of parliamentary seats. To avoid an embarrassing repeat during the spring 2002 municipal elections, NDP leaders engineered very limited supervision, leaving 37,410 auxiliary polling stations unmanned by bench judges. Sure enough, opposition parties boycotted and the ruling party secured all the seats.[7]

The management of the 2000 parliamentary elections had more subtle, though no less significant consequences. Bench judges experienced numerous instances of harassment and obstruction from security agents, and several engaged in verbal and physical confrontations with police as they protested police blockades of roads to polling stations and intimidation of non-NDP voters. Contrary to Law 73's stipulation that it is the prerogative of the supervising judge at the polling station to determine the station's periphery, security agents essentially trapped judges inside polling stations while violence and harassment raged outside.[8] Bench judges' negative

---

7   *Al-Ahram Weekly*, April 4–10, 2002.

8   In preparation for the 2005 elections, Judges' Club board member Ahmad Sabir detailed his and other judges' experiences in 2000. See Ahmad Sabir, "Judges Supervise Elections Despite the Absence of Guarantees," *al-Quda* (September 2003–August 2004) [Arabic].

experiences in 2000, coupled with the unresolved controversy over what constitutes a judicial body, laid the groundwork for the fierce electoral contention of 2005.

"WE SEE YOU"

The 2005 elections merged two parallel judicial struggles: the quest for clean elections and the quest for judicial independence. Egypt's judges have a long history of struggling for independence from the all-powerful executive branch. Executive–judicial relations got off to a good start at the beginning of Mubarak's tenure with the passage of Law 35/1984, returning the Supreme Judicial Council (SJC) after its abolition by the Nasser regime in 1969. The SJC is a liaison institution between executive and judiciary that each branch naturally seeks to tweak to augment its own power. Judges invoke its historical pedigree as an independent institution of judicial peers who manage judicial appointments and promotions, with an autonomous budget and full control over disciplinary affairs, away from the designs of the Ministry of Justice. The executive, for its part, has always sought influence over the institution by controlling its composition and mandate. The Judges' Club (established in 1939) was born in this tug of war between the two state branches as a vehicle to aggregate judicial opinion and forward negotiation with the Ministry of Justice.

Executive attempts to control the judiciary began in earnest in the 1990s, with the SJC under the strict control of the Ministry of Justice. By 2005, reformist judges amplified their demands for a new law that would overturn the practice of appointing judges to the SJC by the Ministry of Justice, and replace it with election by judges themselves. The core goal of the judges was an autonomous, elected SJC that would manage the affairs of the judiciary while retaining their Judges' Club as a separate professional association.[9]

The government began its legal maneuvering a year before the 2005 elections, moving to shut down the controversy over who gets included in the definition of a judicial body. In a highly publicized request for interpretation, President Mubarak referred the matter to the SCC. On March 7, 2004, the SCC, headed by Mubarak loyalist Mamdouh Mar'i, returned an opinion that shocked legal experts. Mar'i argued that government attorneys and administrative prosecutors were indeed part of legitimate judicial bodies and as such could be entrusted with supervising elections. Meanwhile, on March 12, judicial discontent reached fever pitch with an extraordinary general assem-

---

9   Interview with Judge Hisham al-Bastawisi, Cairo, December 26, 2005.

bly convened to deliberate on an unprecedented intra-judicial incident. Fathi Khalifa, president of the SJC, had issued a written "warning" (*tanbih*) to senior judge Husam al-Ghiryani for "disparaging the decisions of the SJC." Judges were affronted by the transparent attempt to silence an esteemed judge, and al-Ghiryani received a prolonged standing ovation. The incident rekindled debate over the purview of the SJC and the stage was set for conflict.

In April 2005, the judges' first public signal that they would have no truck with fraudulent elections came in a rousing general assembly meeting of the Alexandria Judges' Club, in which al-Ghiryani and others took the podium to assert that they would stand firm against falsifying voters' will. A month later in Cairo, on May 13, thousands of judges from all over Egypt met in an extraordinary general assembly to specify their conditions for clean elections ahead of the May 25 referendum on amending Article 76 of the constitution.

On referendum day, the violence against protesters of the Kifaya (Enough) movement captured international headlines, but the government insisted on the orderliness of polling in the rest of the country and claimed a turnout of 54 percent. The day's events led to weekly protests on Wednesdays by Kifaya and its supporters that lasted throughout the summer, drawing much media attention and varying levels of popular participation. What was soon dubbed "Black Wednesday" by the opposition spawned two additional instances of election-related mobilization. English teacher Ghada Shahbandar founded a cyber-savvy, independent citizen monitoring group called Shayfeenkom (We See You) to oversee the autumn presidential and parliamentary poll. Then, in July, the Judges' Club issued a report based on its fact-finding mission on conduct of the referendum, the first report of its kind. The nine-page document challenged government turnout figures and claims of full judicial supervision, finding that auxiliary polling stations were still manned by government clerks and that real turnout ranged from 3 to 5 percent. The report included testimonials by some judges and legal officers who admitted to faulty procedures.[10]

Amending the constitution to allow for direct multi-candidate presidential elections was the centerpiece of the Mubarak government's political strategy in 2005, though no one in Egypt or abroad expected a real contest. The surprises lay elsewhere: in Ghad Party president Ayman Nour's garnering of second place with 7 percent of the vote, and the enormous fuss raised over the election management body. While the state-owned press reveled in the simple citizens who expressed gratitude and delight with President Mubarak by filing applications for presidential candidacy (including one

---

10   The report was widely published in independent and opposition newspapers and on the Internet. See the full text in *al-'Arabi*, July 3, 2005.

woman), domestic monitoring groups and the opposition pored over the details of election procedure. Law 174/2005 on presidential elections established a Presidential Election Commission (PEC) headed by the self-same Mamdouh Marʻi, four judges and five "public figures known for their impartiality," to be chosen by both houses of Parliament. Critics charged that not only was the inclusion of "public figures" a transparent move to pack the PEC with government loyalists, but that the PEC's absolute immunity from any form of oversight by any institution (Article 12) violated the constitutional right of litigation (Article 68).

Two highly controversial actions by chairman Marʻi galvanized public mistrust of what came to be called the "imperial" PEC. First, Marʻi inexplicably decided to exclude some 1,700 judges from supervising presidential elections. Then, he made a public statement disregarding the September 6 administrative court ruling allowing civil society groups to monitor the vote. A day later, Marʻi reversed his decision. That one of Egypt's three most high-ranking judges would cavalierly dismiss a widely hailed court ruling, and then abruptly backtrack, reinforced suspicions that the PEC was a legal front to dilute full judicial supervision rather than an impartial management body designed to bolster election integrity. As with the May 25 referendum, the Judges' Club issued a report in November detailing its criticisms of the presidential elections. A report of the International Republican Institute argues that the Club's report "deserves credit for some of the procedural changes that were made in advance of the parliamentary elections, including the removal of polling stations from police stations, reducing the number of voters assigned to each polling site to facilitate voting, and the use of indelible ink in all polling stations."[11]

The parliamentary elections from November 9 to December 7 saw unceasing action by judges and monitoring groups to ensure a clean vote, especially during the second and third phases when violence by NDP supporters and security forces against opposition candidates and voters led to eleven deaths. The leadership of the Judges' Club consistently communicated its concerns to Minister of Justice Mahmoud Abu al-Layl (head of a new Parliamentary Elections Commission), monitored the situation on the ground in particularly hard-fought districts, and vigilantly invoked proper electoral procedures. One dramatic instance of this came on November 22, when the Judges' Club issued a widely publicized statement framed as "Egypt Judges Seek Army Protection."[12] In fact, the statement was invoking

---

11   2005 Parliamentary Election Assessment in Egypt (Washington, DC: International Republican Institute, 2005), pp. 10–11.

12   United Press International, November 23, 2005.

Article 26 of Law 73/1956, which empowers the head of a polling station to call in police or armed forces to maintain order. The statement surmised that since police "were unable or unwilling to perform their duties, the Judges' Club calls on the Election Commission to seek aid from the armed forces to secure the conduct of elections."

But the highest election drama came in districts like Damanhour in Buhayra province, where, despite the judicial efforts at monitoring, the regime pulled its various tricks to fix the results. In Damanhour, security forces barricaded polling stations, helping the government's candidate to beat the opposition candidate, a Muslim Brother. A legal official who monitored the Damanhour vote, Nuha al-Zayni, published an account describing the forgery of the final tally.[13] Together with the Brothers' unprecedented electoral success, the exposure of such shenanigans called into question the Mubarak regime's ability to perpetuate its rule at the ballot box.

GEARING UP

Egypt's power elite thus approached the 2010 parliamentary campaign exceptionally motivated to control the outcome. As soon as the 2005 elections concluded, the regime began a systematic restructuring of the political arena, changing the constitution and electoral laws, weakening the Muslim Brothers, and strengthening the NDP's party organization. The aim was not simply to crush the Muslim Brothers at the polls, but to do so with finesse, in order to project anew the image of effortless government control that was so besmirched in 2005.

Three alterations in electoral procedures further skewed the playing field. First, the regime did away with full judicial supervision of elections, again amending Article 88 of the constitution. The revised text replaced monitoring by judges with oversight by an electoral commission composed of "current and former members of judicial bodies," an amorphous category allowing the government greater leeway in selecting pliant personnel. The regime's salesmanship for this maneuver is on display in a WikiLeaks cable summarizing a 2005 meeting between Gamal Mubarak and Elizabeth Cheney, then a State Department official with responsibility for Middle East democracy promotion. The cable says that Mubarak "blamed the low turnout in the presidential election (about 7 million voters or 23 percent) on overzealous judges supervising the September 7 ballot who had, allegedly, refused to allow more than one voter at a time into polling stations, and thereby diminished turnout." The amended Article 88 also stipulated that

---

13   *Al-Masry al-Youm*, November 24, 2005.

voting take place on a single day, for the first time since the 1995 elections. Now the opposition could not use the first phase to test outreach tactics and gauge voter response, an important signaling mechanism that was a byproduct of judicial supervision.

The second rule change reprised President Anwar al-Sadat's invocation of state feminism to ornament an authoritarian maneuver. In 1979, Sadat dissolved Parliament to cleanse it of vehement opposition to his foreign policy, and called early elections under new rules that introduced thirty seats reserved for women. The SCC struck down the women's quota in 1986. In 2009, Gamal Mubarak's Policies Secretariat passed through Parliament a law adding sixty-four new parliamentary seats reserved for women. The set-aside is due to expire after the 2010 and 2015 election cycles. NDP spokesmen billed the measure as the empowerment of women to enter national politics, but the opposition called it an increase in seats for the NDP in the guise of women's rights.

The third rule change built in a safeguard in case the above adjustments failed to thwart Islamist gains. A little-noted but significant item in the raft of constitutional amendments passed in 2007 gave the president the power to dissolve Parliament without a referendum, a right he did not have before.[14] Should the 2010 Parliament become unruly, Mubarak could simply shut it down. At the same time that it fixed the electoral framework, the regime siphoned off the material and symbolic resources that sustained the Muslim Brothers. First, in 2007 the authorities arrested and referred to a military tribunal several leaders of the organization, most important among them Khayrat al-Shatir, a key financier and strategist. Other Brother-owned businesses were closed and their assets frozen, on charges of money laundering and attempting to revive the Brothers' 1940s-era military wing. The Brothers' candidates in student union elections on university campuses were also targeted, with police using the same violence against voters that they had previously reserved for national elections. Next, the 2007 constitutional amendments banned political parties based on "any religious frame of reference," to short-circuit attempts by the Brothers to form a political party. In 2008, municipal elections that the Muslim Brothers tried to contest were summarily fixed, sealed, and delivered to the NDP, without a single place allowed the Brothers out of 52,000 seats.

The regime was also keen to ruin the Brothers' reputation for competence and clean hands. To tarnish the Brothers in the popular imagination, state television used the peak viewing season of Ramadan to air a slickly produced miniseries about the Brothers in their founding years.

---

14   Nathan Brown, Michele Dunne, and Amr Hamzawy, "Egypt's Controversial Constitutional Amendments," Carnegie Endowment for International Peace, March 23, 2007.

Written by leading screenwriter Wahid Hamid and featuring a star-studded ensemble cast, the serial faithfully related the tale the government has always told about the Muslim Brothers: they are a shifty, secretive, violent, opportunistic cult that is poised to take over Egypt. And to create mistrust of the Brothers' strong suit, the government targeted six of their parliamentary deputies for involvement in alleged corruption. The six were among fourteen legislators, including six from the NDP and two from the Wafd, accused of diverting for personal use state-funded medical treatment reserved for constituents.

The regime gamed the system and undermined its main competitor, but it also turned inward, restructuring its main election vehicle to make it a leaner, more efficient vote-getting machine. Over the past four election cycles, a trend had emerged showing declining performance on the part of the NDP's official candidates: 58.8 percent of these candidates won in 1990, compared to 52.6 percent in 1995, 38.9 percent in 2000, and 32.8 percent in 2005. A corollary was the fierce intramural competition between official and unofficial NDP candidates—the "independents." Aware of an image problem, especially relative to the Muslim Brothers' discipline, the NDP's new leaders moved to erase the party's reputation as a menagerie of self-seekers who compete against one another and split the party vote.

Ahmad 'Izz, a steel magnate and an associate of Gamal Mubarak in the Policies Secretariat, shoved aside NDP election kingpin Kamal al-Shazli to promulgate his own strict rules for candidacy, marketing the new procedures as the "institutionalization" of the NDP. As before, aspiring candidates had to pay a nonrefundable, minimum application fee of £E 10,000 (around $1,750), but now they also had to sign affidavits vowing not to run as independents if they were not selected to front the NDP. As insurance, 'Izz and Co. instructed the Ministry of Interior to issue only one copy of a candidate's criminal record, which is required of anyone who wishes to declare electoral candidacy. Since the sole copy of this record was to be submitted to the NDP, jilted would-be candidates were not able to reapply as independents.

"RIGGING WITH A HINT OF ELECTIONS"

The meaning of ending judicial supervision was immediately made clear on election day. If the iconic image from the 2005 elections showed elderly female voters climbing makeshift ladders to enter polling stations blocked off by police but staffed by judges, the defining image from 2010 was a surreptitiously shot four-minute video of a voter-free polling station in the Bilbays district of the Delta province of Sharqiyya. Two poll workers calmly filled out ballot after ballot, stacks of which were then carried off by other civil servants to be stuffed in boxes off camera.[15] As Muhammad Badi', leader of the Muslim Brothers, quipped, "These were not elections with rigging; it was rather rigging with a hint of elections."[16]

By the early afternoon of November 28, the day of first-round voting, and in defiance of the Higher Election Commission's strict ban on cameras inside polling stations, hundreds of videos were being posted on YouTube and Facebook capturing the fraud-producing methods of yore. The clips are a valuable documentary record; it turns out that the ballot stuffing of Bilbays was ubiquitous. Videos also picture clusters of NDP voters huddled over ballot boxes, collectively filling out ballots while uniformed police look on; opposition candidates and their representatives heatedly arguing with polling station heads who refused them entry, citing eleventh-hour rule changes; opposition voters assembled in front of closed-off polling and counting stations, chanting slogans against the cheating; and incensed citizens storming polling stations and hurling stuffed ballot boxes out the windows.

The most widely discussed incident of fraud involved Judge Walid al-Shafi'i, who went to the press with his election-day experience. Al-Shafi'i was assigned to the Badrashin district in the October 6 province outside Cairo as one of the drastically reduced corps of jurists overseeing the polls. On the afternoon of the voting, he made his way to an auxiliary polling station to investigate reports that it was blocked off to voters. As soon as he arrived at the station, he was detained and his ID card confiscated by Ahmad Mabrouk, head of the Badrashin State Security Investigations Department, who barked at him, "You step aside." While in police custody, al-Shafi'i saw no voters at the station but did see poll workers sitting at desks in a classroom filling out empty ballots. A hapless worker came up to him with a pile of completed cards, saying, "I'm finished, sir."[17]

Why did the Mubarak regime abandon what was thought to be its trademark asset, namely the calibration of election rigging to let in some legislative opposition, polish its image, and thereby stabilize its hold on power? The oft-made claim that the regime needed total control of Parliament to stage-manage the scheduled 2011 presidential election is unconvincing. Even with a quarter of the seats, a parliamentary opposition could not field a contender for executive office. The rules laid out in the amended Article

---

15   The clip is available online at youtube.com/watch?v=T4HBUKkXyIc.
16   Reuters, December 23, 2010.
17   *Al-Masry al-Youm*, November 30, 2010.

76 in Egypt's constitution were expressly designed to block the presidential candidacy of anyone outside the regime.[18]

Both NDP members and their critics attributed the 2010 election outcome to the party's new guard, headed by Assistant Secretary-General Gamal Mubarak and his right-hand man, Ahmad 'Izz. Regime apologists deployed the rhetoric of superior organization and dogged constituency service to portray the government party's dominance as a "sweeping win." As the NDP court intellectual, Abdel Moneim Said, insisted: "The NDP had begun to prepare for this campaign five years ago, applying a minutely calibrated scientific approach that involved thorough studies of all the electoral constituencies."[19] Opposition writers agreed that the election was the handiwork of the NDP's junior elite but gave them a negative cast, depicting Gamal Mubarak and 'Izz as political neophytes with a zero-sum view of politics.[20] Writing on the BBC website, the novelist Alaa al-Aswany drew a nostalgic contrast with the grizzled old guard represented by Kamal al-Shazli, the consummate horse trader whose death shortly before the elections symbolized the complete takeover of the NDP by the crony capitalists surrounding the younger Mubarak.

A focus on the crew of NDP forty-somethings who steered the Egyptian ship of state before the 2011 revolution should not obscure the deeper social dynamics that drove their calculations. As the new guard commandeered public assets for delivery into private hands, Parliament moved to center stage as the site where the legal framework for the transfer was to be hammered out. As with any exclusive club, membership of Parliament allowed entry into new networks of privilege created by the economic shift, but it also enabled access to information about economic rearrangements that was routinely hidden from public view. NDP hangers-on sought Parliament for the profits, while the

---

18   Article 76 laid out two paths to presidential candidacy. The first path ran through membership in a party, provided that the party had been in existence for at least five consecutive years before the date of candidacy and had at least 3 percent representation in both the lower and upper houses of Parliament. In addition, the presidential candidate had to have been a member of the party's high council for at least one consecutive year. A built-in exception exempted an existing party from the threshold, allowing it to field a candidate even if it has only one parliamentary seat. Four regime-created opposition parties received one seat each in the 2010 elections. The second path to the presidential palace was for "independents," who had to obtain the signatures of at least 250 elected officials distributed as follows: sixty-five from the lower house and twenty-five from the upper house of Parliament, and ten members of every municipal council in at least fourteeen governorates. The upper house and municipal councils were entirely dominated by the NDP.

19   Abdel Moneim Said, "Last Word on the Elections," al-Ahram Weekly, December 16–22, 2010.

20   'Imad al-Din Husayn, "A Palace Coup in the NDP," al-Shurouq, December 8, 2010, and Dia' Rashwan, "Who Gave the Order and Why?" al-Shurouq, December 27, 2010. [Arabic]

opposition sought Parliament for knowledge and proximity to the bureaucracy controlling public services. Because of its visible size, at 121 deputies, and its representation of normally excluded interests, the combined opposition in the 2005 parliament was able to clamor for the information and services that the NDP wanted to reserve for itself. So as to forestall a reprise, the regime decided to shutter Parliament as a place to do politics, reallocating the opposition's valuable seats to a wider net of NDP dependents.

UNDER THE ROTUNDA

Egypt's opposition parliamentarians had no illusions about their clout under the rotunda. The NDP's overwhelming majority drowned out even their loud voices in debates over legislation, and parliamentary rules prevented them from blocking government policies. So they ramped up their problem-solving and monitoring functions instead, channeling goods and services from the bureaucracy to their constituents, and activating mothballed legislative oversight instruments to funnel information to the public about controversial bills and policies.

One of the most intense confrontations between government and opposition inside the chamber concerned the state budget. In the March 30, 2010 plenary session to vote on the budget, ninety-eight Brotherhood and secular opposition deputies tabled a written protest accusing the government of manipulating revenue figures. Budget Committee Chairman 'Izz angrily pounded on the podium and shook his fist at fellow committee member and Muslim Brother MP Ashraf Badr al-Din, spluttering: "I know more than you do! This is just an attempt by the ignorant to instill public doubt in the state budget!"[21] Not surprisingly, in an extended rationalization of the NDP's "victory" after the elections, 'Izz targeted the Brothers' parliamentary performance. "The overall attitude of MB representatives over the past five years was to reject every single draft of legislation and every article—and every paragraph in every article—of draft law, for no logical reason," he wrote in the quasi-official *al-Ahram* newspaper. "Our MPs debated, amended, and passed legislation allowing the private sector to participate in infrastructure projects so our country can reduce budget spending, but none of them agreed."

When their views were rendered moot inside the chamber, opposition deputies simply took them to the sidewalk outside. Bearing signs and wearing sashes emblazoned with slogans over their suits, the protesting opposition parliamentarians were a novel sight for eager news photographers. The

---

21   *Al-Masry al-Youm*, March 31, 2010.

deputies staged walkouts on a host of domestic and foreign policy matters, including the Israeli bombing of Lebanon in 2006, the wholesale constitutional amendments of 2007, President George W. Bush's visit to Egypt and the exclusion of opposition candidates from municipal elections in 2008, the renewals of emergency law in 2006 and 2008, and the undemocratic amendments to the law on the exercise of political rights in 2010. They joined forces with the extra-parliamentary opposition, participating in the May Day protest demanding an increase in the national minimum wage and sitting cross-legged on the ground with the protesters who camped outside Parliament during the spring of 2010, listening to their grievances and attempting to broker negotiations with government officials. The parliamentary opposition represented a much wider social base than the Mubarak regime was prepared to deal with in an official institution.

Everyone knew that elections under Mubarak were fraudulent affairs, a combination of violence and vote-rigging. The significance of the elections was not their outcome, but the way in which Egypt's judges, dissident parliamentarians, and social movements turned them into arenas of intense struggle for greater representation.

CHAPTER 13

Controlled Reform in Egypt: Neither Reformist nor Controlled

Issandr El Amrani

Drawn out over five weeks in November and December 2005, Egypt's parliamentary elections gripped a country normally jaded about formal politics—and produced some surprising results. While the ruling National Democratic Party retained a large majority of seats in the legislature when the votes were counted, more than half of its candidates went down to defeat. The secular opposition parties, already weak, were crushed, losing most of their seats. Candidates associated with the outlawed Muslim Brothers, meanwhile, surged to an unexpectedly strong showing. These developments, along with rampant vote buying and violence that claimed the lives of eleven people and wounded hundreds more, kept Egyptians accustomed to yawning at the country's electoral exercises glued to the television screen.

The parliamentary elections were to have been the ultimate test of the government's commitment, after a year of disappointing false starts, to its promises of a "democratic flowering" in Egypt. If the government's conduct during the polling justified skepticism about the prospects of top-down political reform, so did the government's inability to engineer the outcome as completely as in the past. If the regime's path to reform was advertised as controlled political liberalization, the elections showed the path to be neither controlled nor truly reformist. For a small, but increasingly influential group of Egyptian liberals worried by the prospects of authoritarian regression and/or a strengthened Islamist movement over the coming decade, the elections pointed to the regime's failure at managing the reform agenda. They began to look for a solution elsewhere.

PSEUDO-REFORMS

Starting in the early months of 2005, the Egyptian regime stepped up the effort to soften its authoritarian image. The "reform" agenda was set by President Husni Mubarak himself, beginning with his startling announcement on February 26 that he would ask Parliament to amend Article 76 of the constitution to allow for the first multi-candidate presidential election in the country's history. Even hardened opposition figures had to cheer, despite what most regarded as the foregone conclusion that in September Mubarak would win a fifth term in office.

By the time the People's Assembly agreed upon a wording for the amendment, however, much of the initial enthusiasm had evaporated. The amendment, which passed a national referendum on May 25, placed stringent restrictions on who could run for the presidency, practically barring the door to independent candidates, and, beyond the 2005 election, rendering it exceedingly difficult for candidates from the small "legal" opposition parties to get the necessary number of endorsements from elected officials. Leading opposition figures and even some liberal members of Mubarak's National Democratic Party (NDP) expressed their dismay.

Moreover, the conduct of the referendum was flawed in two important respects. Though the regime intended to broadcast the image of a democratizing Egypt, the lasting visuals captured by local and international media depicted the violence with which pro-NDP thugs attacked anti-Mubarak protesters, including women, outside polling stations. Second, the official turnout figure of 54 percent was called into question by civil society organizations and the independent and opposition press, which ran accounts of voters casting multiple ballots and other irregularities. On July 2, the Judges' Club—the professional syndicate of the Egyptian bench that has been vocally campaigning for greater judicial independence—issued a report confirming that turnout figures had been manipulated to exaggerate public backing for the amendment. The judges noted that, in several constituencies, turnout had been officially registered at 100 percent. In the terse words of the report: "Nobody died, nobody traveled, nobody was sick, had to work, or was too lazy to go out to vote?"

The controversy over the referendum was followed by a heated battle in the People's Assembly over amendments to the laws governing, among other things, the formation of political parties, political fundraising, and access to electoral information. Law 175/2005, which amended Law 38/1972, concerned the election directly. In it the government responded to long-standing demands of the opposition, notably stressing that security services should not interfere in elections, banning electioneering in government offices, and confirming the judiciary's right to monitor balloting. As in other laws, however, the NDP added provisions that seemed targeted at the Muslim Brothers, such as proscribing the use of mosques or prayer sites in campaigns. These laws were rushed through Parliament in late June with little attempt at discussion with the opposition, which protested both the laws' content and the manner in which they were passed.

MORE AT STAKE

Swallowing their disappointment at these pseudo-reforms, the opposition mobilized for the parliamentary elections, in which they knew a great deal was at stake. The newly amended Article 76 and the new electoral laws had established a prerequisite for government-recognized parties that wanted to field a candidate in future presidential elections: control of at least 5 percent of the People's Assembly. Beyond that, in the July 20 speech launching his campaign, Mubarak had pledged to move ahead with important political reforms in 2006, notably replacement of the Emergency Law in place since 1981 with anti-terror legislation (another goal long pursued by the opposition), and introduction of measures increasing the powers of Parliament at the expense of the presidency. While the presence of a larger opposition bloc would not necessarily guarantee that the opposition would be listened to—the NDP was still certain to control enough seats to pass any law it wanted—an opposition united in its demands could at least contribute to debates and highlight the inadequacies of the regime's legislation.

Officially, the NDP itself encouraged the participation of the opposition. But the ruling party's new leadership, under the president's son, Gamal Mubarak, faced a dilemma. On the one hand, the younger Mubarak justified his entry into party politics after the 2000 elections on the grounds that declared NDP candidates had fared poorly against "independents"—party members who quit before the elections, only to "rejoin" after winning seats. In 2000, in fact, official NDP candidates obtained only 38 percent of the seats in the People's Assembly, and the party only achieved its 90 percent majority when the so-called independents "rejoined." In some cases, these politicians belonged to factions at odds with the party leadership; in others, they were people who simply wanted the seat and were confident they would be taken into the NDP fold to pad its majority. Gamal had to prove that he and his coterie of "reformists" could not only improve the party's image, but also win elections under the NDP banner. On the other hand, domestic and foreign pressure dictated that opposition forces occupy a greater number of seats in the next parliament; a return to 90 percent NDP control of the People's Assembly would be described as a farce no matter how clean the contests.

Before the elections, therefore, there was a general expectation that while the NDP would do well, it would no longer command an overwhelming majority. When party spokesman Muhammad Kamal was asked what score he would like to achieve, for instance, he set the low standard of anything above the official 38 percent of 2000. It was expected that the Muslim Brothers would make gains. (Though the group is officially "illegal" and could not run candidates under its own name, the elections of the 1990s and 2000s were contested by "independents" with widely known Brother affiliations.) In statements to the press prior to the elections, the organization's supreme guide, Muhammad Mahdi 'Akif, predicted that Brother hopefuls would win between fifty and seventy seats, whereas NDP officials did not expect them to win more than forty seats. It was also expected that secular opposition parties, two of which had together secured about 10 percent of the vote in the presidential election, would increase their presence in Parliament.

These expectations, combined with the bolstered legal authority given to supervising judges and the introduction of phosphorus ink and transparent ballot boxes at polling stations, led to a general impression that the 2005 parliamentary elections would be freer and fairer than their precedents. This feeling was reinforced by the release of hundreds of Muslim Brothers detained since May 2005 and the fact that, unlike in 2000, none of the Brothers' campaigners were arrested in the run-up to the first round. On the eve of the elections, Essam al-Arian, a senior Muslim Brother, told *Middle East Report* that there was not a single member of the Brothers in prison for the first time since 1995.

THUGS AND A WHISTLEBLOWER

In practice, during the first round of the elections, held on November 9 with a run-off on November 15, there was markedly less violence and obstruction by security forces than on previous occasions. Incidents of violence did take place, but apparently at the behest of individual candidates who hired thugs to beat up on their opponents' supporters. A far more serious problem was widespread fraud. Independent monitors and journalists reported dozens of cases where public-sector employees were bussed in en masse, as well as confusion about and manipulation of registered voters lists, and open vote-buying. Some reports had would-be voters promising to support certain candidates in exchange for canned food or soft drinks.

Many Egyptian commentators were scandalized to see this chaos, blaming it on the fierce competition for seats and soaring campaign spending, notably by independent businessmen allied with the NDP, but also by the Muslim Brothers. "The Muslim Brothers use religion to impose themselves while the NDP buys votes to maintain its control of Parliament against the people's wishes," noted 'Abd al-Halim Qandil, editor-in-chief of the Nasserist weekly *al-'Arabi*. "A seat in Parliament is the best investment in Egypt: one million spent on a campaign will generate ten million after the election of the candidate, who will use his position to make corrupt gains."

But aside from the cheating, a second trend was emerging. While they were not interfering with the balloting, security forces were guilty of "passive neutrality"—in other words, deliberate failure to intervene to stop those candidates carrying out the fraud and violence, who tended to come from the NDP.

With first-round results showing that the Muslim Brothers had already doubled their number of seats, the regime's tactics began to shift. Analysts had predicted that the Brothers would fare better in the second and third rounds, which were held in districts where they are popular. The first part of the second round, held on November 20, saw the beginning of massive interference by security forces, notably the Central Security riot control troops, which escalated during the run-off of November 26. State violence was selectively employed; some NDP candidates received more help than others. The most egregious incidents took place in the Delta town of Damanhour, even though there were more fatalities in Alexandria.

By the third round, the regime was resorting—again, only in selected constituencies—to closing polling stations altogether, on the grounds that "disruptive elements" were causing violence. According to eyewitnesses, election monitors, judges, and independent and opposition press reports, violence was being caused either by hired goons or voters responding to attacks by Central Security troops. In the meantime, the state press— which since the presidential election had begun to paint a fairer picture of opposition politics—adopted the Interior Ministry's official stance that the violence was mostly caused by supporters of the Muslim Brothers. In the words of a representative Interior Ministry statement: "The incidents of violence witnessed during the election were the product of various candidates, in particular Islamists, and the strict neutrality of the security forces, so strict that they were even accused of 'passive neutrality.' These incidents required that security forces respond sternly to restore order and secure the electoral process . . .[Our warnings] went unheeded by various candidates and their supporters, in particular Islamists, who insisted on abusing the unprecedented climate of freedom which the country is witnessing."

Although independent newspapers, particularly *al-Masry al-Youm*, were reporting daily on violations ignored by the state media, it was one account that finally blew the lid off the official story. In its November 24 edition, *al-Masry al-Youm* carried a front-page article by Nuha al-Zayni, a legal officer who supervised the Damanhour election. Al-Zayni told of the many procedural and other violations carried out by the NDP and security forces. According to Hisham Kassem, the newspaper's publisher, her article had to be reprinted for three consecutive days because issues were selling out so quickly. The paper subsequently increased its print run and received many letters by other whistleblowers wanting to give their testimony. The article also prompted a statement, signed by 120 judges, attesting that the violations described by al-Zayni were common in other constituencies.

Although the third-round run-off on December 8, during which at least eight people were reported killed in altercations with security forces, would prove that a climate of violence and intimidation had taken over the elections, al-Zayni's whistleblower article was the tipping point in public opinion. Magdi Muhanna, the liberal columnist in *al-Masry al-Youm*, concluded that "whatever the result of the parliamentary elections, it is now clear that the violence and bias of the security forces have seriously dampened political reform in Egypt."

A RULING PARTY IN CRISIS?

On the surface, the NDP emerged yet again as the dominant party in Parliament, with 316 seats, or about 73 percent of the total. This supermajority not only allowed the NDP to pass any law it wanted (assuming party discipline), but also gave it enough votes to approve constitutional amendments, lift the parliamentary immunity of individual MPs, and empower the executive branch to approve major contracts (particularly defense contracts), among other prerogatives.

Technically, however, the ruling party lost the elections. Exactly as in the 2000 legislative elections, NDP candidates only obtained 38 percent of the seats—in other words, only 149 out of 444 NDP candidates actually prevailed in their respective races. The remaining 167 seats belong to NDP members who were not selected as official candidates but ran as "independents." The irony is that, for several years, the revamped NDP of Gamal Mubarak had claimed that it would no longer tolerate "rebels" challenging its favorites. Gamal had also insisted on the need to bring new blood into the party that would appeal to voters more than the entrenched apparatchiks.

In the run-up to the election, the NDP made a big show of its democratic and scientific candidate selection process, even requiring prospective candidates to take an exam to determine their suitability for office. In reality, a small cabal of party leaders—from both the new and old guards—handpicked the slate. In some respects, the "new NDP" stuck to its promises: when Husni Mubarak, in his capacity as party president, announced the NDP's list on October 13, 136 of the party's 444 candidates were new faces, something party leaders pointed to as proof of their seriousness about internal democracy. But these claims were belied by frequent reports in the independent press of disagreements among senior party leaders over which candidates to pick. Later, during the elections, there followed accusations that some members of the old guard were backing rebel "independents" against the party's official candidates.

The problem became obvious in the Qasr al-Nil district in central Cairo, where the incumbent Husam Badrawi, often considered one of the few true liberals in the Gamal Mubarak camp, was defeated by "independent" Hisham Mustafa Khalil. Badrawi had been one of the most vocal advocates of barring independents from rejoining the party before the election, and even engaged in a public spat with party spokesman Muhammad Kamal over the issue. He was believed to be disliked by the old guard, which was rumored to have backed Khalil, and was one of the few NDP members to talk openly of the need to remove what he said were "corrupt" elements of the ruling party.

"It was my opinion that we should not allow the independents back, even if it meant fewer seats," said 'Abd al-Mun'im Sa'id, a political scientist and a pro-reform member of the Policies Secretariat—the NDP's think tank. "That would have made the NDP smaller but much stronger and more appealing to other political forces, with which it could have made a coalition." That sentiment was echoed by key figures in the Egyptian intellectual establishment, such as influential *al-Ahram* columnist Salama Ahmad Salama. But it was largely ignored by the leaders of the party's old guard, notably Secretary-General Safwat al-Sharif, who led the effort to draw the independents back into the fold—in some cases, without even asking for their permission beforehand. For the first time, some who ran as independents said they would not rejoin the party.

This issue clearly divided the reformist camp of the NDP, many of whom grumbled about being ignored by the party's leadership. Yet in the elections, it tended to be members of the old guard, associated with the party's reputation for corruption, who lost. The 2005 parliamentary elections saw the fall, among others, of senior NDP members such as Ahmad Rashid, the dean of Alexandria University; Yusuf Wali, once a powerful minister of agriculture; and Amin Mubarak, a relative of the president. Official NDP candidates won no seats in three governorates (Suez, Ismailiyya, and Matruh) and very few in three others (Sohag, Daqhaliyya, and Qina). More generally, the 2005 elections have seen the entry of first-time politicians to the People's Assembly: 77.5 percent of elected MPs are new arrivals, with only ninety-eight incumbents re-elected. The vast majority of those who lost were NDP members.

Overall, the performance of the NDP in the 2005 elections suggests that little had changed since 2000. Although new bodies such as the Policies

Secretariat attracted a few genuine liberals, the political machine remained in the hands of a sclerotic elite. The NDP, in other words, remained mostly a party of opportunists who joined it for access to state resources and regime networks. Gamal Mubarak's purported efforts at "party-building," hailed in the past three annual party conferences and in the aftermath of the presidential election, were revealed as hollow. The younger Mubarak's role was a central problem, as it was unlikely that the NDP could ever evolve into a real party as long as it was considered by the regime to be an extension of the presidency. This was most clearly evident in the fact that key personalities responsible for the elections (from both the old and new guards) remained in place despite their poor performance.

TRIUMPH OF THE MUSLIM BROTHERS

The Muslim Brothers' success at the ballot box did not merely reflect the growing popularity of the Islamist group. It also marked a fundamental change in the Brothers' strategy, of working toward active political participation rather than merely seeking to survive. In a January 2, 2005 interview with *al-Masry al-Youm*, Supreme Guide 'Akif all but endorsed the re-election of Mubarak, even invoking the Qur'anic principle of *wilayat al-amr*, which says that Muslims should obey their leader. That spring, a rift seemed to be widening between 'Akif's cautious older generation of Brothers and the more assertive "middle generation" who made inroads into professional syndicates and Parliament in the 1980s and 1990s.

The assertive tendency won out. While other parties focused on the presidential election, the Muslim Brothers, along with their network of supporters and campaigners out of jail, set about building grassroots support for the legislative contests. As analyst Mohamed el-Sayed Said noted, the group lavished money on charity and social projects during the month of Ramadan, a few weeks before voting commenced. Although, as 'Akif pointed out, the Brotherhood competed in fewer than 170 constituencies, it put up a vigorous fight wherever it campaigned. In a testament to the group's popularity and organizational skills, it managed to win twelve seats in the third round, despite the security forces' closure of polling stations and targeting of Brothers for arrest. By the end of the balloting, 'Akif claimed, at least 1,300 of the group's supporters had been detained.

The Brothers' attention to planning went beyond electioneering. As it became clear that the 2005 People's Assembly would contain a large Islamist contingent, the Brothers launched a media offensive to assuage fears that they had hostile intentions toward secularists and Christians. The campaign came partly in response to wild alarmism in much of the Egyptian press, as well as concerns voiced by prominent Copts, notably intellectual Milad Hanna's prediction, in the quasi-official daily *al-Ahram*, that many wealthy Copts would leave Egypt rather than accept a Brother-dominated government. Brother spokesmen appeared for the first time on Egyptian state television, as well as on pan-Arab satellite channels, and published editorials in the Arab and international press, seeking to reassure the world, as the November 23 *Guardian* headline put it, that there is "no need to be afraid of us." In these interviews and articles, senior Brothers repeated again and again that they were committed to the democratic process and wanted to focus on political reform, rather than the Islamization of Egypt.

A meeting with the press to introduce the Brothers' eighty-eight new MPs began with a Qur'anic recitation, but then moved to chants of "Reform!" The guests of honor were 'Aziz Sidqi, a former prime minister who had formed a nominally secular reform movement with the Brothers, and Rafiq Habib, a Coptic politician formerly associated with the post-Islamist al-Wasat movement. 'Akif told those gathered that he would instruct the MPs to push for democratic reforms, chiefly reducing the powers of the presidency and placing a term limit on the head of state. Most strikingly, he also announced in an interview with the independent weekly *al-Dustur* that he would seek to modify the Brothers' internal regulations to limit the term served by the supreme guide to four or five years, renewable once. The supreme guide enjoyed a lifetime appointment.

Leading Brothers also stated unambiguously, for the first time, that they sought to formalize their political role by creating a political party that would exist separately from the traditional *da'wa* (proselytizing and charity) functions of the organization. Confirming what many had long suspected, the 2005 elections enthroned the Brothers as Egypt's second political force and only truly effective party.

BIPOLARITY

The secular opposition parties introduced after the abolition of the single-party system in 1977 were not set up to perform well. They were led by aging, uncharismatic autocrats and lacked the money and organizational skills of the NDP and the Brothers. The scant voter enthusiasm for established opposition leaders was clear after the presidential election, when Nu'man Guma'a, head of the liberal Wafd Party, finished third with less than 3 percent of the vote, despite being described by the state press as Mubarak's only serious opponent.

The Ghad Party headed by former Wafdist politician Ayman Nour might have been an exception if half of its senior leadership had not rebelled, apparently at the behest of the NDP, throwing the party into disarray. Nour, who was put on trial on a trumped-up election fraud charge after the polls and received a prison sentence, lost his seat in Cairo's Bab al-Shar'iyya district. The NDP clearly devoted much effort to humiliating Nour, appointing a former police general as its candidate in his district to intimidate Nour supporters, and, according to reports by election monitors, illegally registering over 2,000 pro-NDP voters on the day of the election.

Other prominent oppositionists were also defeated, including Khalid Muhi al-Din, leader of the "legal left" Tagammu' Party, and Munir Fakhri 'Abd al-Nour, head of the Wafdist parliamentary delegation. Only the Wafd managed to keep its strength in parliament, with six seats, while the Tagammu' won two and the rebel faction of Ghad and the Ahrar Party each garnered one. For the first time since its formation in 1977, the Nasserist Party did not win a single seat, although a breakaway faction, Karama (then still in the process of forming a party), did win two seats. Although to a less spectacular extent than the Brothers, legal opposition candidates also suffered from fraud and election-day thuggery.

Alongside the rise of the Brothers, these paltry results—a total of twelve seats for the legal opposition, Karama included—underlined the need for reform inside the opposition parties. 'Abd al-Nour of the Wafd was dismissed from the party after he called for Guma'a's resignation. He was believed to have the backing of other senior Wafdists, who protested his sacking. Nasserist leader Dia' al-Din Dawoud announced that he would not stand again in the party's internal elections, which were brought forward as rumors of major splits in the party emerged. Other parties saw similar clashes along ideological and generational lines in the ensuing months.

The implosion of the secular opposition and resentment among NDP liberals led to renewed speculation that a new party gathering reformists from across the political spectrum could emerge. In light of the disappointment with the NDP's handling of the election and secular Muslim and Coptic trepidation about the Brothers, such a party might have united the opposition more effectively than the half-hearted attempt at a "National Front" before the 2005 elections, particularly if the party could draw the support of leading businessmen unhappy with the NDP. The travails of Ayman Nour throughout 2005, however, sent a chilling message to would-be liberal leaders that the regime would not tolerate the emergence of a populist-liberal alternative.

The 2005 parliamentary elections created a bipolar dynamic in Egyptian politics, pitting the NDP against the Muslim Brothers under the rotunda of the People's Assembly and in the marketplace of clientelism and patronage. Both sides were bidding for the reformist mantle, but in light of the NDP's conduct and the Brothers' efforts to moderate their discourse, the Islamists were making the more convincing case. For Egypt's secular-minded leftists and liberals, this was seen as the most dangerous scenario: their place as a nominal alternative to the status quo had been usurped, leaving them on the outside looking in.

CHAPTER 14

The Muslim Brothers in Mubarak's Last Decade

Samer Shehata and Joshua Stacher

The 2005 parliamentary elections catapulted the Muslim Brothers of Egypt into their most visible—and most scrutinized—position ever. At Cairo dinner parties, members of the secular elite speculated that the Brothers' electoral gains would embolden the organization to impose an intolerant interpretation of Islam upon Egypt, repressing women and the country's Coptic Christian minority. A sense of security returned to the table when, nearly unanimously, the dinner companions agreed that since the Muslim Brothers were only eighty-eight out of 454 members of a body still dominated by the ruling National Democratic Party (NDP), they could not pass legislation. The conclusion for many of these elites: tacit support for a regime for which they otherwise had little affection.

The state was also unnerved by the Brothers' success at the polls. The Islamist organization, founded in 1928, was officially banned. Yet affiliates of the Brothers had run as independents in local and parliamentary elections since 1984, with increasing success, despite various state stratagems to depress their vote. In 2005, voter intimidation and ballot stuffing failed to stop the Brothers' affiliates from winning a historic eighty-eight seats, and it was not long before security forces resumed arbitrary arrests, partly in an attempt to keep the new deputies in line. Yet, even as the crackdown proceeded, the Brothers' parliamentary bloc drew notice for its work across ideological lines to serve constituents and increase its collective knowledge of local, national, and international affairs. The delegation did not pursue an agenda of banning books and legislating the length of skirts, but one of political reform. The Brothers' work in Parliament revealed the group to be the closest thing to a real political party in Egyptian politics under Mubarak.

BROTHER PARLIAMENTARIANS BAND TOGETHER

The mood was not festive at the Intercontinental Hotel in Heliopolis four days after the 2005 elections' final round, when Mahdi 'Akif, then the Brotherhood's general guide, introduced the new bloc to the press corps.

In many ways, the large contingent was a fresh organizational challenge for the Brothers. Many of the new MPs were complete strangers to each other until they met under the parliamentary rotunda. Complicating matters, the Brother MPs made a point of living in their districts—in twenty-one of Egypt's then twenty-six provinces—in order to work their jobs, provide social services, and maintain their constituents' trust.

The Brothers' small office in Cairo's al-Manyal neighborhood no longer afforded enough space for all the deputies to meet, given the five-fold increase in their numbers. So the MPs stayed in the four-star Ma'adi Hotel when Parliament was in session. "When Parliament meets, we forget our houses," said 'Ali Fath al-Bab, the only one of the deputies to be elected three times. "We take our suitcases—even those who live in Cairo—and stay in the hotel."[1] The MPs roomed and ate together, and discussed the following day's agenda in the hotel's conference halls. They also chatted informally and attended plenary lectures by speakers from outside the organization.

Yet the Ma'adi Hotel also performed a more basic function: giving the MPs a place to stay so they could attend parliamentary sessions regularly. Fath al-Bab noted the difference from the 1995–2000 term, his first, when he was the only Brother MP. Nominally, half of all MPs, or 228, had to be present to constitute a quorum. If the number fell below 228, however, the session was still considered lawful, as a simple majority of those present was sufficient to pass legislation. Recalling his first term, Fath al-Bab explained, "By the end of the night, there might be thirty NDP MPs left and they would still be passing legislation." But the Brothers' regular attendance changed that: "The NDP now has to have 100 people in Parliament at all times to maintain their majority." As Husayn Muhammad Ibrahim, vice chairman of the bloc and a twice-elected MP, noted, "Our presence has had another effect. The NDP MPs are forced to be more critical toward the government and better prepared. It has changed how they act, but not how they vote." The quasi-official daily al-Ahram concurred that the "Islamic trend" played a "noticeable and distinguished role that cannot be denied" in legislative sessions.[2] The parliamentary sessions of 2005–10 were the most serious of any in Mubarak's tenure.

While the Brother MPs could not pass or block legislation by them-selves, the delegation's attitude of taking Parliament seriously spoke to a wider goal. Brother MPs worked under the guiding principle that

---

1   Unless otherwise noted, all quotations of Muslim Brothers are from interviews conducted by the authors in Cairo in March–April 2006 and April 2007.

2   Al-Ahram, August 4, 2006.

Parliament would be the engine of political reform in Egypt. As Ibrahim stated, "We want people to see Parliament as a place where steps can happen. Before, the MPs were asleep." Hazim Farouq Mansour, a deputy from Cairo's Shubra neighborhood, agreed: "We want to reform the country from top to bottom by working within the existing institutions—be they Parliament, laws, civil society, or the constitution." Egypt's parliament had a reputation for being a rubber stamp for the regime. That remained the case until Mubarak fell. Yet from 2005 to 2010, the Brothers' MPs showed that flawed political institutions could be transformed into an arena of political contestation and struggle.

IN THE KITCHEN

According to several Brother MPs, being a parliamentarian was not all it was cracked up to be. As Ibrahim griped, "Egyptian MPs are *masakin* (downtrodden). There is not enough time for our legislative duties, our role as government's watchdog, and the demands for constituent services." So that their MPs might fill their multiple roles, especially those of legislating and keeping the government accountable, the Brothers created an organ that was part research arm and part think tank.

This "parliamentary kitchen," as the Brothers called it, was divided into specialized teams that gathered information about issues before the People's Assembly. "In Parliament, you have access to a library and a central information office," explained Ibrahim. "Neither is useful. A kitchen is a necessity, and all the blocs need one. Its job is to use civil society and consult experts to organize information we use in Parliament." The parliamentary kitchen has been around since 2000, when seventeen Muslim Brothers were elected to the People's Assembly. But as the size of the bloc increased, the kitchen was forced to expand the scope of its activities. The result was that Brother MPs were better prepared and informed about the issues than their counterparts in the ruling party.

The parliamentary kitchen had a second, and in many ways more important, function. Whether researching public health, judicial matters, or environmental problems, the kitchen reached out to society at large when gathering information. "We think that anyone who has knowledge is approachable," Fath al-Bab stated. "We don't just rely on Brother sources." The kitchen was responsible for organizing the MPs' seminar series, which featured non-Brothers speakers such as Dia' Rashwan of the al-Ahram Center for Political and Strategic Studies, NDP Higher Policy Council member Hala Mustafa, and the chairman of Cairo University's Political Science Department, Hasan Nafa'. While this outreach benefited Brother

MPs first and foremost, it also encouraged civil society activists, whom the regime and ruling party ignored at best and smothered at worst, simply by providing an attentive audience.

The organizational focus served up by the kitchen was sharpened by the bloc's internal organization. Brother MPs served on two or three of the bloc's nineteen committees, which covered a range of issues such as education, health, economics, and the environment. The range of the MPs' professional expertise—the Brothers have historically drawn many of their members from the professions—gave the bloc in-house specialists to rely upon when Parliament took up technical issues. Brother MPs included, among others, doctors, dentists, engineers, lawyers, scientists, academics, and legal experts. According to Ibrahim, "As eighty-eight, we have specialists from all fields and we are better able to support one another and facilitate cooperation."

The increased numerical strength of the Brothers in Parliament was felt unmistakably when the government published its annual Government Statement on budgetary and policy priorities in February 2006. Fath al-Bab described the process: "MPs only get five minutes each to respond to the Statement. This is a document that includes economic, agricultural, social, foreign, domestic, and youth affairs. So we decided to write and publish a response. Our response was 300 pages." While the Statement passed with the NDP's safe majority, for the first time a few NDP MPs voted against it, revealing the influence of the Brothers' bloc.

Many governments, journalists, and academics view the Brothers with an unfounded amount of suspicion. The front page of the independent weekly *al-Fajr* on November 21, 2005—in the middle of the parliamentary elections—depicted the group's general guide dressed in Nazi uniform. As the elections proceeded, observers repeated clichés implying the Brothers' dubious commitment to democracy. Steven Cook of the Council on Foreign Relations argued: "They've clearly embraced the procedures of democracy, but it's unclear that they have internalized the principles of democracy."[3] 'Adil Hammouda, editor-in-chief of *al-Fajr*, went much further, saying: "The next step after the Brothers reach Parliament is the cancellation of democracy."[4] While skepticism toward any political organization is healthy, commentary on the Brothers has frequently leapt to unsubstantiated conclusions that paint the group as a monolith bent on oppression and rule by force.

---

3   Sharon Otterman, "Muslim Brothers and Egypt's Parliamentary Elections," Council on Foreign Relations Backgrounder, December 1, 2005.

4   Quoted in *al-Masry al-Youm*, November 27, 2005.

Hence, the argument about Brother MPs was that they take orders from the group's Cairo headquarters, as mere servants beholden to the whims of the Guidance Office. The way the Brothers acted in Parliament belied this image. Second-term MP Akram al-Sha'ar, from Port Said, contended, "Our priorities and strategies are from the same model as the group's. But the Brothers sent us as MPs, not toys . . . We do not do everything they tell us, and we do not tell them everything we do."

Subhi Salih, a freshman Alexandrian MP, said the primary point of contact between the Brothers' headquarters and the MPs was the parliamentary department, headed by former MP and Guidance Office member Muhammad Mursi.[5] While it is reasonable to think that the Guidance Office oversaw Mursi, there is no evidence that MPs took orders and acted accordingly. As Salih told it, "We are all in agreement over our principles and strategy but there are rules that govern our disagreements. In Parliament, we disagree and vote differently among ourselves all the time." Salih's example was that Brother MPs voted differently on consumer protection legislation during a session in May 2006. While the Brothers' bloc stuck together on major issues, opposing the extension of the emergency law, judicial authority law, and press legislation, Brother MPs did not necessarily march in lockstep. Nor was the bloc dependent on one powerful personality. On May 18, security services beat and arrested Muhammad Mursi, who was protesting in solidarity with Mahmoud Makki and Hisham al-Bastawisi, two pro-reform judges who were dragged in front of a disciplinary hearing after they criticized election fraud. The bloc insisted that its activities were unaffected. Said deputy Muhammad al-Fadl, "The Brothers are an organization and an institution. There is no effect. If Muhammad goes to jail, then someone takes his place."

HANDLING CRISES

When the first Egyptian cases of H5N1 virus, also known as bird flu, were reported in mid-February 2006, rumors fueling collective hysteria spread throughout the country. One rumor claimed that the nation's drinking water was contaminated because dead and infected chickens had been thrown into the Nile. As the government could not convince the public otherwise, the $2.9 billion Egyptian poultry industry, which employs upwards of 2.5 million Egyptians, faced devastation. *Al-Ahram Weekly* reported that

---

5   By the end of the 2010 parliamentary session, Salih had become one of the Brothers' better-known MPs. He was later named to the eight-person committee the SCAF charged with drawing up constitutional amendments in February 2011.

the poultry industry had lost $217 million and that 1 million people had lost their jobs. "Poultry exports have collapsed," the paper reported, "and 35 percent of poultry farms have closed down as the industry faces losses of up to £E 10 million [$1.7 million] a day."[6]

Health experts, the media, and the opposition roundly criticized the Egyptian government for underestimating the threat of avian flu, being insufficiently prepared, and mishandling the crisis. By May, six people had died and thirteen others were infected with the virus. The Brother MPs, meanwhile, applied immediate pressure on the government to devote greater attention to avian flu in order to lessen the impact on the nation's economy. Drawing on the group's organizational resources, the Islamist parliamentarians spearheaded a nationwide campaign to inform Egyptians about bird flu, calming nerves and dispelling rumors about the disease. Days after the first Egyptian bird flu case was announced, dozens of Brother MPs stood outside Parliament eating grilled chicken while photographers snapped pictures.

On February 26, more than 500 angry poultry farmers and traders demonstrated in front of the state Radio and Television Building to protest their losses, as well as newspaper reports of government plans to import frozen chickens and continue culling local birds. Poultry farmers also demonstrated in front of Parliament. When Brother MPs learned of the protest, a number of them left the morning's session to meet with the farmers. The MPs listened to their concerns and arranged for them to present their complaints to the People's Assembly. Afterward, according to MP Hamdi Hasan, a group of his peers invited the poultry farmers to the Assembly's garden, where they lunched on chicken while discussing the crisis.

In addition to eating chicken and eggs and drinking tap water in front of the cameras to allay public fears, the MPs visited poultry-producing areas and met with representatives from the poultry industry in Daqhaliyya, Damietta, Sharqiyya, Gharbiyya, Cairo, Minya, Port Said, and other governorates. Brother parliamentarians held press conferences and public meetings about the disease. The Brothers' campaign, which drew on the services of public health experts, microbiologists, doctors, veterinarians, and other specialists, presented medically supported facts about bird flu in addition to explaining how to cook chicken properly so as to avoid the disease. The group also distributed tens of thousands of pamphlets about bird flu throughout the country; their outreach to the public was clearly superior to that of the government.

---

6   *Al-Ahram Weekly*, February 23–March 1, 2006.

A second instance of crisis mobilization concerned the Emergency Law, under which Egyptians had lived since 1981. The law granted the executive and security forces wide-ranging powers to limit freedom of assembly, dissent, and political activity. Emergency rule also permitted the detention of individuals without trial and the arbitrary closure of newspapers. Although the law was set to expire at the end of May 2006, several weeks before this date Mubarak hinted at the possibility of extending the law for an additional two years. Nine months earlier, during the country's first multi-candidate presidential election, the president had promised voters that, if re-elected, he would replace the despised law with anti-terrorism legislation.

Muslim Brother parliamentarians mobilized to forestall any attempt at renewal of the politically stifling legislation. Beginning in mid-April, Brother MPs initiated a "network of parliamentarians" opposed to the Emergency Law and encouraged fellow legislators to join it. On April 19, the front page of the independent daily *al-Masry al-Youm* reported on the newly formed network's first meeting in the People's Assembly. The group, "Representatives Against the Emergency Law," totaled 113 members and consisted of all eighty-eight Muslim Brother MPs and three ruling-party deputies, as well as other independent and opposition party parliamentarians. In addition to signing a petition against the renewal of the law, the group declared its intention to work with all trends in Egyptian society opposed to emergency rule. The network specifically mentioned the street protest movement Kifaya, as well as university professors.

Brother MPs vowed to publicize the names of parliamentarians who voted in favor of renewing the unpopular legislation. They also encouraged citizens to convey their views about the Emergency Law to their elected representatives—a practice that had been unheard of in Egypt, where the primary function of an MP was thought to be helping constituents find jobs or secure services, rather than representing their opinions. Despite the network's efforts, it could not prevent extension of the law.

Egyptians had no idea on April 29 that the next morning Mubarak's government would ask the People's Assembly to extend emergency rule for an additional two years. But Brother MPs learned from reporters that high-ranking NDP parliamentarians and government officials were secretly preparing this maneuver. "It was a surprise," recalled MP Muhammad Saad al-Kitatni. "The agenda that came for that day was different, and had to do with farming and the Ministry of Agriculture."

On April 30, nearly 100 parliamentarians—not just Brother MPs—walked into the Assembly and donned black sashes that read "No to

Emergency." The prime minister and the interior minister, who rarely attended parliamentary sessions, were present in the chamber. The first order of business was the government's request to renew the Emergency Law. Only seven opposition MPs were allowed to speak against the proposal—three of whom were from the Brothers. Twenty NDP parliamentarians, by contrast, spoke on behalf of renewing the legislation. Each speaker was allotted just three minutes. Confronted with the extension's inevitability, the Brothers' bloc relied on parliamentary procedure to ensure a degree of transparency. The bloc presented a petition signed by twenty MPs requesting that the vote be taken individually, as opposed to the usual "yea" or "nay" collective vote. This measure required the speaker to go through the entire list of MPs and register individual votes publicly. While the vote was taking place, Brother MP Akram al-Sha'ar spotted an NDP MP trying to record a "yea" vote for an absent colleague (who was in Syria at the time), as well as the incorrect recording of another parliamentarian's vote on the measure.[7] The final tally was 257 in favor and ninety-one opposed to renewing the Emergency Law.

ADVENTURES WITH THE JUDICIARY

Working with independents and other opposition party MPs, the Brothers' parliamentary bloc also led a charge against the detested minister of justice, Mahmoud Abu al-Layl. Abu al-Layl served as the head of the Parliamentary Election Commission, considered responsible for much of the fraud that marred the 2005 legislative elections despite the supervision of Egypt's well-respected judges. As minister of justice, he oversaw the referral of senior judges Mahmoud Makki and Hisham al-Bastawisi to an internal disciplinary hearing after they publicly criticized vote rigging and other irregularities.[8] Al-Bastawisi and Makki became national heroes and came to personify the judiciary's struggle for independence and reform.

To mark the hearing's final two sessions—on May 11 and 18—the Brothers' rank and file, along with Kifaya supporters and others, protested in support of the two judges. Already for two weeks, semi-spontaneous protests had erupted around Cairo as Muslim Brothers and others gathered in solidarity with al-Bastawisi and Makki. Downtown Cairo was transformed into a military zone, with thousands of security personnel deployed around the High Court, the Judges' Club, the Press Syndicate, and other buildings.

---

7   *Al-Masry al-Youm*, May 1, 2006.
8   Hisham al-Bastawisi is now contemplating a presidential run. If he runs, he will be among the top tier of serious candidates for the Egyptian presidency.

The area was described as "under occupation" by the country's independent and opposition press. Over 700 protesters were arrested between April 24 and May 18. The Brothers bore the brunt, as over 85 percent of the arrests came from their ranks, including such leading figures in the movement as Essam al-Arian and Muhammad Mursi.[9]

The group's MPs also got into the action, actively supporting Makki and al-Bastawisi, as well as the principle of judicial independence, on the streets and in Parliament, throughout the spring and early summer of 2006. When the disciplinary hearing concluded on May 18, over twenty Brother parliamentarians stood outside the High Court in solidarity with the judges. Under the Cairo midday sun, the MPs stood wearing black sashes across their chests that read "The People's Representatives with Egypt's Judges." Nearly four hours later, the disciplinary board found Makki innocent and slapped al-Bastawisi with a reprimand. Afterward, the Brother parliamentarians walked several hundred meters, past thousands of security forces, to the Judges' Club, where they received a round of applause from the Club's membership. In early June, the Brothers' bloc presented the Judges' Club version of a new judicial authority law in Parliament (although of course the ruling party's version passed later that month).

The bloc's mobilization against Abu al-Layl was not confined to showing solidarity with his targets among the judges. In late April, 102 members of Parliament, led by the Brothers' bloc, called for a vote of no confidence in the justice minister because he was "abusing his position," trying to subsume the judiciary under the executive. Long-time Assembly speaker and NDP parliamentarian Fathi Surour disallowed the vote, claiming that proper parliamentary procedure had not been followed. Surour argued that the parliamentarians relied on a law pertaining to a sitting minister's criminal misconduct—under which category "political matters," like Abu al-Layl's interventions against the judges, do not fit. He also stated that the law which the MPs attempted to use in bringing their vote of no confidence required that members of the court trying the minister hail from both the "southern" and the "northern" regions of the country.[10] When this law was passed in 1958, Egypt and Syria were nominally conjoined in the United Arab Republic—an arrangement that ended in 1961.

Such legalistic machinations did not deter the Brothers' attempts to inject seriousness into the legislature. The bloc constantly lodged informational requests and interpellations, proposing legislation, responding

---

9   Mursi became the head of the Brothers' newly founded Freedom and Justice Party.
10   *Al-Ahram*, May 1, 2006.

to the state budget, and criticizing government. One researcher estimated that during the parliamentary session from December 2005 to July 2006, 80 percent of all parliamentary activity came from Brother parliamentarians.[11] Like any opposition party, the Muslim Brothers' parliamentary bloc used the People's Assembly in Egypt as a stage for criticizing the powers that be and as a vehicle for promoting their ideas. But they demonstrated that they took Parliament seriously as an institution. In fact, Brother MPs took the institution more seriously than any other political force in the country—including the ruling party. In a sense, the Brothers became victims of their own success, for starting in 2006, the Mubarak regime moved swiftly to put them back in their box.

BLACKENING THE BROTHERS

The crackdown intensified after a student demonstration at Cairo's al-Azhar University on December 10, 2006. Dressed in black, their faces covered with matching hoods whose headbands read *samidun*, or "steadfast," several dozen young Muslim Brothers marched from the student center to the university's main gate. Six of the masked youths, according to video and eyewitnesses, lined up in the middle of a square formed by the others and performed martial arts exercises reminiscent of demonstrations by Hamas and Hizballah.

Around 2,000 students were present for the show, which lasted approximately twenty-five minutes. Riot police immediately unloaded from trucks outside the university gate, massing only a few feet away from the unarmed demonstrators, but there were no clashes. No one was injured or arrested, and the protesters returned to the student center without incident. Classes were not canceled. Nevertheless, Egyptian state television and Arab satellite stations treated the demonstration as major news, repeatedly broadcasting footage of what they had labeled "the al-Azhar militias." Independent newspapers such as *al-Masry al-Youm* asked what the incident implied about the Muslim Brothers, while the government-controlled press, running close-up photos that exaggerated the demonstration's size, launched a campaign alleging that the Brothers were a violent organization with a paramilitary wing. *Ruz al-Yusuf*, a pro-government daily that frequently targeted the regime's critics, featured close-ups of the black-clad karate performers on the front page, under the ominous headline "The Brothers' Army."

---

11   Noha Antar, "Political Reform and Political Islam: The Case of Egypt," paper presented at the World Congress for Middle East Studies, Amman, June 14, 2006.

Four days after the al-Azhar demonstration, 124 students as well as seventeen senior Brothers—including Khayrat al-Shatir, the second deputy guide and the organization's third-highest-ranking official—were arrested in predawn raids. Police confiscated three personal computers, two mobile phones, and £E 60,000 in cash (slightly over $10,000) from al-Shatir, a wealthy businessman. Al-Shatir's son-in-law, who worked in the organization's media division, was also arrested. In the ensuing days and weeks, police rounded up several hundred Muslim Brothers from around the country. It was a fortuitous turn of events for the regime, coming just before Mubarak's proposal of sweeping amendments to the Egyptian constitution. The Brothers' reputation with the public was soiled at the precise moment when the regime was introducing new legal measures to rein in its most powerful domestic opponent.

The stage for sharper confrontation was set in early November 2006, when student union elections in the national universities were raising Cairo's political temperature. Campuses became increasingly tense as various university administrations, in concert with State Security, sought to control the elections while students—including members of the Muslim Brothers, socialists, and independents—resisted the interference. The troubles began at Cairo University, where the university administration and State Security combed through the lists of nominees and arbitrarily disqualified students affiliated with the Brothers. The pattern was repeated at Helwan, 'Ayn Shams, and al-Azhar Universities. Well over 200 candidates were thus barred from running.

At Cairo University, Brother students accused the administration of fraud and staged largely peaceful sit-ins within the university's gates. Word spread to students at other national universities. A 2005 initiative sponsored by the Brothers called Free Student Unions (FSU) regained momentum as the students attempted to establish independent unions free from regime influence. Socialist students joined in solidarity, in an infrequent instance of cross-ideological political activity. Yet as the FSU mobilized, the election campaigns became increasingly violent.

When 'Ayn Shams University held elections on October 29, the Brothers and FSU students standing outside polling stations to protest electoral manipulation met with a response usually reserved for national parliamentary elections. Thugs reported to be in the employ of State Security, as well as pro-government students, arrived at the polling stations with knives, clubs, bottles, and pipes to discourage others from congregating there. They also tore down signs supporting Brother candidates. Scores of young men faced off, and in the ensuing three days of bloody confrontation, three students were hospitalized. Images of the clashes made their way onto Egypt's political blogs, as well as Brothers' websites.

Two weeks later, the FSU organized alternative and unsanctioned elections at 'Ayn Shams that, again, drew the ire of State Security and pro-government students. Two more days of clashes added fuel to the fire. Student union elections became more violent as they progressed from one university to the next. While Egyptian NGOs, socialist groups, and the Brothers published statements condemning the violence, elections had still not taken place at al-Azhar—the oldest and, arguably, the most important religious university in the Arab world.

Al-Azhar University's troubled experience with student union elections is important for understanding the martial arts demonstration that took place on December 10. Al-Azhar students had not chosen their own representatives since 1992. As one Brother medical student, Yahya Ibrahim, put it, "We would go home for a holiday and return to an appointed student union." In the winter of 2006, following the Brothers' success in the 2005 parliamentary elections and the formation of the FSU, students were in a mood to defy the usual administration shenanigans.

Ahmad al-Tayyib, president of the university, added something new to the tactics employed to exclude the Brothers on other campuses. During the first week of December, he expelled six Brother medical students for their FSU activities. Students responded by trying to meet with al-Tayyib as well as organizing in solidarity with their dismissed classmates. At one point in the students' mobilization, according to Ibrahim, the State Security representative at the university, Hisham 'Abd al-Mun'im, told them that if they did not desist, they would be treated "like 'Ayn Shams." The students understood his words as a physical threat.

The Brothers students met to discuss their options: How should they register their protest? Ibrahim says the option of a martial arts performance was chosen to show that they were not afraid of State Security's thugs. At that point, the Brother student organizers claimed, students from the physical education department volunteered to demonstrate their karate skills. The Brother students contacted the media and requested that they cover the performance. It is unclear how much coordination took place between the al-Azhar students and the national Brothers. Though a member of the Guidance Office served as head of the group's student affairs department, the Brothers' senior leaders denied that they knew about the martial arts display, and the students confirm the leaders were not told.

Egyptian state media, however, went into overdrive. In addition to *Ruz al-Yusuf*'s dramatic banner headline, regular front-page stories about the

Brothers appeared in the flagship daily *al-Ahram*. The stories reported on the arrests of Brothers from around the country and aired allegations of illegal Brothers financial networks, money laundering activities, and links to international terrorist financiers.[12] Editorials cited the Brothers' militant past as evidence for its inherently violent character.

Recurring stories about the "al-Azhar militia" and illegal financial networks cast a shadow upon the group's image as a largely peaceful organization committed to working within the system. The tone of public discourse about the Brothers changed, with some beginning to wonder whether at least some of the state-run media's allegations could be true. The martial arts demonstration, notwithstanding its disavowal by senior Brothers, was a surprising mistake by a group known for its internal discipline.

THE REGIME STRIKES BACK

But the regime did not wait for the media to blacken the Muslim Brothers' image before rounding up the 124 al-Azhar students, including medical student Yahya Ibrahim, and seventeen other Brothers in the wee hours of December 14. According to Ibrahim, State Security and police stormed the dormitory shortly after 3 am, rousing the sleeping students on their list, blindfolding them, and binding their hands. The students heard the officer in charge communicating with his superior over a walkie-talkie, expressing confusion over the list of names. "Should I [just] bring them all?" he asked, to which the response was, "Yes, quickly." Not all of the hooded demonstrators were arrested, Ibrahim says, because "State Security did not know who they were, because their faces were covered." The students would spend seventy days in prison, without being formally charged, before being released on February 21, 2007. Yet their reintegration into the university did not proceed smoothly. Ahmad al-Tayyib expelled sixty of them, explaining at a meeting with the students that al-Azhar was a place for education—not for political activity.

The seventeen senior Brothers arrested on December 14, such as Deputy Guide Khayrat al-Shatir, were less fortunate still. They were eventually charged with money laundering, financing banned political activities, and trying to revive the Brothers' paramilitary wing. A month after the arrests, on January 28, Egypt's prosecutor-general froze al-Shatir's assets, along with those of twenty-nine others. Businesses owned by Brothers, including several publishing houses and import/export firms, a

---

12   See *al-Ahram*, January 15, 2007.

pharmaceuticals manufacturer, and a construction company were closed, the merchandise confiscated. The frozen assets were valued at tens of millions of dollars.

The next day, a judge in a Cairo criminal court dismissed the charges against al-Shatir and his codefendants and ordered them freed without delay, but police simply rearrested al-Shatir and the sixteen others. Then, on February 6, President Mubarak intervened by ordering that al-Shatir and thirty-nine other Brothers be tried in front of a military tribunal. It was to be the first time that Egyptian civilians would face military tribunals since the regime employed them against the Brothers in 2001. Although a protest petition circulated among Egyptian politicos and intellectuals, in the following months there were more arrests. One group that seems to have been targeted was the "parliamentary kitchen." According to one MP, Muhammad al-Baltagi,[13] nineteen kitchen aides were arrested shortly after the events at al-Azhar. It seems very unlikely that these staffers had anything to do with the student affairs department, student union elections, or the al-Azhar demonstration. Another, more political logic was at work.

On December 26, 2006, Mubarak formally proposed thirty-four amendments to the constitution. Ostensibly, the changes aimed to modernize the constitution by limiting presidential powers, enhancing multiparty competition, and eliminating anachronistic references to socialism. In reality, the amendments, which were subsequently approved by Parliament and ratified on March 26, 2007 in a national referendum, further solidified the legal underpinnings of authoritarianism in Egypt.

Article 5 explicitly banned political activity based in any way upon religion. Months earlier, in mid-January, the Muslim Brothers had announced plans to establish a political party. Brother officials declared the party would be a civil political entity with a religious *marja'iyya* (foundation). The revisions to Article 5 prohibited the possibility of such a party, and provided the regime with further legal tools for curtailing the Brothers' activities. Article 76, relating to presidential nominations, was modified to ease the restrictions on nominating presidential candidates from legally recognized parties. This article, first amended in 2005, made Egypt's first-ever "presidential election" possible. (Previously, the president had been chosen by yes/no referenda on a single candidate.) The 2007 modification did not, however, alter the requirements for nominating independent candidates.

---

13   At the time, al-Baltagi was a rising star among the Brothers. He gained still more prominence as one of the most visible Brothers that participated in the revolution. Today, he is a leading personality in the Freedom and Justice Party.

The restrictions on independents were so severe, in fact, that it was practically impossible for such candidates to stand in presidential elections. These restrictions were aimed, in large part, at preventing the Brothers from ever being able to nominate one of their own for president. The changes to Article 88 eliminated the system of judicial supervision of elections that began in 2000 ("one judge for every ballot box"), replacing it with an "electoral commission" composed of sitting and retired judges, partly chosen by the regime, and further stipulating that balloting occur on a single day. This amendment was widely seen as an attempt to remove Egypt's independent judges, who had proven troublesome for the regime in the past, from the electoral process.

The amendments to Article 179 proved to be among the most controversial. Marketed as the "Egyptian PATRIOT Act," this article embedded wide-ranging anti-terrorism measures in the constitution. The amendment empowered the president to refer cases to military and exceptional courts, and allowed the police to search homes and conduct surveillance—including wiretaps and other electronic intrusions—without warrants.

The amendments also enabled potential changes to Egypt's electoral system. Before 1990, elections were held under a "party-list" or modified "slate" system that limited the opportunities for independent candidates. Egypt's Supreme Constitutional Court ruled the system illegal in 1990. From that point forward, legislative elections were conducted under an "individual candidacy" system by which hopefuls were not required to belong to legally established political parties. The Brothers ran their members as independents, even though they campaigned openly as affiliates of the organization. Under the pretext of strengthening political parties and enhancing the role of women and minorities in political life, the 2007 constitutional amendments enabled the return to a "party-list" system with a limited number of seats reserved for independents. The real purpose of the change, however, was to reduce significantly the ability of the Brothers to compete in elections. The Mubarak regime went further than the usual electoral engineering—changing the constitution in order to mold the electoral law to its liking.

When the thirty-four amendments were first proposed, some opposition parties withheld judgment, while others accepted some of the proposed changes in principle.[14] But when the amendments, especially Articles 88 and 179, took their final form, all segments of the opposition (including the citizen protest group Kifaya) called for a boycott of the national referendum needed to approve them. The Muslim Brothers were among the first

---

14   *Al-Masry al-Youm*, January 10, 2007.

to criticize the proposed amendments. In interviews, Muhammad Habib,[15] Deputy Guide at the time, characterized the proposed amendments as "a move backward with regard to freedoms." Muhammad Saad al-Kitatni, chairman of the Brothers' parliamentary bloc, declared: "The primary goal of the amendments is to intensify authoritarianism and to prepare for inheritance of power [by Husni Mubarak's son Gamal] and the curtailment of the opposition in general."

The constitutional referendum took place ten days earlier than originally scheduled. Egyptians overwhelmingly stayed home. The government reported 27.1 percent voter turnout, while the Egyptian Organization for Human Rights estimated the figure at less than 5 percent. Other civil society and rights groups put the figure even lower, with widespread reports of vote-rigging and deserted polling stations.

Events in the region also facilitated a broader crackdown on the Brothers. Hamas's performance in the January 2006 Palestinian elections and the outcome of the summer 2006 war between Israel and Hizballah produced an international environment less hospitable to Islamist groups. American pressure on the Mubarak regime, which had greatly decreased as the results of Egypt's 2005 parliamentary elections became apparent, ceased entirely after Hamas's victory. Washington remained silent as the Mubarak regime arrested hundreds of Brothers and transferred dozens to military courts. Despite meetings that took place in April between al-Kitatni and House Majority Leader Steny Hoyer (D–MD) at the Egyptian parliament and the US ambassador's residence in Cairo, the Bush administration never softened the traditional US hard line against the Brothers.

Intensified repression notwithstanding, the Muslim Brothers did not exit Egyptian political life. The group had to adjust to a new reality, however. As Habib stated, "The repression is as strong as in the 1960s and the 1990s but now they [the regime] are much smarter and plan better. They know better where to hit us." Among these smarter regime sanctions were the severe financial measures aimed at the organization's ability to provide social services, which many believe to be the backbone of the Brothers' popular support. Seizing the assets of major financiers such as Khayrat al-Shatir was intended to discourage others from funding the organization.

---

15   Habib lost re-election to the Brothers' Guidance Office in December 2009. He subsequently resigned as deputy guide, claiming that the Brothers had violated their internal election procedures. Habib resigned from the organization altogether in July 2011, and joined a newly formed political party made up of former Brothers (al-Nahda).

Ibrahim al-Hudaybi, a grandson and great-grandson of two general guides of the society, was quoted in the American press arguing that the late 2000s crackdown was "the worst attack on the Brothers since the 1950s."[16] Yet the overwhelming consensus within the leadership of the Muslim Brothers was that, at worst, comparing crackdowns is difficult and, at best, the repression was nothing like that of the 1960s, when Brothers were routinely subjected to torture and many were forced to flee the country. As parliamentary department head Muhammad Mursi concluded, "In the 1960s, they [the government] were trying to destroy [us] completely. Now, that is impossible. There are more roots than anyone can completely pull out from the streets."

Authoritarianism increased during the last years of Mubarak's rule. But even the repression of the regime's security forces, and its legal machinations, could not expunge the Brothers from the country's politics. The Society of Muslim Brothers remained the best-organized and most powerful opposition force in Egypt. They worked tirelessly against the regime's monopoly of power. They railed against government corruption, campaigned against the Emergency Law, and exposed the regime's fraudulent elections. Ultimately they proved more durable than Mubarak, but the organization (and its members) paid a high price for its activism.

According to now ex-Brother Habib, the repression changed the composition of the Guidance Office and made the organization more conservative in its outlook. Indeed, on the eve of the January 25 uprising, the Brothers refused to participate in the planned demonstration. Youth members joined the initial days of protest but the Brothers only fully committed once the scale of the uprising became apparent. And when the Brothers concluded that if the regime survived, they would pay the ultimate price, the organization became fully committed to the "revolution." Indeed, the group's participation was indispensable to helping the protesters finish off Mubarak's rule.

Yet the group's limited coordination with the protesters ended shortly thereafter. Indeed, the Brothers have played a complicated and sometimes contradictory role since the uprising. On the one hand, they have repeatedly supported the SCAF against the demands of liberal activists and youth protesters. On the other hand, the group has also smartly moved on from sustained protests and demonstrations and begun working to enter the political landscape as a formal actor. With the creation of the Freedom and Justice Party in July 2011, the Brothers are operating for the first time largely (although not entirely) above ground. In Egypt's fundamentally

16   *Christian Science Monitor*, May 2, 2007.

new political context, we can expect significant transformation within the organization. Its role in Egyptian politics will also likely change. But the Muslim Brothers will remain one of the most important political trends in Egypt as the country moves forward with its transition.

CHAPTER 15

The Gama'a Islamiyya:
From Impasse to Opportunity

Ewan Stein

In the early 1990s, the security forces of Egypt were embroiled in a low-grade civil war with the Gama'a Islamiyya (Islamic Group), an uncompromising outfit committed to the violent overthrow of the government. The Gama'a, like the even more radical Egyptian Islamic Jihad and al-Takfir wa al-Hijra, grew out of study circles reading the works of Ibn Taymiyya and Sayyid Qutb, the intellectual godfathers of *jihadi* groups across the Muslim world, including al-Qaeda. Qutb taught that *jahili* (pagan) governments and social elites had usurped the entire realm of Islam. For his more extreme followers, war was not only permitted, but also mandated, to restore the Muslim world to righteousness. The enemy was everywhere; the Gama'a did not distinguish between the Egyptian regime and its "infidel" US and Israeli allies, or between armed police and camera-toting tourists.[1] The Muslim Brothers, whose ranks had included Qutb, had betrayed their past, he claimed, in the interest of accommodation with the regime.

In the summer of 2009 I interviewed the then de facto leader of the Gama'a Islamiyya, Najih Ibrahim, for *Middle East Report*. At the time, the Gama'a had won the international security community's attention for its pioneering ideological "revisions" (*muraja'at*), in which it renounced jihad against the Egyptian regime, violence against civilians, and other forms of terrorism. Much of the revisions literature, which ran to over twenty books, was written by Ibrahim, who reexamined Islamic sources to construct new justifications for the peaceful and conciliatory course. The works were vetted and approved by the Islamic Research Academy at al-Azhar, and attracted praise from such prominent clerics as Yusuf al-Qaradawi.

But despite the Gama'a's new status as poster child for de-radicalizing jihadists around the world, as a social and political movement within Egypt it had reached an impasse. Although most of the founding

---

1   See the interview with former Gama'a leader Tal'at Fu'ad Qasim, "What Does the Gama'a Islamiyya Want?" *Middle East Report* 198 (January–March 1996), pp. 42–3. Egyptian security men killed Qasim in 1998.

members (known as the "historic leadership") had been freed from prison, along with thousands of lower-echelon cadres, the Mubarak regime kept the group on a tight leash. It was permitted to maintain a website but members were banned from preaching in mosques, speaking in public, or giving TV interviews. Leaders like Najih Ibrahim could not travel within, let alone outside, Egypt without approval from the security apparatus. Deprived of opportunities for *da'wa* (proselytizing), and with an aging and dispirited core membership, it seemed the Gama'a might simply wither on the vine.

The fall of Mubarak in February 2011 yielded a substantial dividend for Islamists of all stripes, despite the secondary role the Muslim Brothers, the *salafis*, and the Gama'a Islamiyya played in the revolution itself. The Gama'a, like these other groups, exudes a new self-confidence as it seeks to position itself as a credible mainstream—and vote-worthy—political and social movement that understands the material and spiritual concerns of the Egyptian masses.

But the Gama'a, perhaps more than any other player in Egypt's new political ferment, struggles to free itself from a checkered past. On the one hand, many Egyptians hold painful memories of the civil strife of the 1990s in which over 1,000 people lost their lives and in which Gama'a zealots terrorized Copts, women, intellectuals, and anyone else they deemed out of step with their vision of a proper Islamic society. On the other, many who may otherwise be sympathetic to the group's social agenda deride its leaders for the apparently self-serving deal they made with the Mubarak regime in the early 2000s, helping to bolster tyranny in order to save their own skins. Ibrahim's attitude to the protests that began on January 25 was one of extreme reticence. Following Mubarak's woeful speech on February 1 he called on demonstrators to return home and to respect the president's record as a "fighter" for Egypt. He argued that "constitutional legitimacy" was more important than "revolutionary legitimacy." This stance merely confirmed suspicions that the Gama'a and the regime were in cahoots.

It is interesting, from the vantage point of mid-2011, to recall the positions and predicament of the Gama'a in the late Mubarak period. Although the Gama'a, like other Islamic groups, is threatened by schism, the largely peaceful nature of the January 25 revolution has vindicated the group's decision to renounce violence as a means of effecting political change in Egypt. This is particularly important for those among the membership who, suffering in the stultifying atmosphere of the late Mubarak period, may have doubted the wisdom of the new course and begun to consider other options.

THE PREACHER OF BAKUS: ALEXANDRIA, JUNE 2009

The historic leaders of the Gamaʿa, as well as the bulk of its rank and file, were released from prison, but they remained under close watch as of 2009. The official head of the group, the Alexandria-based Karam Zuhdi, suffered from several chronic medical conditions and kept a low profile in comparison with others, particularly the Minya-based political chief ʿIsam Dirbala and Najih Ibrahim.

Now in his fifties, Ibrahim is the author of most Gamaʿa literature (both pre- and post-revisions) and emerged as the group's main spokesman. Ibrahim hails from the province of Asyout in Middle Egypt, but settled in the bustling popular neighborhood of Bakus in Alexandria—his wife's hometown—after his release from prison. A garrulous, paternal, and personable figure, Ibrahim oversees and writes for the Gamaʿa website (the group's only officially tolerated outlet before Mubarak fell) while earning a living as a dermatologist, a profession he continued to pursue throughout his twenty-four years behind bars. The study in Ibrahim's comfortable sixteenth-floor apartment commands sweeping views of the Mediterranean Sea and, with the windows flung open and the cool sea breeze blowing in, feels like a hard place in which to think angry thoughts.

Ibrahim's book collection attests eloquently to his intellectual formation. On the lower shelf sits a neat row of tomes, whose familiar green-and-red binding and gilt calligraphy identify them as collections of Islamic law. Above them is a more haphazard assortment of paperbacks, including many works of Egyptian political and intellectual history. Alongside volumes from his own series *The Correction of Concepts*, the names of major Egyptian secular writers leap out: Abdel Moneim Said, Anis Mansour, Muhammad Hasanayn Haykal. Propping up the books on one end is a stack of volumes containing the complete papers of seminal—and ideologically composite—Egyptian nationalists Mustafa Kamil and Muhammad Farid. Does the erstwhile theoretician of jihad now fancy himself a present-day Saad Zaghloul, the revered hero of the Wafd whose statue strides purposefully toward Europe a few miles down the Corniche?

Not quite. But Najih Ibrahim comes across as every inch the Egyptian patriot. An hour into our meeting he disappeared to return with a tray of fried sardines, rice, and salad, proudly and unequivocally announcing that Egyptian food is the best on the planet. More pertinently, he pointed out (clearly not for the first time) that the world's first Islamist movement, the Muslim Brothers of Hasan al-Banna, was Egyptian, and now the first Islamist movement to admit to its mistakes is also Egyptian. Asked whether he thought Egypt remained the beacon of the Islamic world, he nodded slowly: "For the Sunnis you have Egypt and you have Saudi Arabia." Saudi Arabia is important because of Mecca and Medina, but in Egypt the quality of the preachers sets the country apart: "Egyptian imams can do their sermons by heart, whereas the Saudi ones need to read from notes."

The conceptual frame of reference for the pre-revisions Gama'a Islamiyya, as with most Islamist groups, transcended the nation-state. As reflected in Ibrahim's older titles, such as *The Charter for Islamic Action* (1984) and *The Inevitability of Confrontation* (1987), the worldview of the Gama'a was relatively simple: the Islamic caliphate had been carved up and replaced by "statelets" ruled by secular-minded "infidels," in league with Crusaders and Jews. These infidels would never re-establish the caliphate, essential to the revival of Islam, and must therefore be toppled via jihad. At the same time, Muslim societies had to be purged of incorrect and deviant practices via "enjoining good and forbidding evil," or *hisba*. (The Gama'a did not go so far, as did al-Takfir wa al-Hijra and Egyptian Islamic Jihad, as to declare almost all of society to be infidel.) This direct action on behalf of religion would increase the efficacy of ceaseless proselytizing (*da'wa*) to bring society back to the true religion of God.

These three elements of the Gama'a program (*jihad, hisba,* and *da'wa*) remain at the core of the "revisions" literature, but Najih Ibrahim was keen to stress the following: *jihad* is a means to an end, and the end does not necessarily justify the means. The duty of violent *jihad* falls into abeyance if the costs outweigh the benefits. The Islamist movement erred seriously when it tried to overthrow regimes, which, no matter how decadent, cannot be declared infidel. The harming of civilians, Muslim and non-Muslim, is forbidden in Islam. The duty of *hisba* must be discharged in coordination with the state. *Hisba* is now more a set of guidelines for neighborly behavior, authorizing, at most, a kind of citizens' arrest, than the vigilante doctrine of old. Finally, *da'wa* is the prime concern and *raison d'être* of the Islamist movement. No step should be taken that may prejudice the goal of guiding humanity to salvation.

THE POLITICS OF RELIGION

After three hours of discussion, Ibrahim had to go to work. He asked his teenage son (conjugal visits were allowed in jail) to show me around Alexandria until it was time for me to catch my train. Looking down from Stanley Bridge at the beach packed with revelers, with the sun setting over the broad expanse of the Mediterranean, it was hard to believe that this city is the epicenter of Egypt's closed-minded *salafi* trend, which some believe is the wave of the political future in Egypt and beyond.[2] Owing much to the strictly fundamentalist teachings of Muhammad Ibn 'Abd al-Wahhab and his followers in the Arabian Peninsula, the Egyptian version apparently also has its own momentum. The Gama'a itself was influenced by the austere orthopraxy picked up by the Egyptian multitudes returning from stints of employment in Saudi Arabia and the Gulf states.

Although the Gama'a Islamiyya would at one time have appeared near the top of the list of Egyptian (and Arab) *salafi* groups, in 2009 Ibrahim gave the *salafi* trend a mixed report card. On the plus side, the *salafis* tenaciously uphold the Islamic creed. And they are right to shun politics, particularly at the level of the state.

Ibrahim's reasoning here revealed a distinctly realistic (if not realist) view of international relations, as well as cynicism regarding the benefits of ruling Egypt. "Islamists can never take power," Ibrahim insisted, adding that those who, like some of the Muslim Brothers, think otherwise are deluded. "Whether they try to do so by force or through elections," Islamists will fail. "Were the Brothers to win power in Egypt," he predicted firmly, "Israel would immediately reoccupy the Sinai and the United States would impose economic sanctions." An Islamic state is one of several means to the end of bringing people to their religion, but should never be an end goal. In reality, for Ibrahim, the Islamic state is a misnomer. The state that Islamists really want is a civil state governed by Islamic rules—which has, give or take a law or two, been achieved already in many places, including in Egypt. Rather than aspiring to more, it is much safer and more beneficial for Islamist movements to leave states in the hands of secularists and be allowed to pursue peaceful *da'wa* under their protective shield.

Ibrahim said that refusal to be content with this setup was the Gama'a's pivotal mistake. Although President Anwar al-Sadat had allowed nearly boundless freedom for *da'wa*, the young activists were greedy (Ibrahim was twenty-seven when Sadat was assassinated in 1981). "We also wanted the state. So we killed Sadat and lost the state and the *da'wa*!" The freedom of the 1970s was intoxicating for these young activists who, filled with a false sense of their own power, thought that anything was possible. For Ibrahim, the "revisions"—writings full of cautious pragmatism and advising against "over-exuberance" in religion—are largely about reclaiming the space for *da'wa* that he and his brothers squandered in their youth.

---

2   Interview with Husam Tammam, Sixth of October City, Egypt, June 7, 2009. Since the fall of Mubarak the *salafi* trend has energetically entered the political fray, represented by two political parties, al-Fadila (Virtue) and al-Nour (Light).

A THIRD WAY?

Salafis, however, in their obsession with emulating every detail of the world of the Prophet Muhammad, fall short in Ibrahim's view when it comes to real-world issues. The Gama'a embraces existing customs and social norms so long as they do not contradict Islamic law (*shari'a*). In this regard, Ibrahim commended the Muslim Brothers for the excellent connection they enjoy with "life" and the pressing concerns of modern society. But "they put politics before religion, and that's wrong." In a sense, the Gama'a has maintained this critique since the 1970s. The armed Gama'a Islamiyya emerged from a much broader peaceful student movement. Most of this movement, including future high-fliers like Essam al-Arian and 'Abd al-Mun'im Abu al-Futouh, merged with the Muslim Brothers, whereas those interested in confrontation rather than accommodation remained as the Gama'a. (Arian and Abu al-Futouh revised their ideas to the extent that they are now considered among the most liberal-minded of the Brothers' spokesmen, although Abu al-Futouh was dismissed from the Brothers on June 19, 2011 when he announced he was going to run for president.) Throughout the 1980s and 1990s, the Gama'a maintained a sharply critical stance toward the Brothers' political dances with the Mubarak regime and shifting alliances with secular political forces, like the Wafd.

But one got the sense from talking to Ibrahim that the Gama'a would participate in political life, were it allowed. The security restrictions on Gama'a leaders and members were relaxed after they were released from prison, but before Mubarak's fall they traveled only at the pleasure of the security apparatus. They were not allowed to speak in mosques or otherwise organize.

In 2009, it seemed plausible that the Gama'a could present itself as a middle way between morally unimpeachable but defeatist *salafi* trends and the Muslim Brothers, who have sacrificed their Islamic soul on the altar of secular politics. According to Ibrahim, over 20,000 rank-and-file members had been let out of jail since the ceasefire in 1997 (though, since the vast majority were imprisoned without trial, it is impossible to know the extent of their commitment to the group before, during, or after their incarceration).[3] In any case, the group apparently has representatives in every Egyptian town, and the rows of bearded cadres that filled gymnasia

---

3   A Gama'a lawyer now claims the total number incarcerated was 15,000—a figure of 50,000 was also rumored. The Interior Ministry has promised the Gama'a a general amnesty for those with court rulings against them during the Mubarak regime, and begun paying some compensation to members for mistreatment, including torture. *Al-Masry al-Youm*, June 19, 2011.

to hear the historic leadership as it toured Egypt's prisons to promote the revisions in 2001–02 suggest a buoyant number. Shortly after agreeing to meet me for an interview, Najih Ibrahim dispatched "one of the brothers" from Minufiyya in the Delta to deliver personally to me in Cairo the entire corpus of Gama'a revision literature. The speed and efficiency with which this operation was accomplished suggest that the group's command and control mechanisms remain well oiled.

So could the Gama'a give the Brothers a run for their money? Less than charitable commentators, such as the journalist (and former jihad member) 'Abd al-Mun'im Munib, suggest that the Gama'a made a deal with the regime, that the regime was grooming the Gama'a as a weapon to wield against the Brothers, and that the Gama'a supported the principle of hereditary succession and believed Gamal Mubarak would have granted them freedom to proselytize.[4] Ibrahim in turn, flatly refuted such accusations.[5]

At the same time, it is true that as an apolitical (and relatively marginal) religious group the Gama'a posed no threat to the Mubarak regime. It did not challenge state policy on either domestic or foreign issues, and criticized those who did so. It opposed not only the Brothers' contestation of elections but also the Kifaya opposition movement, which Najih Ibrahim laughingly dismissed as a "cocktail" in reference to its political and ideological heterogeneity. Like the Brothers, the Gama'a was against workers' protests and strikes even as labor unrest swept the country in the years before the 2011 uprising.

THE GAMA'A ISLAMIYYA AND THE JANUARY 25 REVOLUTION

In the wake of the January Revolution the Gama'a Islamiyya shook off its shackles and emerged as a key component of a resurgent Islamism, routinely listed with the Muslim Brothers and the *salafis* as one of the movement's three main prongs. But the Gama'a's new rise is not without public relations difficulties and ambiguities of purpose. The popular movement that brought the Gama'a in from the cold was not of any Islamists' making, and nor was it of a predominantly religious complexion. And

---

4   'Abd al-Mun'im Munib, "Why Doesn't Najih Ibrahim Give His Honest Opinion of Gamal Mubarak?" *al-Dustur*, July 8, 2009.

5   Najih Ibrahim, "King Farouk Was at His Weakest When He Killed al-Banna, and Nasser Executed Six Muslim Brothers, So Why Would the Mubarak Regime Need Us to Strike the Brothers?" *al-Dustur*, July 8, 2009. Whatever the veracity of these accusations, Ibrahim and others within the Gama'a were quick to attack the corrupt privatizers and their champions within the National Democratic Party when Gamal's supporters were purged from government by Mubarak at the end of January 2011. This was a way for the group to celebrate the gains of the revolution without attacking the president directly.

whereas in the wake of mass protest in the late 1970s some Islamic activists felt the time was ripe to spark revolution and seize power, the Gamaʿa leaders today are under no illusions that this constitutes a viable or even desirable option.

After Mubarak's departure, yet more Gamaʿa leaders and members were freed from prison or allowed to return from exile—most notably the cousins ʿAbboud and Tariq al-Zumur. These two, previously of Egyptian Islamic Jihad, were at the heart of the plot to assassinate Sadat and, though members of the Gamaʿa Shura Council, supported the 1997 ceasefire but not the subsequent ideological revisions. Najih Ibrahim's praise for the president at the height of the demonstrations alienated him from the unfolding revolution and put the group on the back foot. As with other Islamist groupings, being on the wrong side of the revolution has aggravated fissures within the Gamaʿa itself. Ibrahim's stance prompted a challenge to him and Karam Zuhdi from ʿIsam Dirbala and his protégé Safwat ʿAbd al-Ghani, both of whom were temporarily suspended from the group in mid-March. But Zuhdi has stepped down and Ibrahim become increasingly sidelined. In a sign of the times, Gamaʿa positions are now publicized via the Shura Council's Facebook page, rather than on Ibrahim's website.

In June, the Gamaʿa held its first-ever Shura Council elections. As a result, Dirbala—a somewhat less "liberal" figure than Ibrahim—is now president of the council and emir of the Gamaʿa. Dirbala, while still emphatic about abstaining from violence and not disavowing the revisions literature, lacks the contrition of Ibrahim, who stresses the need for Islamists to admit and learn from their mistakes. Dirbala, like others, explains the group's previous violent tack not so much as jurisprudential misunderstandings but as the only option left for young Muslims relentlessly persecuted by the Mubarak regime. In this narrative, the January 25 revolution is the culmination of the Gamaʿa's own long struggle against tyranny and oppression. But the leaders are careful to praise and cultivate links with the Supreme Council of the Armed Forces (SCAF). They oppose continued protests and strikes.

The newly dominant trend appears to gravitate further toward Salafi ideas, while Ibrahim and his followers represent a more tolerant, and perhaps flexible, direction for the group, true to the spirit of the revisions that advocated openness toward state and society. Ibrahim himself was elected to the Shura Council but refused any administrative office (he was apparently offered the *daʿwa* committee). But Ibrahim is not allowing the new leadership to proceed unchallenged. In late June, the Shura Council announced a prohibition on Gamaʿa members appearing on TV chat shows hosted by unveiled women, a ban that Ibrahim pointedly violated a few days later by appearing as a guest on the unveiled Rula Kharsa's *Life and People* show on the Life Channel.[6]

So what might the future hold for the Gama'a Islamiyya? In the most striking break with the past, it has formed a political party, Hizb al-Bina' wa al-Tanmiya (Construction and Development Party), led jointly by Tariq al-Zumur, Safwat 'Abd al-Ghani, and Mahmoud Taha. The party is open to forming election coalitions with other forces and will, like any party, seek to influence the legislature according to its own ideological vision. And the party gives the mother group legitimacy. But at least as important as seeking political influence via the ballot box, the Gama'a appears set on continuing its tacit alliance with the military regime and serving as its extension in society. Dirbala has called for the formation of a religious police in Egypt. Ibrahim, for his part, called for expanding the remit of existing vice squads to cover adultery and sodomy.[7] The Gama'a was active in helping the SCAF rein in sectarian violence in Imbaba in early May 2011, reflecting a continued penchant for social control. And if it does not intend to return to its previous practice of changing errant behavior by force, it can at least serve as the regime's moral eyes and ears.

Where the Gama'a will likely seek to broaden its popular appeal is the issue of crime and social decay. Even before the revolution, petty crime was widely perceived to be on the rise, and the resulting need to confront endemic thuggery (*baltaga*) and deteriorating public security looms large in Gama'a and *salafi* discourse. The Gama'a's Taliban-style approach to combating crime was a key factor in its rise before being crushed by the Egyptian security forces—and in certain parts of the country the security forces worked with the Gama'a. As Ibrahim recalled in 2009, the Gama'a was attractive because of its energy and goals, but it also offered protection and retribution to victims of theft or assault. Such services were particularly useful for the dislocated laborers and students for whom the traditional tribal structures were unavailable. The police, then as now, were of no use in such situations, especially in rural and slum areas. The Gama'a, Ibrahim argued, was to rid the streets of drug pushers, thugs, and an ever expanding list of undesirables that came to include, for some, unveiled women, artists, musicians, and Copts.

As Egypt's poor continue to fall through the cracks, the Gama'a may be around to help clean up the mess. The question then would be how far it can or will go. The group's new prescriptions on *hisba* may advocate nothing

---

6   Najih Ibrahim, "I Examine Women in My Clinic, So How Can I Decline an Appearance with Rula Kharsa?" *Al-Quds al-'Arabi*, July 4, 2011. [Arabic]
7   *Al-Masry al-Youm* (English edition), April 3, 2011.

more than firm advice to the concerned citizen, but the old literature on the same topic was not very precise about using force, either, and, as with any political organization, there is always scope for the rank and file to interpret written directives. To the extent that the Gamaʿa wants to offer more than the apartness of the *salafis*—or, for that matter, the Sufi orders—some elements of the group may end up returning to the more proactive vigilantism of old, particularly in those districts where the state fears (or can be induced not) to tread. But too much security entrepreneurship might anger the authorities, as happened in the 1980s. Could the Gamaʿa become loosely incorporated into the state as a quasi-official militia, in the style of the Iranian Basij? Currently this move seems unlikely, but given the uncertainty of Egypt's future in the post-Mubarak era, the regime's historical predilection for such co-optation, and the growing unmanageability of Egypt's urban spaces, the possibility should not be discounted.

Even as the Gamaʿa re-establishes itself as a social movement, then, it is doubtful that in its present form it would adopt a revolutionary course. Aside from having learned the hard way the consequences of rebellion, the Gamaʿa is socially and economically conservative, espousing much the same socio-economic vision as the Muslim Brothers. In the rural sphere, the Gamaʿa supported the unraveling of Nasser-era land reform, in particular the Law on Rents for Agricultural Land that benefited the rural aristocracy and rich property speculators, even though (or, more cynically, because) the Gamaʿa fed off those forced to leave the land and flock to urban slums because of the liberalization of rents in the 1980s and 1990s.

The Gamaʿa does not offer a progressive social agenda to lift Egyptians out of poverty, and adopts a paternalistic attitude toward the Egyptian poor. The group shares with conservatives everywhere the conviction that society's problems are due mainly to lax morals, not an unjust economic system. In a proper Islamic society, the poor will be taken care of through the benevolence and piety of the rich, who will conscientiously meet their charitable obligations. State intervention in this and most other realms remains, for Ibrahim and many others, counter to Islam, a vestige of the communistic Nasser years. Social justice consists of eliminating bribery, corruption, and "bad management" as the middle classes perform their duties as Muslims.

One of the main outcomes of the January revolution has been the opening of the political field to a variety of old and new actors. And now that parties with religious bases are being licensed, the heterogeneity and fluidity of Islamist politics is particularly striking. Although the Muslim Brothers may still be the most organized and effective political force in Egypt, their continued hegemony in Islamist circles is far from certain. The Gamaʿa Islamiyya in its heyday was a major social movement and genuine alternative to the Brothers. But in seeking to combine its more familiar *da'wa* activities with engagement in the political sphere, the Gama'a must articulate a meaningful and distinctive political program. Such pressure has created splits within the Brothers and *salafi* movements and will undoubtedly continue to cause divisions within the Gama'a. The future is far from certain. But as things stand, the sterner direction that the new leadership configuration appears to be taking may consign the Gama'a Islamiyya to the status of hard-line pressure group, rather than the more mainstream and collegial movement apparently favored by Najih Ibrahim.

CHAPTER 16

Cross and Crescent in Post-Mubarak Egypt

Mariz Tadros

January 2011 was a tumultuous month from the start. The suicide bombing on January 1 in the Two Saints Church in Alexandria, which left twenty-five dead and over 200 injured, precipitated protests by hundreds of youth in Cairo, Alexandria, and across Egypt.[1] While the Kifaya movement, Islamists, and others had instigated hundreds of protests in previous years, there was something distinctive about the demonstrations in the aftermath of the Alexandria church bombing. These protests were led by Copts, the group conventionally considered the most passive and inward-looking in the country among Egyptian intellectual and political circles. If the section of society that the regime had counted on to be most compliant was in the streets, displaying unparalleled personal animosity toward President Husni Mubarak, then what of groups that historically had been far less yielding? The Coptic protests thus opened a deep fissure in the culture of fear that had discouraged average Egyptians from defying the status quo. They were also entirely youth-organized and led, in contrast to previous actions led by more senior figures. In another development that presaged the January 25 revolution, the Coptic uprisings in the first week of January began in the Cairo neighborhood of Shubra and made their way to the city center.

In many respects, then, these Copt-led protests are as important as the Tunisian revolution in anticipating and precipitating Egypt's January 25 revolution. Yet very few accounts of the revolution say so. Such collective amnesia is characteristic of the Egyptian public's general response to sectarian matters. Sectarian attacks elicit a stream of rhetoric calling for social cohesion and national unity, but then it is back to business as usual. The ouster of President Mubarak may yet remake state–society relations in many respects, but there is little evidence that transitional justice will occur in Muslim–Christian relations. To the contrary, there is a strong belief, voiced during the uprising and afterwards, that Mubarak's government fomented sectarian tensions and so

---

1   For details of the church bombing and its aftermath, see Mariz Tadros, "A State of Sectarian Denial," *Middle East Report Online*, January 11, 2011.

religious prejudice will subside in post-Mubarak Egypt. Yet this has clearly not been the case.

In the first 100 days after Mubarak's resignation on February 11, there were no fewer than ten confirmed attacks on Christian places of worship or property, as well as other incidents of sectarian violence. These incidents included: an army raid on a monastery; the arson of churches in Rafah, Sol, Atfih, Dayr Mawas, and Imbaba; the looting and burning of property belonging to Copts in the villages of Badraman and Abu Qurqas; the assault on Christians in al-Qamadir, and the excision of a Coptic citizen's ear in Qina. On February 22, in the village of al-Shuraniyya in the Upper Egyptian province of Sohag, a number of homes were set afire and property inside destroyed when rumor spread that local Baha'is, who had been expelled from the village in 2009, had returned.[2] There were repeated attacks by *salafis* on tombs belonging to Sufi orders.

The escalation of sectarian attacks contrasted starkly with the spirit of national unity in Tahrir Square, where Egypt's "January 25 revolution" seemed to bring together the Muslim majority and the Christian minority. The global media foregrounded images of Muslims kneeling in prayer, encircled by Christians protecting them from the incursions of pro-regime thugs, and Muslims returning the favor during the celebration of Sunday mass. The slogan "Muslim, Christian, one hand!" was chanted frequently and fervently. There was not a single attack on a church during the eighteen days of revolutionary activism across the country, despite the withdrawal of police and security forces from the streets. In the euphoria, many were quick to pronounce the end of sectarianism in Egypt. Since Mubarak's regime had incited tensions between Muslims and Christians as part of its divide-and-rule strategy, the revolution seemed to herald a new era of social harmony and coexistence.

Yet the spirit of Tahrir Square was bounded in space and time. The downtown plaza had a moral economy of its own, a social solidarity across lines of class, gender, and religion that stopped at the impromptu checkpoints. Outside the square, social divides were as concrete as ever, and the joyful days preceding the ouster of Mubarak cannot be recaptured. The reason is as simple as a cartoon published in *al-Masry al-Youm* in which

---

2   *Al-Sharq al-Awsat*, February 24, 2011. The Baha'i faith, like Christianity and Islam, follows the teachings of a divinely inspired messenger, in this case the nineteenth-century Persian nobleman turned prophet Baha'ullah.

the revolutionary moment is marked by the Egyptian flag, while the phases before and after fly the cross and crescent. The January 25 revolution reinforced a key lesson of the history of Muslim–Christian relations in Egypt: national unity is strongest at times when citizenship is mediated by a common Egyptian identity, and weakest when citizenship is mediated by religion. The emphasis on Egyptian-ness in Tahrir Square was highly effective in uniting rather than dividing. Had the rallying cries been religious in character, the Christian minority (some 10 percent of Egyptians) would not only have turned away, but turned against the revolution, if not visibly then inwardly. The increasing Islamization of politics in post-Mubarak Egypt has badly damaged the democratic credentials of the revolution by deepening the inequities between Muslims and Christians—and creating new ones.

NEW ACTORS, OLD STRATEGIES

The sectarian attacks of March, April, and May 2011 have shocked many Egyptians who believe that Egypt has no problem with religious intolerance, only with leaders who whip up displays of it for their own purposes. With Mubarak gone, many insist that Muslim–Christian tensions are orchestrated by members of the former ruling party in association with disgraced State Security officers. Yet analysis suggests the involvement of others as well: *salafis*, the Muslim Brothers, ordinary citizens, and, not least, the army.

Security remains lax after the fall of Mubarak and the dissolution of his regime's secret police as well as many regular police units. Egyptians of all faiths complain of the rise in street crime and the slow response of the authorities to reported muggings and assaults. Disputes escalate to blows, as the army has proven an inadequate substitute for a proper gendarmerie. Yet in cases of religiously motivated attacks, the army seems to practice a policy of studied non-intervention, if not outright complicity with the attackers.

A case in point is that of Ayman Mitri, a Copt from the Upper Egyptian town of Qina whose ear was cut off by a gang of locals who falsely accused him of running a prostitution ring. The toughs claimed to be applying the penalty prescribed by the *shari'a*. Mitri filed a police report against the perpetrators, but was pressed to withdraw it during a "reconciliation committee" meeting attended by the army's local second-in-command. The sheikh of al-Azhar also met with Mitri to express his deep regrets, but no prosecution ensued.

Later, a local thug with a 200-man militia took over the villages of al-Badraman and Nazlat al-Badraman in Minya, another Upper Egyptian province, expelling some Copts, kidnapping others and demanding a ransom from many, while expropriating the lands of still others and impos- ing a levy on Copts for several weeks. He called the levy *jizya*, the name of the poll tax paid by protected non-Muslims (*ahl al-dhimma*) to Muslim rulers before the mid-nineteenth century. Forty-three human rights organi- zations wrote to the Supreme Council of the Armed Forces (SCAF) asking for action against the would-be sultan, but none was forthcoming. Shortly afterward, in the first week of April, Muslim villagers in Minya's al-Qamadir protested the planned repair of the church of Mari Yuhanna, built with offi- cial sanction in 2001 and serving about 2,500 worshippers. The parishion- ers sought a restoration permit from the army when the building began to collapse. Local Muslims objected, saying they were offended by the church's location in front of their mosque (built in 2010). With no intervention from the authorities, another "reconciliation committee" meeting resolved to move the church premises to a smaller building on the village outskirts, stipulating that it could display no religious markers like a bell or a cross.[3]

On two other occasions, the army itself was the aggressor. In an under- reported incident on February 22, soldiers attacked the monastery of St. Bishoy in Wadi al-Natroun with tanks and live ammunition, injuring four. The army accused the monks of building a fence without a permit (though the land legally belongs to them), and later released a statement insisting that only barriers built on state-owned land were razed. Yet, as the blogger Muhammad Mar'i asked, why target the monastery for illegal construction when thousands of unlicensed residential structures pop up all the time?

March 4 saw the better-documented church blaze in Sol, a village in the vicinity of Helwan south of the capital. Amidst Coptic protests around the country, rumor spread in the Cairo neighborhoods of Sayyida 'Aisha and Khalifa that the Christian garbage collectors (*zabbalin*) living in the nearby Muqattam hills were raping Muslim women in their church and were on their way to burn the Sayyida 'Aisha mosque. Thugs armed with guns and knives set upon the *zabbalin*, who threw back bricks and glass to defend the approaches to their settlement. The attacks left six dead—including one Muslim resident of the *zabbalin* community who had descended the hill to defend his Coptic friends and neighbors—and dozens injured, some in serious condition. The wounded garbage collectors claimed that the army arrived and took the side of the attackers. "The thugs and those attacking us were hiding behind the army's tanks, and both were shooting at us," said one *zabbal* who was shot through the jaw with a live round, which he says

3   Yusuf Sidhum, "Will the State Quail Before the Terror of the *Salafis*?" *Watani*, April 17, 2011.

bore the Defense Ministry's engraving.[4] The state prosecutor is investigating the matter.

THE QINA CONUNDRUM

Over the course of ten days in mid-April 2011, life in much of Upper Egypt came to a virtual standstill.[5] The crisis began on April 14, when the government announced that 'Imad Mikha'il, a Copt and a general in Mubarak's security apparatus, was appointed governor of Qina province. Angry Qinawis demanded his immediate resignation, holding rallies and moving to halt railway transport from Qina north to Suhag and south to Aswan. The protests only subsided on April 26 when the cabinet announced a three-month freeze on the governor's term, during which a Muslim official would undertake his duties. The protesters, however, vowed that they would continue to push for Gen. Mikha'il's resignation. The standoff exposed cracks in state–citizen relations as well as the ideological struggles between forces vying for power.

When the cabinet announced its list of governors, there was prompt opposition to Mikha'il on account of his association with the Mubarak regime. The January 25 revolution coalition argued that he was responsible for repression of the uprising in his previous capacity as deputy security head of Giza. In Qina, large protests erupted after Friday prayers on April 15 and continued for several days, preventing civil servants from entering the governorate premises and blocking the rail lines. Three days later, the prime minister sent Gen. Mansour al-'Isawi, the minister of interior (and a Qinawi) and Gen. Muhsin al-Nu'mani, minister of local administration, to hear the people's grievances. The meeting ended in frustration, and shortly afterward, the deputy prime minister refused to accept the letter of resignation that Mikha'il presented. The protesters threatened to shut off the supply of water to the Red Sea governorate and cut electricity to the sugar refineries. Some also warned the governor of death should he set foot in Qina.

The national press has been sympathetic to the Qinawis' stance: historically, the government has neglected the southern governorates, which have some of the lowest human development profiles nationwide and have been marginalized from the centers of decision-making. Abu al-'Abbas Muhammad, a Qinawi, wrote in the state-run magazine *Ruz al-Yusuf* that Prime Minister Sharaf should have shown the same regard for Qina that

---

4   Interview with an injured person, Muqattam, April 28, 2011.
5   A much-abridged version of this section appeared in the *Arab Reform Bulletin* on May 11, 2011 under the title "Egyptian Democracy and the Sectarian Litmus Test."

he showed for Tahrir Square when he visited the plaza upon his appointment and told the crowds that his legitimacy derived from them: "I say it
bluntly: those who conjured these spirits should release them. The government brought this crisis about and the government should bring an end
to it."[6] Indeed, delegating the Qina listening tour to two generals—one of
them the interior minister, to boot—was redolent of the old regime's ways,
treating political crises as security matters. Renowned author Alaa Al
Aswany described the premier's message to Qinawis as follows: "I decide,
and whether you like it or not, you will accept my dictates in a state of
submission."[7]

But to read the Qina events as a case of citizens confronting authoritarianism would be too simple. Around the same time, demonstrations
began in several other provinces, including Alexandria, Asyut, Minya,
Daqhaliyya, and Bani Suwayf, against the appointment of generals from
Mubarak's police state as governors. These protests, however, were notably
smaller, in the hundreds, while in Qina they numbered in the hundreds
of thousands. It was surely not coincidental that Qina was the only province whose appointed governor was to be a Christian. What happened
there involved a constellation of actors: tribal leaders, *salafis*, the Muslim
Brothers, Sufis, and members of the dismantled NDP and state security
agency, who, according to some reports, helped to idle the railways. The
common objective was not the demand for a civilian governor, but for a
Muslim one.

Qina had been assigned a Christian governor once before. This figure,
Magdi Ayyoub, was loathed by Coptic Qinawis for being so keen to appear
unbiased that he discriminated against Christians. It was during his tenure
that Egypt witnessed one of its bloodiest sectarian attacks to date—the
shootings of Nag' Hammadi parishioners leaving Christmas Eve Mass
in 2010. Muslim Qinawis also disliked Ayyoub, complaining that he was
a weak leader overly afraid of stepping on toes. But there was another
complaint as well, namely, that he could not participate in Friday prayers.

As for Mikha'il, a group calling themselves "intellectuals of Qina" issued
a statement contending that local forces had striven to channel opposition
to his appointment in a sectarian direction. According to the statement, a
Muslim Brother by the name of 'Abd al-'Aziz reached an agreement with
Qina's director of general security to delay the trains for two hours, and was

6   Abu al-'Abbas Muhammad, "Egypt Is Not Just Tahrir Square," *Ruz al-Yusuf*, April
23–29, 2011.
7   Alaa Al Aswany, "When We Speak, You Must Listen," *al-Masry al-Youm*, April 26,
2011.

then surprised when protesters occupied the tracks for several days. Muslim Brothers and *salafis* led the protests, but later the more established Islamists retreated. The statement (corroborated by journalistic accounts) highlighted that opponents of Mikha'il put forward an alternative slate to rule Qina as an Islamic emirate, consisting of two *salafi* sheikhs and a former NDP local councilman. According to several press reports, the town's mosques became platforms for calls to reject the Christian governor on the grounds that a non-Muslim has no authority (*wilaya*) over a Muslim.[8] Among the popular slogans raised in the protests were: "Islamic, Islamic, not Christian, not Jewish," "Raise your head up, you are Muslim," and "There is no God but God, the Nazarene is the enemy of God." ("Nazarene" refers not to Jesus but to Mikha'il, being a Muslim designation for Christians intended as a slur.)

The Islamist intellectual Fahmi Huwaydi cautioned that Islamists should not be lumped together,[9] but the Qina crisis shows that, in particular political settings, various Islamist factions can and do synchronize their efforts toward a common goal. The Muslim Brothers, the Gama'a Islamiyya and assorted *salafis* set up loudspeakers in front of the governorate, threatening to take up arms if the cabinet did not heed their demand for a Muslim governor. In front of al-Wihda mosque in the town center, *salafis* raised the Saudi flag and called for the establishment of an Islamic emirate. Political activist Hamdi Qandil interpreted this act as Saudi meddling in Egyptian affairs, employing thugs under the cloak of religion.[10] But the flag may not have symbolized counterrevolution so much as the strength of Wahhabi ties with *salafis* in Egypt.

Commentator Dia' Rashwan argued that since Christians were among the first to oppose Mikha'il's appointment, the protests were not motivated by sectarian sentiments.[11] Yet the clout of the *salafis* and other Islamists was conspicuous early on. When the two ministers visited Qina, the majority of the forum's attendees were *salafis*. "When the minister of interior asked about Copts, he discovered there was no representation and two priests were brought in for a meeting to be held with the minister afterwards," noted one journalist.[12] Also present were the Gama'a Islamiyya, the Muslim Brothers, and "NDP figures." A *salafi* sheikh rose and chanted, "We want it Islamic," to which neither minister responded.

---

8   *Al-Masry al-Youm*, April 21, 2011 and *Watani*, April 22, 2011.
9   Fahmi Huwaydi, "Talk of Lies and Hatred," *al-Shurouq*, April 27, 2011.
10   Hamdi Qandil, "Generals, Make the Decrepit Interior Minister Resign and Hit the Thugs of Saudi Arabia," *Sawt al-Umma*, April 25, 2011.
11   Dia' Rashwan, "A Vision and Possible Solutions for the Qina Crisis," *al-Shurouq*, April 25, 2011.
12   *Ruz al-Yusuf*, April 23–29, 2011.

The greatest evidence that the primary objection to Mikha'il was his religious identity, not his military rank, came after the government froze his assumption of office. The protesters released a statement saying they had blocked the railways for legitimate reasons, namely that they do not want Qina to fill the "quota" for Copts in government.[13] The Qina crisis is symptomatic of the dilemmas facing the transitional government in Egypt should the *salafis*, the Gama'a Islamiyya, the Muslim Brothers, and other Islamist forces continue to grow in mobilizing power.

OF "HONOR" AND SECTARIANISM

The attacks on the churches in Sol and Imbaba had something in common: both were ignited by perceptions of damaged communal "honor" due to a claimed loss of women's virtue. In Sol, Muslims burned the church in retaliation for an alleged relationship between a Christian man and a Muslim woman, whose father had been killed by his family because he refused to kill his daughter to cleanse the family's "honor." In Imbaba, on May 7, 2011 attacks on two churches in Imbaba, a poor quarter of Cairo left fifteen dead and over 200 injured. The crisis began when a crowd of some 2,000 *salafis* (and unknown others) agitated to "liberate" 'Abir, a Christian woman who they claimed had converted to Islam, married a Muslim and then been abducted to a building belonging to the Mari Mina church.

The timing of the 'Abir protests is noteworthy. Islamists had mounted rallies on consecutive Fridays since the summer of 2010 demanding the "release" of Camillia Zakhir, a priest's wife who they claimed had also converted to Islam before being detained by the Coptic Orthodox Church.[14] On April 29, a *salafi*-led coalition of "new Muslims" held a large demonstration in front of the cathedral where the Copts' Pope Shenouda resides, demanding her release and the pontiff's removal. On May 7, Camillia Zakhir appeared on television, in the company of her husband and her young son, to emphasize that she had left home after a marital dispute: she had not converted, or been held by the Church. Mere hours after the broadcast, bearded men believed to belong to the *salafi* movement were heading to the Mari Mina church, where 'Abir's husband had informed them that his wife was being held against her will. It was a case of "never mind Camillia, take 'Abir," as Khalid Muntasir wrote in a scathing column.[15]

---

13   *Al-Shurouq*, April 27, 2011.
14   For a detailed account of the Camillia crisis, see Mariz Tadros, "Behind Egypt's Deep Red Lines," *Middle East Report Online*, October 13, 2010.
15   Khalid Muntasir, "Never Mind Camillia, Take 'Abir," *al-Masry al-Youm*, May 10, 2011.

At the church, three sheikhs were allowed to inspect the premises, and they confirmed that 'Abir was not present. In the meantime, however, the large crowd outside aroused fears of an assault on the church, and clashes erupted with neighborhood Copts, including an exchange of gunfire. Property belonging to Copts was burned and looted, and the mob proceeded to set St. Mary's church ablaze as well. A fact-finding mission from the National Council for Human Rights attributed the violence to the deficient response of security forces, and accused NDP remnants of instigating social strife to abort the revolution. The council's report also pointed to extremists trying to reconfigure Egyptian society so that Copts have no rights except as *ahl al-dhimma*.[16]

After the Imbaba incident, Ahmad al-Tayyib, the sheikh of al-Azhar, warned Egyptians that sectarian strife could culminate in civil war. Public opinion was quick to pick up on this fear, but remains in overall denial of the dynamics of violence against non-Muslims in Egypt. Sectarianism is blamed on foreign enemies and a "deviant few" Egyptians. How these marginal actors are able to galvanize hundreds of Egyptians to take part in attacks in the name of defending religion is not explained.

There is also a pattern of presenting sectarian attacks as conflicts between two equal parties. An impassioned column by 'Abd al-Fattah 'Abd al-Mun'im, for instance, read: "We have sacrificed the revolution and Egypt so that the *salafis* and the Church can flex their muscles. They are backed up by militias capable of destroying the country in less than ten minutes, and there is no force in Egypt capable of overcoming them, not even the army. They speak in the name of Allah or the Lord. If the case of Camillia is resolved, 'Abir is her substitute. What counts is that the fires of sectarian sedition remain alight."[17] Of course, neither the Church nor independent groups of Copts ever launched an assault on a mosque or property belonging to Muslims during this wave of sectarian unrest. The Islamists and some secular nationalists, however, perceive the lobbying of external Coptic groups for international protection of minority Christians as a provocation, and a principal cause of sectarian incidents.

Any expression of Coptic demands, in fact, seems to be regarded by public opinion in Egypt as provocative, even if it is addressed to Egyptian authorities rather than the West. The protests in front of the National Radio and Television building were led by organized youth, a significant proportion of whom participated in the January 25 revolution. The

---

16   *Al-Dustour*, May 12, 2011.

17   'Abd al-Fattah 'Abd al-Mun'im, "Let Egypt Die and Long Live the *Salafis* and the Church," *al-Yawm al-Sabi'*, May 11, 2011.

demonstrations met a highly negative reaction, replete with arguments that religion-based demands undermine national unity and Egypt's economic recovery. Contrast this response to the general sympathy for the Qinawis who stopped rail traffic to the tourism centers of Luxor and Aswan for ten days straight. The Maspero protests, moreover, were organized independently of the Coptic Orthodox Church and in defiance of an order from Pope Shenouda to desist. It is perplexing that Copts, who have long been criticized in the media for retreating to the Church's "cocoon," should be reprimanded for breaking out of it.

WHAT KIND OF MAJORITARIAN DEMOCRACY?

If the public response to sectarian attacks is reminiscent of the pre-revolution period, so is the handling of the crisis by the armed forces and transitional government. Only in the case of Imbaba have the perpetrators of attacks been held for trial. By and large, the army has resorted to the same mechanism used by Mubarak's state security officers to paper over sectarian conflict—"reconciliation committees"—except that now, *salafi* sheikhs are key players therein. These committees only serve to thwart legal recourse for wrongdoing, and perpetuate inequality. In the first meeting held in Sol after the church arson, it was agreed (with the army's blessing) that the church should be rebuilt in a different location, preferably on the edge of town, to avoid offending majority sensibilities.[18] Following massive protests led by youth coalitions and Copts at Maspero, the army volunteered to rebuild the church. Leading Islamists such as Sheikh Muhammad Hasan and Sheikh Muhammad Higazi, known for his Muslim Brother sympathies, were tapped to participate in the meeting in Sol and then in Qina. The army deflected criticism of these moves by saying it called in Sheikh Hasan "because people listen to him."[19]

Yet the army's choice of strategic partners is dangerous in view of the vision of majoritarian democracy that *salafis* promote. Sheikh Hasan and his peers reassure Copts that they have nothing to fear from the rise of Islamist forces because they are guaranteed protection under Islam—rather than under a constitution enshrining the rights of all citizens, irrespective of religion. In the ninety years since Egypt's constitution was promulgated in 1922, the terms "Nazarenes" and "*ahl al-dhimma*" have been so prominent in public discourse only once before, during the resurgence of Islamist movements in the 1970s.

---

18   *Al-Wafd*, March 7, 2011.
19   *Al-Dustour*, May 11, 2011.

Muslim–Christian relations in Egypt will not be improved through national dialogues and reconciliation committees. What is needed is the political will to administer justice consistently and in compliance with universal rights, rather than power hierarchies and normative values on the ground. Yet there will no doubt be cases where *vox populi* clearly favors exclusionary practices, as with the expulsion of Baha'is in Sohag. Legal justice is necessary but insufficient to transform social relations: with the slogan "Raise your head high, you are Egyptian" replaced in many locales with "Raise your head high, you are Muslim," it is difficult not to sense that the revolution has been hijacked. Is there popular will to seize it back? This is one of the pressing questions facing Egypt.

A view of downtown Cairo, across the Nile from the
Cairo Tower. © Teun Voeten / Panos Pictures

Part IV

ECONOMIC REFORM, DEMOGRAPHY,
AND ENVIRONMENT

CHAPTER 17

Economic Reform and Privatization in Egypt

Karen Pfeifer

Egypt's economic history, from the abdication of King Farouk in 1952 to the abdication of Husni Mubarak in 2011, can be divided into three grand stages: the era of state-led development, the gradual erosion of state-led development, and the blossoming of neoliberalism. The period from 2008 to the present (July 2011), that is, from global financial crisis and recession to fragile recovery, may be a fourth stage—entailing at least the erosion of neoliberalism and, perhaps, the beginning of an era of more balanced growth with a more equitable distribution of benefits.

STATE-LED DEVELOPMENT

The era of state-led development, from the 1950s to the 1970s, was characterized by an enlarged role for government in the economy, with public investment in physical infrastructure, industrial production, agrarian reform, and human development. (See Figure 17.1 showing Egypt's score on the Human Development Index in comparison with the Arab countries as a group and the world as a whole.) This process was accompanied by fundamental changes in society and the class structure. The role of foreign capital was circumscribed, while domestic private capital was subordinated and confined to the interstices of state-run institutions and state-owned enterprises (SOEs). The landlord class was shrunk by land reform and a commercialized peasantry and rural working class cultivated in its place. With the expansion of ostensibly universal public education, including at the college level, a growing middle class of urban professionals and civil servants arose, including women in the ranks of the college-educated and salaried labor force. The urban working class burgeoned, in industry, services, and public-sector firms and agencies. The state recognized the contributions of the professional and working classes and their right to form syndicates and unions, but controlled both the leadership and the finances of these institutions from the top, forbidding actions such as strikes. A social compact prevailed in which the state provided legal protection for workers' wages, benefits, and job security, as well as universal access to public services, welfare, and subsidies for basic necessities, in exchange for political quiescence and devotion to a common project of nation-building.

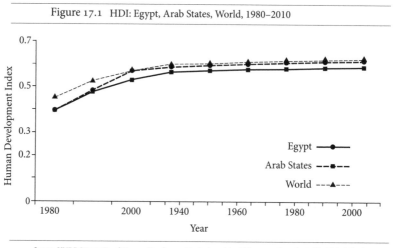

Figure 17.1   HDI: Egypt, Arab States, World, 1980–2010

Source: UNDP, International Human Development Indicators, http://hdrstats.undp.org/en/tables/default.html

The institutional fabric of state-led development gradually eroded over the 1970s and 1980s, due to both external pressures and internal contradictions. The two wars with Israel, in 1967 and 1973, were exorbitantly expensive for a low-income country and closed the Suez Canal for some years. The collapse of oil prices in the 1980s led to stagnation in neighboring countries where Egyptian migrant laborers worked. The heavy hand of central planning became overbearing and unwieldy. The complex agenda imposed on SOEs and other public-sector employers, including the absorption of all high-school and college graduates, eventually rendered many SOEs inefficient and economically unviable. The conflict between, on one hand, supporting peasant agriculture to raise rural incomes and, on the other hand, requisitioning key commercial crops at low prices to feed the urban population and to sell for hard currency grew so severe that it drove peasants into producing unregulated, but socially less rational, crops such as clover to feed cattle. The educated middle class began asserting demands for civil liberties and respect for human rights. When economic problems worsened and opposition arose, top-down authoritarianism turned brutal and repressive, in particular toward the organized working class and left-leaning political formations. Finally, the purchase of essential imports, such as inputs for industry and food to replace what was no longer produced domestically, was made increasingly difficult by the slow growth of exports, and this led to rising government deficits and international debt.

EROSION OF STATE-LED DEVELOPMENT

In response to emerging economic constraints, the regime of Anwar al-Sadat turned to the policy of *infitah*, or opening to foreign capital. While a private domestic capitalist class remained in the shadow of the state, the *infitah* helped to create a new wealthy comprador class, serving as the local agents for import/export companies and as representatives and junior partners of foreign capital. Following Egypt's peace treaty with Israel in 1979, the United States became Egypt's largest trading partner, source of foreign investment, and aid donor.

But the effort to curry favor with foreign capital was made without giving up the core role of the state and without major structural change in the Egyptian economy. The state economic enterprises, social contract with labor, and other promises of the Nasser era were left intact, and queues lengthened for public-sector jobs as the growth of the public sector slowed. This system was sustainable only as long as inflows of foreign currency continued apace—from aid, oil exports, foreign direct investment (mostly into the oil sector), Suez Canal tolls, international tourism, remittances from émigré workers, and a build-up of public debt to foreign lenders.

As oil prices and oil revenues declined in the mid- to late 1980s, the internal contradictions of state-led development and the region's dependence on declining oil revenues and labor remittances came together to generate a crisis. The state's industrialization strategy had relied on importing Western technology wholesale in large chunks of capital-intensive investment. This meant that growth in the early decades had been based on additions to capital and labor, with little technological innovation or long-term expansion in the demand for industrial labor. The combination of stagnation in agriculture and industry led to rising unemployment, rapid rural–urban migration, and expansion of the informal sector. Furthermore, in contrast to the East Asian model—Egypt is often compared unflatteringly to South Korea—protection for domestic industry had been allowed to go on for too long, with little expectation that these firms would "pay back" state support with innovation that would make their products competitive in world markets and earn their own share of foreign exchange.[1] And,

---

1   See John Waterbury, *Exposed to Innumerable Delusions: Public Enterprise and*

finally, the promise of jobs in the public sector for all graduates, and the job protections that formal-sector labor had won as part of the state-led social compact, led to overstaffing, wasted time and resources, and declines in real compensation as inflation overtook nominal wage growth.

Consequently, Egypt's economic growth, national saving, and public spending all plummeted in the later 1980s. Real per capita GDP growth fell from an average 4.7 percent per year during the 1980–85 period to 0.3 percent per year from 1985 to 1990, and public spending was reduced steadily from its peak of 55 percent of GDP in 1985 to a low of 26 percent in the year 2000.[2] This combination of internal crisis and the new reality of declining oil revenues and remittances made the Egyptian state more vulnerable to political influence from the emboldened class of importers and financiers who had flourished under the *infitah*, and more susceptible to pressure from the international financial institutions (IFIs).

ADVENT OF NEOLIBERALISM

International financial institutions, in particular the World Bank and IMF, were able to introduce neoliberal ideas ("the Washington consensus") to Egypt through the role they played in tackling Egypt's debt crisis. Structural adjustment programs required shrinking the role of the state, first through "stabilization" measures to cut government spending, reduce public deficits, and curb inflation, then through "liberalization" measures to reduce subsidies, remove price controls, and lower tariffs, and finally through "privatization" measures to sell off public-sector enterprises. Without cushioning the blows, all of these measures would create a fair amount of pain for working- and middle-class families and lead to strikes and protests.

Prior to 1990, neoliberal reforms had not made much headway in Egypt, due to resistance from organized labor and the possibility of escape for émigré workers. In reward for participating in the 1991 war to expel Iraqi forces from Kuwait, however, Egypt received a record amount of aid, $4.8 billion, in 1990–91, of which $3 billion came from the Gulf oil exporters. In addition, international creditors canceled $13 billion of Egypt's international debt. This financial relief facilitated the

---

State Power in Egypt, India, Mexico, and Turkey (Cambridge: Cambridge University Press, 1993), p. 235; and World Bank, *World Development Report 1995*, pp. 103–8.

2   Hossein Askari, *Middle East Oil Exporters: What Happened to Economic Development?* (Northampton, MA: Edward Elgar, 2006), pp. 97, 122.

regime's agreement to an IMF-led structural adjustment program that would not cause immediate pain to the citizenry or generate strong opposition.[3]

The crisis years of the later 1980s and early 1990s had been a period of increasing poverty for Egypt. Yet in the early 2000s, income inequality and poverty measurements showed a less dire situation than simple per capita measures of economic growth suggested, indicating that some institutions must have been providing significant income and consumption support to the poor.[4] As the state's role was shrunk under the "stabilization" program, these functions had increasingly come to be provided by the non-profit private sector, mostly in the form of Islamic charities.[5]

As Egypt reduced the ratio of government spending to GDP by half from 1985 to 2004, public-sector employment declined from 39 to 30 percent of the labor force. As the government liquidated holdings in 189 of 314 state economic enterprises, employment in that sector was halved, from 1.08 million employees (about 6 percent of the labor force) to less than a half-million.[6] At first this appeared to validate the success of the privatization program, as the official unemployment rate fell from 11.7 to 8.3 percent and employment in the formal private sector rose 6 percentage points to 27 percent. By 2006, however, it was clear that it had been the informal sector, rather than the private formal sector, that had expanded the most, absorbing 75 percent of new labor force entrants, accounting for 61 percent of actual employment, and producing between one third and one half of officially measured GDP.[7] The safety valve of labor emigration was as important as ever: in 2005–06, 2.3 million Egyptians worked abroad, and their remittances rose from an average of $3 billion from

3   Joel Beinin, "Late Capitalism and the Reformation of the Working Classes in the Middle East," in Israel Gershoni, Hakan Erdem, and Ursula Woköck, eds. *Histories of the Modern Middle East: New Directions* (Boulder, CO: Lynne Rienner, 2002), pp. 116–17.

4   As of 2000–02, Egypt's Gini index for consumption was 0.34, and Egypt's Human Poverty Index (HPI-1) value of 20 and its rank of sixty-first in 2005 were significantly better than its HDI and GDP per capita ranks.

5   World Bank, *World Development Report 2006*: Tables A1 and A2; UNDP 2007/2008: Country Page Egypt.

6   Carana Corporation, "Special Study: The Results and Impacts of Egypt's Privatization Program," *Privatization in Egypt: Quarterly Review* (April–June 2002), pp. 8–11.

7   Heba Nassar, "Temporary and Circular Migration: The Egyptian Case," Analytic and Synthetic Notes, Circular Migration Series (Florence, Italy: European University Institute, Euro-Mediterranean Consortium for Applied Research on International Migration, 2008), p. 6; Ragui Assaad, "Labor Supply, Employment, and Unemployment in the Egyptian Economy, 1988–2006," Economic Research Forum, Working Paper Series N. 0701 (Cairo, 2007), pp. 1, 12–13.

2000 to 2003 to more than $5 billion in 2004 and 2005, as indicated in Figure 17.3 on page 219.

DILEMMAS OF PRIVATIZATION

After decades of delay, privatization in Egypt was accelerated in the second half of the 1990s, as 119 of 314 state-owned enterprises (SOEs) were fully or partially sold.[8] These firms were mainly manufacturing ventures, but the government pledged to expand the privatization program to include utilities, public-sector banks and insurance companies, leading tourist hotels, and maritime and telecommunications firms. In May 1998, the International Monetary Fund, long skeptical of the Mubarak regime's commitment to privatization, pronounced itself satisfied with the program's progress, as measured by the proceeds going into the central treasury.

These developments generated controversy over capital ownership and social welfare. Between 1992 and 1996, financial markets expanded and trading volume in Egypt's stock market increased ninefold. The number of companies actively traded grew from 111 in 1985 to 354 in 1996, and the International Finance Corporation listed Egypt in its emerging markets index. Recognizing that the proponents of privatization had won the day, leftists, workers, and recalcitrant state bureaucrats sought to slow the pace of the sell-off, while progressives tried to grapple with how Egypt's transition from state to private-sector capitalism would evolve.

HOW TO PRIVATIZE?

There are several methods by which to transfer the ownership of SOEs to the private sector. Firms can be sold directly, and in total, to another company for a negotiated price. A second option is sale through a competitive bidding process on stock offerings, either to an "anchor firm" or "strategic investor," or to the public, without granting any single bidder a controlling interest. A third method is a voucher program, through which entitlements

---

8   The discussion of late 1990s privatization below is based on Marsha Pripstein Posusney, "Egyptian Privatization: New Challenges for the Left," *Middle East Report* 210 (Summer 1999). Unless otherwise noted, information on Egyptian privatization from 1996 to 1999 was drawn from *al-Ahram Weekly*, *Middle East Economic Digest*, and *Business Monthly*. On privatization battles before 1996, see Marsha Pripstein Posusney, *Labor and the State in Egypt: Workers, Unions, and Economic Restructuring* (New York: Columbia University Press, 1997).

to purchase shares are allocated on an equal basis to all adult citizens, who may then choose either to hold their shares or to sell them. Finally, employee stock ownership plans (ESOPs) allow workers to purchase a stake in the firms that employ them.

Egypt employed a combination of these methods. By July 1998, nine firms had been sold to strategic investors, and another thirty-seven had a majority of shares floated on the stock market, while nineteen companies saw 30–40 percent stakes floated. Many of these cases had 5 to 10 percent of their sales reserved for employee purchases, with employee shareholder associations (ESAs) set up for this purpose; fifteen establishments, mostly land reclamation companies, had a full or majority stake given to employees. Twenty-five firms were liquidated and their assets sold.

Typically, neoliberal economists and lending agencies evaluate these methods according to their measure of the resulting efficiency and profitability of the firm. The underlying assumption—supportable in some but not all cases in Egypt—is that SOEs are inefficiently run, with a bloated workforce producing inferior products, all at a cost to the state. In this context, the arguments in favor of direct or strategic sales are twofold. First, they result in management by a capitalist firm presumably operating according to efficient market principles; second, the anchor should be able to infuse the firm with new capital to modernize equipment and production techniques. While some Western economists see value in broader stock distribution, on the grounds that spreading property more evenly through the society is more egalitarian and enhances popular respect for property rights, the World Bank and the American Chamber of Commerce in Egypt promoted the anchor firm model,[9] with its tendency to concentrate ownership in the hands of established companies.

FEAR OF FOREIGN HANDS

A narrow focus on efficiency criteria ignored fundamental questions about the nationality of capital. Given Egypt's prior experience with colonialism, there was widespread concern about turning over the country's strategic assets to foreign hands. Both the direct and anchor sale models privileged foreign buyers, because—although consortia that pooled local capitalists' resources were being organized—Egyptian businessmen generally lacked sufficient capital to bid for large purchases.

---

9   World Bank, *Bureaucrats in Business* (New York: Oxford University Press, 1995), p. 202.

Efficiency criteria also obscured concerns about the welfare of workers in privatized parastatals. In theory, ESOPs would increase workers' influence over management decisions, thereby leading to more humane working environments, and less resort to lay-offs. ESOPs would also ensure that capital remains in national hands, and could increase workers' incomes. Certain Islamists advocated giving workers a controlling interest in their firms.[10] While most labor activists interviewed by my colleague Marsha Pripstein Posusney in 1995 saw this as complicity in privatization, a few supported experimentation with ESOPs.

Ordinary workers expressed varied responses to these programs, most of which limited them to minority ownership. At one large textile factory, workers opposed participation in a proposed ESA because it appeared unlikely to empower them to remove corrupt and incompetent state managers.[11] In addition, to the degree that ESOPs benefit only former parastatal workers, the new structure would exclude the rest of the citizenry, who were theoretically the collective owners of Egypt's SOEs.

DOMESTIC OR FOREIGN CAPITAL?

In the 1990s, privatization dramatically increased the presence of foreign capital in Egypt. Foreign portfolio investment accounted for about 30 percent of the total market capitalization of $20 billion in 1997, with foreign investors owning roughly 20 percent of negotiable shares on the exchange. More than 700 foreign institutions and funds were involved in the Egyptian market, and several international investment funds were established to concentrate exclusively on Egyptian securities. Even government officials expressed fears that a high proportion of foreign holdings in the stock market were merely speculative, and thus could be injurious to the country's long-term development goals.

Anxieties about multinational penetration infused the debate over how the proceeds of privatization should be used. Under advice from multilateral lenders, the government dedicated a large proportion of the proceeds directly to retiring the public-sector debt held by state-owned banks, a policy that would make the banks themselves more attractive to buyers. Others argued that the proceeds could be better spent helping to modernize and restructure some of the remaining SOEs, rendering them more competitive and hence no longer in need of sale.

---

10   *Al-Sha'b*, April 19, 1994.
11   Samer Shehata, *Shop Floor Culture and Politics in Egypt* (Albany, NY: State University of New York Press, 2009).

Difficulties arose when foreign purchasers attempted to cooperate with local firms in submitting bids. Such a dispute scuttled plans to sell a majority stake in the Ameriyah Cement Company. France's Lafarge Coppée was slated to make the purchase with ASEC, an Egyptian firm that provides specialized management services to the cement industry, but the deal collapsed over ASEC's objections to Lafarge positioning itself as the lead bidder. As the minister of industry in the early 1990s, ASEC chairman Muhammad 'Abd al-Wahhab was seen as the cabinet's most outspoken SOE defender. He resigned from government in 1993, trailed by rumors that he belonged to a cartel of corrupt state managers making illicit profits from the cement industry's liberalization.[12]

Albeit using sometimes noxious anti-Semitic language, some opposition parties claimed that parastatals would be purchased by Israelis and then deliberately managed to ensure that Egypt remained technologically backward. This specter surfaced in a debate over privatizing maritime facilities, since the Israeli ambassador had earlier revealed some Israeli companies' interest in purchasing a state-owned stevedoring company. Initially, these concerns led 'Atif 'Ubayd, the public enterprise sector minister, to restrict share sales in maritime companies to 10 percent, but the government subsequently decided to postpone maritime privatization altogether.

Finally, suspicion of foreign intentions fostered disputes over the pricing of firms to be sold. Sharp disagreements between government officials and international consultants hired to evaluate the firms delayed the start of the program. Even after intense bidding for some strategic sales and oversubscription of some public offerings, a number of Western economists charged the government with demanding unreasonably high prices, while domestic critics accused it of undervaluing Egypt's assets.[13]

All of this controversy resurrected and refocused historic debates on the relationship between class and nation. Was there still an Egyptian "national project" to further industrialize? And, if so, could private domestic capitalists realize it better than state managers had done? Rather than futilely opposing privatization, should leftists support Egyptian capitalists in their struggles to limit sales to foreign investors?

---

12 The last point was contributed by John Sfakianakis.

13 For more on valuation controversies, see Sophia Anninos, "The Value of Privatization," paper presented at the 1998 Middle East Studies Association conference.

SOCIAL WELFARE CONCERNS

Leftists also opposed privatization because of its potentially deleterious consequences for workers' well-being. In "mixed economies" like Egypt prior to liberalization, civil servants and public-sector workers enjoyed protection against lay-offs, access to pensions and social insurance, and even company-provided housing and day care. Along with food subsidies and price controls, these protections and benefits constituted a form of welfare. Ostensibly to ease the strain of this welfare system on government budgets, privatization typically entailed an end to guaranteed employment schemes, and was associated with broader structural adjustment programs that subjected basic necessities to market pricing mechanisms. Thus, reforms threatened to remove existing social safety nets, usually before any alternatives had been established.

Before a new labor law was passed in Egypt in 2003, which would permit mass lay-offs in both the public and the private sectors, the government promoted early retirement schemes as a means to shrink parastatals' workforces prior to sale. Egypt's early retirement program was paid for by a social development fund financed by foreign donors and privatization proceeds. It offered workers an up-front cash payment based on their anticipated salary losses, along with a monthly stipend. But the stipend could be less than half the pension the worker would have received under the old system. Workers claimed that it was insufficient to meet regular expenses, and that their prospects for finding new employment to supplement the stipend were bleak. The rationale for the lump-sum approach was that recipients could invest in a small business or in stocks, and thus foster economic growth. But many were tempted to spend the money on essential large-scale expenses, such as their children's weddings. Those who did so, or whose investment schemes failed, would thus face a dismal future. Workers also wondered whether their jobs could be saved if the government instead invested the early retirement funds in modernizing their factories.

Reports in 1997 indicated that program enrollment was falling short of government targets, and labor activists charged that some workers were pressured into enrolling under threat of wage cuts or transfer. The rate of acceptance was rising by 1999, however, as workers increasingly feared that once a new labor law was enacted, they would risk being fired with no compensation whatsoever in a country that lacks unemployment insurance.

This controversy raised key questions about Egypt's "moral economy." Were jobs a right that required the government to be an employer of last resort? Or should leftists push for Western-style unemployment and welfare systems to protect workers from the ravages of capitalist labor markets? In principle, there was no reason for progressives to oppose the replacement of universalistic protection schemes with targeted programs—why should governments subsidize the well-off? But effective social safety nets require accountable and efficient governments. In the 1980s, when the Mubarak regime considered replacing food subsidies with cash grants and ration cards for the poor, some economists voiced legitimate objections that corruption and bureaucratic incompetence would prevent the aid from reaching the truly needy. These same problems would confront any program to provide unemployment relief.

IMPACT OF PRIVATIZATION ON WOMEN WORKERS

The status of women improved significantly under state-led development, albeit from a very low base. Female literacy in 2001 was just 45 percent, but female gross school enrollment was 72 percent in that year. Women workers had fared relatively well in the public sector, where there was no formal discrimination by gender, with adequate provisions for maternity leave, nursing breaks, on-the-job child care, and equal pay for equal work. With structural adjustment and privatization, however, public-sector employment shrank, and social pressure against women pursuing a career increased, with reports that early retirement schemes in the public sector were actively targeted at women.

Furthermore, in the private sector—the alleged engine for future growth—there was a 40 percent differential between male and female earnings, and private-sector employment was becoming defeminized, resulting in higher unemployment rates for females. While more than a third of women were in the labor force in 2001 (45 percent of the male rate), the female unemployment rate rose to four times that of men by 2004, with the trend more pronounced among educated women.[14] The result, as Eric Denis shows in Chapter 19 of this volume, was that fertility rates rose among stay-at-home wives.

---

14   Marsha Pripstein Posusney and Melani Cammett, "Labor Market Flexibilization and Labor Standards in the Middle East," paper presented at conference on "Globalization and Labor in Developing Countries," Watson Institute for International Studies, Brown University, December 10–11, 2004.

CONTESTING THE LABOR LAW OF 2003

Under the labor law that prevailed until 2003, all permanent employees in large establishments (those employing a minimum of fifty workers) were entitled to job security and social protection.[15] Egyptian labor legislation, dating from the 1950s and 1960s, was extensive. It required formal written employment contracts, guaranteed social insurance to permanent, full-time workers, and rendered dismissals difficult. Special labor offices were charged with ensuring compliance with the law, and labor courts were created to handle disputes. Employees received pensions, health and accident insurance, and, in some cases, access to public housing. These positions were offered to high-school and college graduates as a way to encourage education, and came to be viewed by students and their families as an entitlement.

Laws were more consistently enforced in the public sector than the private sector, however. Domestic private firms often found ways to evade the labor laws. The most common form of evasion was to force workers to sign undated resignation letters at the time they were hired, falsely stating that they had received their severance entitlements. Some business owners also bribed labor inspectors to report fewer than fifty employees on their payrolls, thereby reducing their mandatory insurance contributions and impeding unionization. Foreign multinationals, however, were under more scrutiny, as with the public sector. Labor markets therefore became segmented between parastatal workers, civil servants, and employees of large foreign-owned firms, who enjoyed legal protections, and private-sector workers who did not.

Organized labor, with its core strength in the public sector, had successfully staved off several efforts by the regimes of Anwar al-Sadat and Husni Mubarak to liberalize the economy and privatize the public sector in the 1970s and 1980s. Egypt's trade unions finally agreed to support the privatization legislation designed by the regime in 1991 (Law 203), only with the proviso that all firms sold under the auspices of this law continue to abide by existing labor legislation, and that subsequent sales agreements contain clauses guaranteeing that work forces would not be reduced. But economists and the multilateral lenders promoting Egypt's structural reform objected that these restrictions undermined the

---

15   The discussion of changes in Egyptian labor law below is drawn from Karen Pfeifer and Marsha Pripstein Posusney, "Arab Economies and Globalization: An Overview," in Eleanor Abdella Doumato and Marsha Pripstein Posusney, eds., *Women and Globalization in the Arab Middle East: Gender, Economy, and Society* (Boulder, CO: Lynne Rienner, 2003), pp. 25–54; and Posusney and Cammett, "Labor Market Flexibilization."

privatization program, in particular, by making public enterprises less desirable for purchase.[16]

The government commissioned another body to secretly renegotiate the labor law, including representatives of the Egyptian Trade Union Federation (ETUF), business organizations, the Ministry of Labor, the legal community, and the International Labour Organization (ILO). The committee's progress was slow. The government and private business sought to restrict the right to strike, with the former apparently fearing that any form of collective protest could have a snowball effect in a time of generalized political tensions.

In essence, the negotiations were a struggle over union power—freedom of association, collective bargaining rights, and the right to strike. Union leaders, under the spotlight of the opposition press, resisted the retraction of job security or other traditional benefits enjoyed by public-sector workers, but gave ground on legal restrictions on work stoppages. Dissidents in the union movement argued that the official union leaders were too close to the government and did not represent rank-and-file workers' concerns, and they opposed the enactment of the law. Ironically, then, the main domestic support for the new labor legislation came from the ETUF's leadership, which gained increased power over their workers with its enactment. After protracted negotiations, the law was finally passed in 2003.[17]

The 2003 labor law was designed to make labor markets more flexible, an institutional change to accompany liberalization and privatization. It aimed to give employers far greater leeway in hiring and firing, changing job assignments, using "temporary" labor, and downsizing the workforce according to "economic conditions." It gave managers greater authority to set lower wages and trim the benefits for new hires, and it revoked the annual cost-of-living adjustment to the national minimum wage. It also made it more difficult for a worker to win an appeal against a termination, and more costly in terms of wages foregone.[18]

The new legislation permitted multiple renewals of temporary work contracts, making it unlikely that any temporary worker could achieve the security of permanent status, or that any new worker would be rehired indefinitely. While retaining the requirement that firms obtain

---

16   Posusney, *Labor and the State in Egypt*; Marsha Pripstein Posusney, "Egypt's New Labor Law Removes Worker Provisions," *Middle East Report* 194/5 (May–August 1995), pp. 52–3, 64.

17   Marsha Pripstein Posusney, "Free Trade and Freer Unions? Globalization and Labor Market Changes in the Arab World," paper presented at Middle Eastern Studies Association Annual Meeting, Montreal, November 2007.

18   Posusney, "Egypt's New Labor Law."

government approval for any mass work force reductions, it signaled a sea change by stating explicitly that employers have the right to downsize, lower the contractual wage, and/or require employees to perform different jobs than they were hired for, for economic reasons. A "grandfather clause" exempted current permanent workers from application of these provisions, but workers who lost jobs due to privatization, and then found new employment, would lose this protection. This clause apparently contributed to the cabinet's reluctance to move the legislation until companies with excess workers had already been rationalized.[19] Finally, in an explicit quid pro quo for the "right to fire," the law recognized labor's right to strike for the first time since 1952, but only under restrictive and tightly controlled conditions.

THE ROARING 2000S

Privatization enthusiasts cheered to see stock market capitalization rise from 35.6 to 105 percent of GDP from 1985 to 2004, but the sobering reality was that the share of the formal private sector in GDP actually decreased between 2000 and 2007, from 70.7 to 62.3 percent, and that private ownership became more concentrated as the number of companies listed and traded on the stock exchange decreased by more than 50 percent—from its peak of 1,151 firms in 2002, to 435 in 2007.[20] However, the new wave of reforms was credited with a surge of economic growth from 2004 to 2008, as seen in Figure 17.2.

The ballyhooed round of additional liberalizing reforms under Prime Minister Ahmed Nazif in 2004 was widely praised by the international business community and the World Bank and IMF as a breakthrough in business-friendly policies. These reforms included the lowering of inflation, taxes, and tariffs and the streamlining of documentation needed to import and export, to register property and start up new businesses, and to access credit for investment.

Long-established businesses were also well placed to benefit from the reforms. As the director of an international automaker producing in Egypt for the Egyptian market told the author in November 2006, "It used to take us days to register an incoming shipment of parts, and now it takes us hours. Nazif's reforms have made our day-to-day operations simpler and more efficient and changed the environment to give hope to what could become a

---

19   *Al-Wafd*, July 19, 2001.
20   American Chamber of Commerce in Egypt, "Economic Indicators" (2008), amcham.org.eg.

Figure 17.2 Real GDP Growth, Egypt 2000–12p

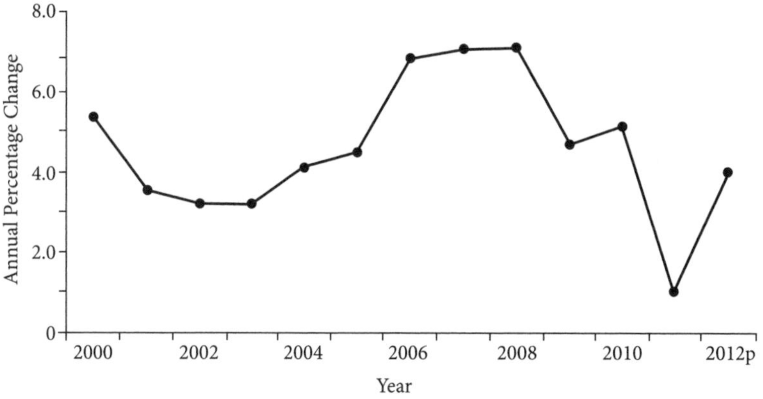

Source: International Monetary Fund, World Economic Outlook Database, April 2011

thriving private sector in Egypt." This company had accordingly expanded its importing of cars and shifted its emphasis in production toward light trucks for sale in the Egyptian market. Its partner in the importing and distribution divisions was none other than the minister of transportation in the Nazif cabinet.

Egypt had liberalized foreign access to almost all sectors of the economy, but with minimal impact on diversification of formal economic activity. The stock of foreign direct investment (FDI) in Egypt rose slowly in the 1990s and early 2000s but was concentrated in the capital-intensive hydrocarbon industry, with US-based oil corporations accounting for three fourths of that stock.[21] Indeed, the energy sector remained the chief draw, with more than half of FDI going into hydrocarbons and related industries in the 2000s. As reserves of oil were dwindling fast but new reserves of gas were being discovered, the growth industries in this sector are natural gas extraction, oil refining and natural gas liquefaction, petrochemicals, and the building of infrastructure for Egypt to broaden its role as a major transmission station for the export of oil and gas from the region to Europe.[22]

Thanks to the 2003 change in labor law and the 2004 reforms,

---

21   World Bank, "Egypt at a Glance," 2008; *World Investment Prospects to 2011: Foreign Direct Investment and the Challenge of Political Risk* (London: Economist Intelligence Unit, 2007) pp. 182–3, eiu.com.

22   For a full discussion of Egypt's role in the oil and natural gas industries, see Anthony H. Cordesman and Khalid R. Al-Khodan, *The Changing Dynamics of Energy in the Middle East* (Washington, DC: Center for International and Strategic Studies, 2006).

Egypt became the object of an unprecedented, but short-lived, wave of foreign direct investment from the world at large and from the Arab Gulf countries. As shown in Figure 17.3 below, FDI from all sources rose by a dizzying factor of 26 in just a few years, from $450 million in 2003 to a peak of $11.6 billion in 2007. Egypt was one of the top three Mediterranean-country recipients of FDI in 2000–08, taking 15 percent of total FDI to the MED-13 (southern and eastern Mediterranean countries) in those years.[23] From 2005 to 2007, FDI to Egypt averaged 15 percent of GDP, or 200 Euros per capita.[24] Foreign participation in Egypt's stock market reached its apogee in 2007, at 31 percent of total trading volume.[25]

On the intra-regional level, Egypt received 7.5 percent of inter-Arab FDI from 2005 to 2009, the fourth largest recipient among Arab countries. Startlingly, Egyptian firms were even the source of 10.4 percent of inter-Arab investment in 2008, the third largest after the United Arab Emirates and Kuwait.[26]

According to one enthusiastic observer writing before the financial crisis of 2008 hit, Egypt was "the most integrated with the Gulf Cooperation Council investment program," receiving about 40 percent of the Arab Gulf states' FDI in the Mediterranean from 2003 to 2007, about $3.3 billion at its peak in fiscal year 2006–07. During that year, Egypt also received $1 billion in remittances from the Gulf states alone, and Egypt's exports to the Gulf states were close to $550 million, including iron and steel, which made up 30 percent of Egypt's non-hydrocarbon exports.[27] Observers also applauded the Gulf states' FDI in infrastructure as well as "manufacturing, organic farming, IGT, financial services, and logistics."[28]

23   Ashraf Mishrif, *Investing in the Middle East: The Political Economy of European Direct Investment in Egypt* (London: IB Tauris, 2010), p. 135.

24   Pierre Henry, Samir Abdelkrim, and Bénédict de Saint-Laurent, *Foreign Direct Investment into MEDA in 2007: The Switch*, (Marseille: ANIMA Investment Network, Study No. 1, July 2008), p. 13, animaweb.org.

25   American Chamber of Commerce in Egypt, "Economic Indicators."

26   Arab Investment and Export Credit Guarantee Corporation, Series "InterArab Direct Investment Inflows," iaigc.net, Dhaman, Kuwait, 2010; Arab Investment Climate 2009, Table 4, iaigc.net.

27   Florence Eid, "The New Face of Arab Investment," in John Nugee and Paola Subacchi, eds., *The Gulf Region: A New Hub of Global Financial Power* (London: Royal Institute of International Affairs, and Washington, DC: The Brookings Institution, 2008), pp. 75–7.

28   Mahmoud Mohieldin, "Neighborly Investments," *Finance and Development* 45/4 (2008), pp. 40–1, imf.org.

Figure 17.3 Remittances, Tourism Receipts, and Foreign Direct
Investment to Egypt, 2001–2010

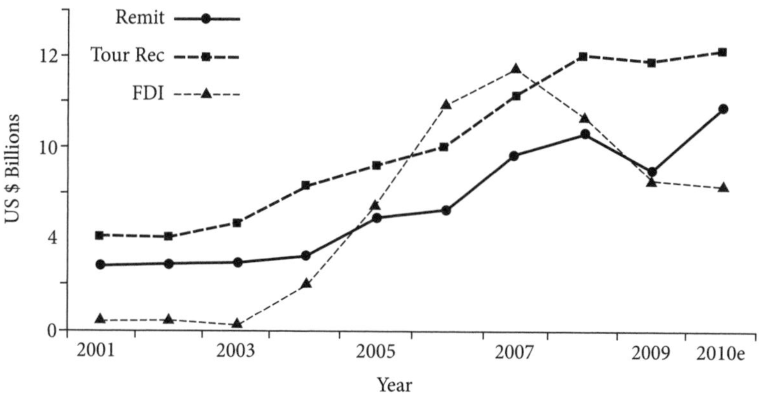

Sources for Remittances: For 2001, World Bank Indicators, worldbank.org. For 2010 estimate, World Bank,
Global Economic Prospects, January 2011: 100, Table R4.2
Sources for Tourism Receipts: World Bank Indicators, worldbank.org. For 2010e: thedailynewsegypt.com
(9.2 for first 3 quarters yields estimate 12.3 for the year)
Sources for FDI: ANIMA Investment Network, 2008: 11; World Bank, Global Economic Prospects,
Jan 2011, Table R4.3, p. 101; World Indicators, worldbank.org

During 2000 to 2007, half of the incoming FDI to Egypt from the
Gulf states went for acquisitions of existing firms rather than new projects.
For example, in 2007 Lafarge of France contracted to purchase Orascom
Construction, an Egyptian corporation that was listed as one of the top 100
nonfinancial transnational corporations (TNCs) from developing countries by UNCTAD in 2006. Some acquisitions entailed purchases of privatized public-sector enterprises, such as the 2007 takeover of the Egyptian
Fertilizers Company by a company from the UAE. Other acquisitions were
purely financial. For example, while Kuwait's stock of investment in Egypt
stood at $25 billion in early 2009, mostly in real estate, two of Kuwait's
biggest investments in 2007 had been the acquisition by the (private)
National Bank of Kuwait of one of Egypt's most successful private banks, Al
Watany Bank, and the purchase by the Global Investment House, a private
equity firm, of a significant stake in the Egyptian private brokerage firm,
Capital Trust.[29]

29   Henry et al., *Foreign Direct Investment*, pp. 22, 35, 67. This source, and subsequent
reports in the ANIMA Invest-in-Med series, provide detailed evaluation of both GCC and
other FDI in the Mediterranean in the 2000s.

CRASH, RECESSION, AND RECOVERY

Liberalization and privatization had clearly left Egypt vulnerable to the ravages of the global financial crisis and subsequent recession that swept the world economy in 2008–09. But Egypt's economy turned out to be more resilient than expected, with growth declining to "just" 4.7 percent in 2009, as indicated in Figure 17.2.

Even before the financial crisis in 2008, the wave of FDI to Egypt had begun to ebb, decreasing by 18 percent from $11.6 billion in 2007 to about $9.5 billion in 2008.[30] The downdraft continued in 2009, at $6.7 billion, and 2010, at an estimated $6.5 billion.[31] The distribution of FDI still favored hydrocarbons, which accounted for 57 percent of FDI in 2008, while finance received 9 percent and real estate and construction 8 percent. Non–hydrocarbon-related industry received 17 percent and services took about 10 percent, but agriculture received 2 percent and ICT less than 1 percent. Of these amounts, new projects and expansions of existing companies accounted for almost one third, while privatization proceeds were about 9 percent. Contrary to the impression given by some observers, over two thirds of Egypt's FDI in 2008 came from the West, with 33 percent from the United States and 36 percent from the European Union. Only 18 percent came from other Arab countries, mostly in finance, real estate, and construction.[32]

The capital market also decreased in value. From its peak in the spring of 2008 to November, Egypt's bourse index dropped 54 percent.[33] Similarly, Egypt's stock market capitalization had peaked at 85.8 percent of GDP in 2007, then declined by half to 41.4 percent in 2009, and foreign participation fell to 19 percent of total trading value.[34] Portfolio flows had already begun to shrink before the global financial crisis took shape. Egypt had experienced a rush of speculative inflows in the boom years of 2005 and 2006, following liberalization of capital markets in 2004. With the slowing of the boom and of foreign investment of all kinds in 2007, however, those speculative flows reversed themselves, creating net outflows of about 3 percent and 7 percent, respectively, in 2007 and 2008.[35]

---

30   World Bank, *Global Economic Prospects*, January 2011, Table R4.3, p. 101; World Indicators, worldbank.org.

31   Ibid.

32   Economic and Social Commission for Western Asia (ESCWA), *Foreign Direct Investment Report* (New York: United Nations, 2009), pp. 8–9.

33   World Bank, *Global Economic Prospects* (Washington, DC: World Bank, 2009), p. 161.

34   American Chamber of Commerce in Egypt, "Economic Indicators" (2008), amcham.org.

35   Michael Sturm and Nicolas Sauter, "The Impact of the Global Financial Turmoil

There was a shift in the number and nationality of companies listed on Arab stock markets. While Saudi Arabia and Jordan added companies to their exchanges between 2007 and 2009, Egypt's listings declined from 435 firms in 2007 to 306 firms in 2009. This drop was likely due to a wave of privatizations of public-sector companies and a strong bout of mergers and acquisitions by Gulf country firms. Egypt, on the other hand, was the main seller, with the value of its sales leaping from $1.7 billion in 2007 to $15.9 billion in 2008.[36] The fact that 30 percent of Egyptian firms disappeared from the stock market from 2007 to 2009 suggests that privatization and mergers and acquisitions may have dampened competition and productive activity, rather than stimulated it.

Egypt's nonfinancial sectors and overall growth were not much affected by the financial crisis but, rather, were shocked by the subsequent recession in Europe and the United States. In 2009, exports decreased 25 percent, Suez Canal fees dropped by over 7 percent, and both fixed investment and remittances declined by 10 percent, while tourism declined only slightly. As indicated in Figure 17.2, aggregate growth declined from the 7 percent rate in 2007 and 2008 to about 4.7 percent in 2009. The IFIs had predicted that it would be much worse, but this rate was still high enough that per capita income did not fall, and unemployment increased by one percentage point, from 8.4 percent in 2008 to 9.4 percent in 2009. What cushioned the blows were Egypt's own peculiar strengths: its domestic informal economy, in which production and demand continued to grow, the quick restoration of remittances and tourism revenues, and a government stimulus package of new investment in infrastructure. FDI, in contrast, was of little help. As shown in Figure 17.3, it decreased by almost 50 percent between its peak in 2007 and the recession of 2009, and did not recover in 2010.

WHAT ECONOMIC PROGRAM FOR THE ARAB SUMMER AND BEYOND?

Before the January 25 uprising, most observers expected Egypt to continue liberalizing, privatizing, and globalizing. Egypt was named as a member of the next round of "emerging markets" by the Economist Intelligence Unit, and listed by Goldman Sachs among the "Next 11" economies predicted to grow faster than average and to become a force to be reckoned with in

and Recession on Mediterranean Countries' Economies" (Frankfurt, Germany: European Central Bank, Occasional Paper Series, No. 118, August 2010), p. 12.

36   Dhaman 2010, p. 13, Table 8, Table 10; 2009, Table 8, Table 10.

the world economy.[37] Following India's model, Egypt developed an apparently successful set of enterprise zones for Internet technology and business process outsourcing, taking advantage of the language skills of its educated population and its proximity to Europe. This sector attracted investment from Microsoft and Vodafone in 2010.[38] Growth in the developing economies of the Middle East was predicted to return to its long-term trend in 2010 to 2012. Egypt, like Turkey, faced good prospects in 2010, having shown that the decline of the vaunted Gulf FDI had not had much of an impact. The major weakness in this picture was the affront to the dignity of the Egyptian people from the high level of corruption and cronyism that this course of liberalized development had entailed so far, and the inequitable distribution of its benefits.

The changes in economic policy already wrought by the "Arab spring" in 2011 and the likely changes ahead will entail neither a total retreat from a market economy, nor a plunge back into full central planning. Rather, to tackle the insulting and embarrassing excesses of liberalization and privatization, and to broaden the benefits of economic growth, the government will subject the market system to greater regulation and supervision, and will give more attention to provision of social goods and reduction in income inequality. As one Egyptian economist noted, "You have to consider that privatization is not only an economic issue; it is also a political issue that has altered the distribution of wealth and power within the society. It also has generated considerable corruption."[39]

To prove its revolutionary mettle in the spring of 2011, the Egyptian investment authority overturned agreements for several direct investments, land sales, and foreign loans. In a dramatic gesture, it reneged on a deal made in 2006 for the purchase of Egypt's famous Omar Effendi department store by Amwal AlKhaleej, a Saudi-owned investment conglomerate. Equally dramatic, and despite the IMF's claim to promote "socially inclusive growth" in the aid and loan packages it organized for Egypt and Tunisia this spring, in June 2011 the government of Egypt revoked its earlier acceptance

37 Bénédict de Saint-Laurent, Jeanne Lapujade, and Zoé Luçon, "The Mediterranean between Growth and Revolution, Foreign Direct Investments and Partnerships in MED Countries in 2010" (Marseille: ANIMA Investment Network, Study No. 21, March 2011), p. 23; Ahmet Akarli, "The GCC: Economic Powerhouse between the BRICs and the Developed World," in Nugee and Subacchi, eds., *The Gulf Region*, p. 48.

38 A. T. Kearney, "Investing in a Rebound: The 2010 A.T. Kearney FDI Confidence Index" (Vienna, VA: Global Business Policy Council, A.T. Kearney Inc., 2010), p. 22.

39 Professor Ibrahim Awad of the American University in Cairo, as quoted in "Arab Spring Undermines Support for Economic Liberalization Policies in the Middle East," Arabic Knowledge@Wharton, July 26, 2011, knowledge.wharton.upenn.

of an IMF loan worth $3 billion.[40] On August 1, the government announced that it was canceling the privatization program for the foreseeable future. The challenge, however, is to determine a coherent and sustainable alternative program to put in its place.

---

40   Ibid.

CHAPTER 18

Dreamland: The Neoliberalism of Your Desires

Timothy Mitchell

Neoliberalism was a triumph of the political imagination. Its achievement was double: while narrowing the window of political debate, it promised from this window a prospect without limits. On the one hand, it framed public discussion in the elliptic language of neoclassical economics. The collective well-being of the nation was depicted only in terms of how it was adjusted in gross to the discipline of monetary and fiscal balance sheets. On the other, neglecting the actual concerns of any concrete local or collective community, neoliberalism encouraged the most exuberant dreams of private accumulation—and a chaotic reallocation of collective resources.

In Egypt, such modes of thinking defined the 1990s as a decade of remarkable success and a vindication of neoliberal principles. Yet accompanying this picture of financial discipline was a contrasting image of uncontrolled expansion and unlimited dreams. The most dramatic example was Egypt's rapidly expanding capital city. While government deficits shrank, Cairo exploded. "Dreamland," the TV commercials for the most ambitious of the new developments promised, "is the world's first electronic city." Buyers could sign up immediately for luxury fiber optic–wired villas, as shopping malls, theme parks, golf courses, and polo grounds rose out of the desert west of the Giza pyramids—but only minutes from central Cairo via newly built bridges and ring roads.

Or one could take the ring road in the opposite direction, east of the Muqattam Hills, to the desert of "New Cairo," where speculators were marketing apartment blocks to expatriate workers saving for their future in the Gulf. They could start payments immediately (no deposit was required) at agencies in Jidda and Dubai. "No factories, no pollution, no problems" was the advertisement's promise, underlined with the developer's logo, "The Egypt of My Desires."[1]

Author's note: The author wishes to thank David Sims, Max Rodenbeck, Boutros Wadie, Kris McNeil, Ethel Brooks, and Lila Abu-Lughod.

1   *Al-Ahram*, January 1, 1999.

The development tracts spreading out across the fields and deserts around Greater Cairo represented the most phenomenal real estate explosion Egypt had ever witnessed. No one had yet mapped what was happening, but a conservative estimate is that within less than five years the area of its capital city doubled.[2]

BUILDING TRADE

The exuberance of these private developers was matched by the state. While speculative builders were doubling the size of Cairo, the government was proposing to duplicate the Nile Valley. In October 1996, President Mubarak announced the revival of plans from the 1950s to construct a parallel valley by pumping water from Lake Nasser in the south into a giant canal running northwards that was intended to irrigate 2 million acres of the Western Desert.[3]

In the meantime, the state also subsidized urban property developers, selling public land cheaply and putting up the required expressways and bridges in rapid time. The state was even involved as a developer, since the largest single builder of Cairo's new neighborhoods, far larger than the builders of Dreamland, was the Egyptian army. Military contractors threw up thousands of acres of apartments on the city's eastern perimeter to create new suburban enclaves for the officer elite.

If one's first reaction was amazement at the scale and speed of these developments, one soon began to wonder about the contradictions. The IMF and Ministry of the Economy made no mention of the frenzied explosion of the capital city, and the state's role in subsidizing this speculative neoliberalism went unexamined. Structural adjustment was supposed to generate an export boom, not a building boom. Egypt was to prosper by selling fruits and vegetables to Europe and the Gulf, not by paving over its fields to build ring roads. But real estate had now replaced agriculture as Egypt's third-largest non-oil investment sector, after manufacturing and tourism.[4] Indeed, it may have become the largest non-oil sector, since most tourism investment went into building tourist villages and vacation homes, another form of real estate.

---

2   For a subsequent study, and maps, see David Sims, *Understanding Cairo: The Logic of a City Out of Control* (Cairo: American University in Cairo Press, 2011).

3   *Al-Wafd*, January 12, 1999.

4   Economist Intelligence Unit (EIU), *Country Report: Egypt*, Third Quarter 1998, p.10.

UNDISCIPLINED CAPITAL

The conventional story is that by 1990 the economy was in crisis, no longer able to support loss-making public industries, an overvalued currency, "profligate" government spending, an inflationary printing of money to cover the budget gap, and astronomical levels of foreign debt.[5] After fifteen years of foot-dragging and partial reforms, the government was forced to adopt an IMF stabilization plan in 1990–91 that allowed the currency to collapse against the dollar, slashed the government budget, tightened the supply of money, and cut back subsidies to public-sector enterprises, preparing to privatize or close them. These "prudent" fiscal policies were implemented more drastically than even the IMF had demanded.[6] But the story was more complex: among the most profligate of the government's expenses was its arms purchases, willingly supplied and subsidized by the US (part of its own system of state subsidies).

An impending default on these military loans, causing an automatic suspension of US aid, helped trigger the collapse in 1990. The crisis was brought on not just by a spendthrift state but by the slump after 1985 in the price of oil—the largest source of government revenue—and by the lost remittances and other income caused by the 1990–91 Gulf conflict. The largest single contribution to Egypt's fiscal turnaround, debt forgiveness, resulted from a political decision of the US and its allies.

Behind this lies a more important story. The crisis of 1990–91 also stemmed from the chaos brought on by deregulated international flows of speculative finance. The financial reforms that followed were not so much an elimination of state support (as the neoliberal version of events would have it), but rather a change in recipients. Since 1974 the number of banks in Egypt had increased from seven to ninety-eight, as commercial banks sprang up to finance the investments and consumer imports of the oil-boom years. The four large state-owned banks made loans mostly to public-sector enterprises. It was estimated that at least 30 percent of these loans were non-performing.[7] But the state banks were also part owners of many private-sector banks, enabling them to channel public funds toward a small group of wealthy and well-

---

5   IMF, *The Egyptian Stabilization Experience*, (Washington, DC: September 1997), p. 5.

6   Ibid., p. 4.

7   Mahmoud Mohieldin, "Causes, Measures, and Impact of State Intervention in the Financial Sector: The Egyptian Example," *Working Papers of the Economic Research Forum for the Arab Countries, Iran, and Turkey*, No. 9507 (Cairo, 1995), p. 20.

connected entrepreneurs.[8] These large private-sector borrowers were also in trouble.

By 1989, 26 percent of private and investment loans were in default— and more than half of these loans belonged to just 3 percent of defaulters. Many of the big defaulters were able to delay legal action, and others fled the country to avoid the courts.[9] The largest default came in July 1991, when the Bank of Credit and Commerce International collapsed. Depositors in BCCI's Egyptian subsidiary were protected by an informal insurance scheme among Egyptian banks, which had to contribute 0.5 percent of their deposits and share the cost of a £E 1 billion interest-free loan to make up the missing funds.[10]

These difficulties signaled that Egypt was increasingly beholden to the interests of a narrow class of financiers and entrepreneurs whose actions it was unable to discipline.[11] As with the 1997–99 global financial crisis, however, and the larger crisis a decade later, the problems of undisciplined capitalism (a better term than "crony capitalism," then in vogue with the IMF, for it points to the pervasive struggle to subject capitalists, within and outside the state, to law and regulation) cannot be separated from the problems caused by speculative global finance, especially currency trading. After international currency controls were abandoned in 1980, daily global foreign exchange turnover had increased from $82.5 billion (1980) to $270 billion in 1986 and $590 billion in 1989 (by 1995 it was to reach $1.230 trillion, and by 2010 $4 trillion).[12] This chaotic explosion of speculation overwhelmed the attempts of governments to manage national currencies according to the local needs of industry and exports.

In Egypt, global deregulation coincided with a surge in private foreign currency transfers as expatriate workers sent home earnings from the Gulf. More than one hundred unregulated money management firms were formed to transfer and invest such funds, five or six of them growing

---

8   Robert Springborg, *Mubarak's Egypt: Fragmentation of the Political Order* (Boulder, CO: Westview Press, 1989).

9   Mohieldin, "State Intervention," pp. 20–1.

10   Ibid., p. 17.

11   On similar problems faced by the Indian state in the same period, and the importance of discipline, see Prabhat Patnaik and C. P. Chandrasekhar, "India: *Dirigisme*, Structural Adjustment, and the Radical Alternative," in Dean Baker, Gerald Epstein, and Robert Pollin, eds., *Globalization and Progressive Economic Policy* (Cambridge: Cambridge University Press, 1998), pp. 67–91.

12   David Felix, "Asia and the Crisis of Financial Globalization," in Baker et al., *Globalization and Progressive Economic Policy*, Table 1, p. 172; Bank for International Settlements, Triennial Central Bank Survey: *Report on Global Foreign Exchange Market Activity in 2010*, December 2010, bis.org.

very large.[13] These Islamic investment companies (so called because they appealed to depositors by describing the dividends they paid as profit shares rather than as interest payments) invested successfully in global currency speculation, later diversifying into local tourism, real estate, manufacturing, and commodity dealing, and paid returns that kept ahead of inflation. The public- and private-sector commercial banks, subject to high reserve requirements and low official interest rates (essential to the government financing of industry), could not compete and were increasingly starved of hard currency.

In 1988–89 the bankers finally persuaded the government to eliminate the investment companies. A law went into effect suspending their operations for up to a year. Companies found to be insolvent (or in many cases made insolvent) were closed, and the remaining companies were reorganized as joint stock companies and forced to deposit their liquid assets in the banks. This protected the banks and their well-connected clients, but provoked a general financial depression from which neither the banks nor the national currency could recover. As a UN report later confirmed, the best predictor of economic crises in countries of the South is not state-led development but the deregulation of finances.[14]

BAILING OUT THE BANKERS

In response to the financial crisis, the centerpiece of the 1990–91 reforms was a gigantic effort to bail out Egypt's banks. After allowing the currency to collapse and cutting public investment projects, the government transferred to the banks funds worth 5.5 percent of GDP in the form of treasury bills.[15] To envision the scale of this subsidy, in the US during the same period the government bailed out the savings and loans industry, transferring a sum amounting to 3 percent of GDP over ten years. The Egyptian bailout was almost twice as large, relative to GDP, and occurred in a single year. Moreover, the government declared the banks' income from these funds to be tax-free, a fiscal subsidy amounting to a further 10 percent of GDP by 1996–97. In 1998, the government attempted to end the subsidy by reintroducing the taxing of bank profits, but the banks thwarted the imple-

---

13   The following is based on Yahya Sadowski, *Political Vegetables: Businessman and Bureaucrat in the Development of Egyptian Agriculture* (Washington, DC: Brookings Institution, 1991).

14   United Nations Conference on Trade and Development, *Trade and Development Report 1988* (New York and Geneva, 1999), p. 55.

15   IMF, *Egyptian Stabilization*, p. 31.

mentation of the law.[16] The banks became highly profitable, enjoying rates of return on equity of 20 percent or more.

The government extended further support to the banking sector by tightening credit to raise interest rates, pushing them initially as high as 14 percent above international market levels. Non-market interest rates brought in a flood of speculative capital from abroad. This was quickly interpreted as a sign of the success of neoliberal discipline. It was nothing of the sort. The money consisted of highly volatile investment funds chasing interest income whose attractiveness was due not to "market fundamentals" but to state intervention. After two years, interest rates were reduced, thus ending the mini-boom.

In 1996, the government engineered another mini-boom by announcing an aggressive program of privatization. It began to sell shares in state-owned enterprises on the Cairo stock market, which it had reorganized to exclude small brokers while eliminating taxes on profits.[17] By June 1997, the government's income from the privatization sales amounted to £E 5.2 billion ($1.5 billion). It used 40 percent of this income to pay off bad debts in the banking sector. The sell-off fattened the banks and the government budget and fueled a short-lived stock market boom. Its outcome was a complicated adjustment of existing relations between public-sector business barons and their partners in the private sector. The press was full of stories of phony privatizations, such as the December 1997 sale of al-Nasr Casting, which had been sold to the public-sector banks. A year later, state officials forced the chairman of the stock exchange to resign after he tried to improve surveillance of company finances and share trading.[18]

The stock market boom lasted less than eighteen months, with the EFG index of large capitalization companies reaching a high in September 1997, then losing one third of its value over the following twelve months.[19] As the stock market slid, the government halted the sell-offs, suspending privatizations after the summer of 1998 and refusing the IMF's demand to begin privatizing the financial sector. Instead, to stem the collapse of the market, the government used its financial institutions to invest public funds. Between December 1997 and October 1998, the large state-owned

---

16   Ibid., p. 35; EIU, *Country Report: Egypt*, pp. 19–20. Other benefits were transferred to the banks in 1991, including a reduction in reserve requirements (a source of fiscal income) from 25 to 15 percent. See Mohieldin, "State Intervention," p. 13.

17   Howard Handy et al., *Egypt: Beyond Stabilization, Toward a Dynamic Market Economy* (Washington, DC: International Monetary Fund, 1998), p. 59.

18   Marat Terterov, "Is SOE Asset-Swapping Privatization?" *Middle East Times* (Egypt), August 9, 1998; *Financial Times,* January 15, 1999.

19   EIU, *Country Report: Egypt*, p. 21; *Business Today* (Egypt) (November 1988).

banks, pension funds, and insurance companies pumped about $600 million into the market, suffering large losses.[20] In the process, the state reacquired shares in most of the companies it had recently claimed to be privatizing. By June 1996, the number of loss-making public enterprises had almost doubled; accumulated losses had risen from £E 2 billion to £E 12 billion.[21] The government had redefined its finances to exclude public-sector companies from the fiscal accounts, however, so this worsening situation was hidden from view.[22] Egyptian policymakers and international financial institutions could continue to claim that the government was replacing deficit spending with a balanced budget.

FAMILY BUSINESS

The neoliberal program did not remove the state from the market or eliminate "profligate" public subsidies. These achievements belonged to the imagination. Its major impact was to concentrate public funds into different, but fewer, hands. The state turned resources away from agriculture, industry, and the underlying problems of training and employment. It now subsidized financiers instead of factories, speculators instead of schools. Although the IMF showed no interest in raising the question, it was not hard to determine who benefited from the new financial subsidies. The revitalized public-private commercial banks lent big loans (tax-free) to large operators. The minimum loan size was typically over $300,000 and required large collateral and good connections.[23]

Leading the pack of those who had good connections were about two dozen conglomerates, such as the Osman, Bahgat, and Orascom groups. These family-owned businesses typically began as construction companies or import/export agents, but most subsequently moved into tourism, real estate, and food and beverages, and in some cases the manufacturing of construction materials or the local assembling of consumer goods such as electronics or cars. They enjoyed powerful monopolies or oligopolies as exclusive agents for the goods and services of Western-based transnational firms.

The Bahgat Group, for example, was the biggest producer of televisions in the Middle East and dominated the Egyptian market, having graduated from assembling Korean sets to making Grundig, Philips,

---

20   Rafy Kourian, "Throwing Good Money After a Bad Market," *Middle East Times* (Egypt), October 25, 1998.

21   Handy, *Beyond Stabilization*, Table 21, p. 50.

22   IMF, *Egyptian Stabilization*, p. 12.

23   *Cairo Times*, December 10, 1998.

and own-name brands. The group's other major interests included hotels and Internet service provision; they were the builders of the Internet-wired Dreamland. Ahmad Bahgat, the family head, was reputed to be a front man for the Mubarak family, which may explain why the express roads out to Dreamland were built in record time. Orascom, a holding company wholly owned by the Sawiris family, controlled eleven subsidiaries, including Egypt's largest private construction, cement-making, and natural gas supply companies, the country's largest tourism developments (funded in part by the World Bank), an arms trading company, and exclusive local rights in cell phones, Microsoft, McDonald's, and much more.

These conglomerates produced goods and services affordable to just a small fraction of Egypt's population. A meal at McDonald's cost more than most workers earned in a day, and a family outing to Dreampark, the amusement park at Dreamland, consumed a month's average wages. The Ahram Beverages Company, which makes soft drinks, bottled water, and beer, calculated its potential market (including expatriates and tourists) to be just 5 or 6 million, in a country of 62 million.[24] This narrow market corresponded to that segment of the population that could afford, or even imagine affording, the country's 1 million private cars—which is why local manufacturers concentrated on assembling Mercedes, BMWs, Jeep Cherokees, and other luxury cars. Beyond the small group of state-subsidized super-rich, modest affluence probably extended to no more than 5 or 10 percent of Egypt's population.[25]

THE SPENDING GAP

What of the other 90 or 95 percent of Egyptians? Real wages in the public industrial sector dropped by 8 percent from 1990–91 to 1995–96. Other public-sector wages remained steady, but could be maintained only because the salaries were less than a living wage.[26] A schoolteacher or other educated public-sector employee took home less than two dollars a day. One sign of the times was the reappearance of soup kitchens in Cairo, offering free food to the poor, which the national press interpreted as a welcome return to the kind of private benevolence among the wealthy

---

24   *Business Today* (Egypt), (November 1998). The company was sold to the Heineken Group in 2002.
25   Osman M. Osman, "Development and Poverty-Reduction Strategies in Egypt," *Working Papers of the Economic Research Forum for the Arab Countries, Iran and Turkey*, No. 9813 (Cairo, 1998), pp. 7–8.
26   IMF, *Egyptian Stabilization*, p. 50.

not seen since the days of the monarchy, in the first half of the twentieth century.[27]

Household expenditure surveys showed a sharp decline in real per capita consumption between 1990–91 and 1995–96. The proportion of people below the poverty line increased in this period from about 40 percent (urban and rural) to 45 percent in urban areas, and over 50 percent in the countryside. Reliable guides to the changing share of consumption by the very wealthy do not exist, since surveys failed to record most of their spending. If household expenditure surveys for 1991–92 are extrapolated to the national level, the figures show the population as a whole spent $15 billion. Yet national accounts give the total expenditure as $30 billion. In other words, about half the country's consumer spending is missing from the surveys. It is plausible that the bulk of these missing expenditures belongs to the wealthiest households. Categorized as those spending over £E 14,000 (at that time about $4,000) per year, in the late 1990s these households represented 1.6 million people, or 3 percent of the population. One estimate suggests that this small group may have accounted for half of all consumer spending.[28]

The inequalities were greatest in the countryside, where neoliberal reforms first began in 1986, directly targeted at those with minimal resources. Neoliberal reforms ended agricultural rent controls and eliminated tenants' security. Reviewing the first decade of agrarian neoliberalism, the reformers acknowledged that its consequences included "growing unemployment, falling real wages, higher prices for basic goods and services, and widespread loss of economic security."[29] They might have added to this list: stagnant agricultural growth (real output in 1992 was lower than in 1986), repeated crises of under- and over-production, the growth of monopolies and price-fixing, a shift away from export crops such as cotton, and a decision by most small farmers to move away from market crops and grow more food for their own consumption.[30] The latter, a decidedly sensible decision, reminds us again of the imaginary nature of neoliberalism's successes.

---

27   *Al-Ahram,* January 1, 1999.

28   The estimate is based on the assumption that all of the missing expenditure belongs to this group. The plausibility of the assumption rests on factors such as the character of the missing expenditures and the relative proportion of incomes that different groups spend on food. Ulrich Bartsch, "Interpreting Household Budget Surveys: Estimates for Poverty and Income Distribution in Egypt," *Working Papers of the Economic Research Forum for the Arab Countries, Iran and Turkey,* No. 9714 (Cairo, 1997), pp. 17–19.

29   Lehman B. Fletcher, *Egypt's Agriculture in a Reform Era* (Ames, IA: Iowa State University Press, 1996), p. 4.

30   For details, see Timothy Mitchell, *Rule of Experts: Egypt, Techno-Politics, Modernity* (Berkeley: University of California Press, 2002), Chapter 8.

REFORM FOR A CHANGE

Alternative strategies to the neoliberal agenda must begin in the country-side. The first priority is a far-reaching land reform program, redistributing land holdings of more than five acres. This would improve living conditions immediately, increase agricultural output, and reverse the growing landlordism and merchant monopolies that were returning the countryside to the conditions of the first half of the twentieth century. Redistributing agrarian resources would provide a powerful stimulus to local investment and wealth creation. At present, with consumption of commodities other than food so heavily concentrated among the affluent and super-rich, much of the country's demand for goods can be satisfied only by imported luxuries. The new wealth of ordinary households would create a vibrant demand for local services and local manufactures. Given the relative importance of workers' remittances from the Gulf (in 1996–97 they amounted to $3.26 billion, more than double the amount of Western portfolio investment and almost five times the paltry level of direct investment by transnational corporations), this is clearly the level at which radical initiatives are needed and can make a difference.[31]

The other priority is political reform. Neoliberalism in Egypt, as elsewhere, was facilitated by a harsh restriction of political rights. Its results included a parliament more than one hundred of whose members the courts declared fraudulently elected, but which announced itself above the law in such matters; and in which the handful of opposition deputies were increasingly deprived of opportunities to challenge the government.[32] Under Mubarak, neoliberalism consolidated a regime that denied Egyptians the right to organize political opposition or hold political meetings, while forbidding the few legal opposition parties to hold public activities. Neoliberalism meant a steady remilitarization of power, especially as control shifted away from ministries, many run by technocrats, to provincial governors, most of whom were still appointed from the upper echelons of the military. And it included the repeated intimidation of human rights workers and opposition journalists by closures, court cases, and imprisonment. Meanwhile, the US refused every appeal to speak out in public on these issues, declaring no interests in Egypt beyond the endurance of the regime and its neoliberal reforms.

---

31   EIU, *Country Profile*, Table 28, p. 54. The World Bank and USAID set up programs to provide loans to the small businesses and micro-enterprises denied access to the formal financial sector. But these programs ignore the question of redistributing wealth to create the demand for such enterprise. See Julia Elyachar, *Markets of Dispossession: NGOs, Economic Development, and the State in Cairo* (Durham, NC: Duke University Press, 2005).

32   *Al-Ahram Weekly,* January 7–13, 1999.

What Egypt most needed was not the emergence of so-called civil society (which often means giving the educated and the well-to-do the opportunity to organize and speak on behalf of those they consider in need of "development"). The real need was to stop those in charge, both inside and outside the regime, from preventing neighbors, coworkers, and communities from getting together, addressing problems, deciding and arguing for what they want, and exposing the corruption, inanities, and injustices of those who hold wealth and power. Like land reform, this was not a new idea; it simply was not visible through the narrow window of the neoliberal imagination.

CHAPTER 19

Demographic Surprises Foreshadow Change in Neoliberal Egypt

Eric Denis

In the Egypt of 2008, half the population had known only one president, Husni Mubarak. And the rate of population growth, at its peak when Mubarak assumed office in 1981, had stopped declining as it had been in the 1990s. A new kind of population increase had begun. Such were the lessons of the provisional results of the Egyptian general population and housing census, conducted in November 2006 in accordance with the regular ten-year cycle. These demographic surprises had important implications for the stability of Egypt and the regime's economic liberalization and structural adjustment program.

One might have questioned, for example, the prevailing assumption that simply enrolling more girls in school would necessarily push fertility rates down for good. Combined with Islamic traditionalists' campaigns against women working, economic restructuring greatly reduced women's job opportunities in the public sector and led to state disinvestment in women's schooling, contributing to impoverishment, degradation, and population increase.

The stubborn growth also underlined the urgency of three continuing crises: the persistent lack of affordable housing, the ongoing enlargement of the work force amid mass reliance upon low-paying, benefits-free jobs in the informal sector, and the unsustainable geographic concentration of the population in a very small part of Egyptian territory. Under Mubarak, the government spent billions to build desert mega-settlements around Cairo, on the seacoasts, and in the invented "Second Nile Valley" plowed through the Sahara. But these projects housed very few people, while the booming working-class population took shelter in self-constructed settlements in the same areas of Egypt that have been most densely populated throughout history. Rather than migrating into the cities close to their jobs, Egyptians were resorting to daily commuting from villages, which are becoming conurbations without urban qualities, or "ruralopolises."

These gender and geographic contradictions of Egypt's neoliberal political economy suggested that issues of population in Egypt were best seen through a pragmatic lens, and not through the polemics of Islamist moralism or state-security hysteria.

In keeping with demographic trends evident since the 1980s, the decade 1996–2006 was marked by a slight drop in the rate of population growth, roughly matching the level measured at the 1996 census. The most immediate consequence of this rate of growth was that between 1996 and 2000, the population of Egypt grew by 13.3 million people. This number is equal to the total number of Egyptians in 1917. During the preceding census period (1986–96), the population grew by 11 million people, compared with 11.6 million people between 1976 and 1986. The negative growth rate during this period, viewed in terms of absolute numbers, was unique in the demographic history of modern Egypt. In the last ten years, by contrast, Egypt witnessed considerable population growth (over 2.3 million more people in terms of absolute numbers), indicating that the downturn in population growth had slowed.

With a total of 72.6 million inhabitants, Egypt now surpassed Iran's 70 million people, despite having twenty times less habitable land (Egypt has 35,000 square kilometers as compared to 730,000 in Iran). If this trend continues, by 2016 the Egyptian population will have topped that of Turkey (currently at 74 million).

The average growth rate of the population between 1996 and 2006 was 2.05 percent, as compared with 2.08 percent for the previous decade and 2.8 percent for the period between 1976 and 1986. The decrease in growth rate was thus a good deal less during the most recent decade than during the preceding one. Moreover, since the preliminary results of the census identified 3.9 million Egyptians living abroad, compared with 2.18 million in 1996 and 2.25 million in 1986 (1.4 million in 1976), demographic growth from 1996–2006 was even stronger: the number of Egyptians living abroad remained stable during the preceding census period (1986–96) and grew by 1.72 million during the next ten years. Even if part of this increase could be attributed to the natural growth of the Egyptian population living abroad (on the order of 480,000 people in ten years, for a growth rate of 2 percent per year), there was still an increase of the Egyptian population during the decade 1996–2006 by 1.3 million people. Thus, the total population can be said to have grown by 14.6 million inhabitants in ten years. If those 1.3 million Egyptians newly living abroad were taken into account, not only did the growth rate not diminish between 1986–96 and 1996–2006, but it could also be said to have increased by 2.2 percent per year.

One factor mitigating the general tendency toward negative population growth was an increase in life expectancy, from an average of 55 years in 1975 to 70.6 in 2004. But the primary factor was the entry into reproductive years of the female population born during the 1970s and at the beginning of the 1980s, when the birth rate had not yet begun to fall. The population boomlet was not simply a natural consequence of an increase in the number of Egyptians capable of bearing children. These women came of age at precisely the time when the Mubarak regime's downsizing of the public sector closed off the main avenue their mothers and older sisters had taken to stable employment. Pushed back into marginal livelihoods, these women likely bore more children so that there were more family members to sustain the household.

UNDER PRESSURE

The changing age distribution of the Egyptian population is quite clear in the data from 1986–96. The significant reduction in mortality also resulted in noticeable growth in the group of those aged forty-five and above: their numbers had increased by 4.8 million by the end of the period.

From 2000–06 (the period when children from 0 to 6 were born) we observe an increase in the birth rate, due to the very large increase in the cohort of women who are between fifteen and forty-five years old (3.3 million more in 2006 than in 1996). The cohort of children under six years old grew by nearly 1.3 million during this time, compared to 1986–96 when it diminished by 360,000.

One positive element of this picture is that the number of school-age young people (between six and fifteen years old) remained stable—a first in the history of Egypt. Hence, there is a favorable climate for the improvement of education, from rates of retention to the modernization of equipment. That said, the last ten years of structural adjustment have also been marked by stagnant education budgets. Given the significant increase in the number of adults in the country, moreover, the pressures on the job and housing markets are intense.

The working-age population, those between sixteen and sixty years old, grew by 1.3 million people. The potential demand for jobs from this group alone was thus equal to the total population of Cairo in 1996, or half of the working-age population in 1976. Egypt faces an impossible equation: underemployment and poverty can only rise, since the public sector has been shrunk and the sell-off of state factories has not succeeded at creating the requisite replacement jobs in the private sector. A recent study shows that "concurrent with the decline of employment opportunities in the public sector, the trend toward informalization of the labor market, begun in the 1990s, is continuing unabated. By 2006, 61 percent of all employment was informal, up from 57 percent in 1998. Moreover, 75 percent of new entrants into the labor market in the first five years of this decade were entering into informal work."[1] Only the service sector has been able to absorb the workers displaced by the destruction of public-sector jobs. The unemployment rate has actually decreased—from 11.7 percent in 1998 to 8.3 percent in 2006—but at the cost of the quality of employment. Most households today cope with job insecurity, low-wage work, and inflation. Domestic consumption has slumped.

Along similar lines, there were 17.3 million households in 2006, 4.5 million more than in 1996. In 2006, there were 29 million men (over eighteen years of age) and women (over sixteen years of age) who were married, 8 million more than ten years previously (compared with an increase of 3.8 million during the decade 1986–96).

The pressure on the housing market has thus increased, even if the annual rate of marriage is trending toward decline. The state is moving away from building public housing, while real-estate developers are moving toward high-end markets and speculation, and so popular demand is satisfied by an informal market that produces modest buildings of three or four stories even in the smallest of villages. The majority of the population, having no alternative, is currently living in such illegal, "haphazard" settlements (the literal translation of their Arabic moniker, 'ashwa'iyyat). These popular encroachments became the norm in the 1990s, when public land was privatized and given over to real estate speculation and the construction of expensive gated communities by a few big contractors. State contestation of the 'ashwa'iyyat is very rare; some are even being legalized, in accordance with a liberal perspective on land titling and enlargement of the land and real estate market. The proliferation of illegal settlements could not be stopped without disrupting the course of economic liberalization; they provided, for instance, a substantial market for the cement and steel tycoons who had also been big beneficiaries of privatization. The popular quarters of the largest cities and provincial towns are also flourishing markets, as they totally lack public services. The masses are reliant upon private initiatives for schooling and access to health care: they have passed from dependency on the whims of the regime to dependency on the whims of the market. Otherwise, only the Islamist charitable societies are offering support to the population, giving a potential social stabilization net to

---

1   Ragui Assaad, *Labor Supply, Employment and Unemployment in the Egyptian Economy, 1988–2006* (Cairo: Economic Research Forum, 2007), p. 1.

the regime at the same time as posing a possible challenge to its claims of legitimacy.

Even as the housing crisis deepens, the licensed production of private housing units routinely surpasses demand. The census counted 10.6 million more dwellings than households in 2006, compared with 1.5 more dwellings than households in 1976. In other words, in Egypt more than 10.5 million housing units sit empty—the clearest proof of the inegalitarian manner in which the revenues generated by the *infitah* have been invested since the 1980s. These results reveal the large demographic disequilibrium and uneven distribution of wealth that weigh upon the social, economic, and political well-being of Egypt.

In the face of these pressing social needs, the regime holds on to its power through authoritarian measures alone while popular outrage simmers. We need only think of the problem of the increased need for food generated by an additional 13 million inhabitants, when half of the demand for wheat in the country is met by purchases on the international markets and bilateral aid.

CONCENTRATION

Besides structural adjustment and economic liberalization, the last decade was also marked by the pursuit of development megaprojects intended to redistribute population, notably the "Peace Canal" in northern Sinai and the perimeter of Toshka to the west of Lake Nasser. Added to this is the boom of investment in the tourist industry along the Red Sea, in the provinces of the Red Sea and South Sinai. With the announcement of preliminary results from the 2006 census, the authorities were pleased to show high rates of demographic growth in these new areas, in which they have invested heavily.

Nevertheless, the cumulative demographic growth of the desert provinces accounts for only 3.5 percent of the total growth in Egypt since 2006. To be sure, this is one percentage point higher than during the two preceding decades, but that translates into only 470,000 people out of 13.3 million. In short, since 1917, the proportion of the population from desert regions has grown from 0.3 percent to 1.8 percent of the total population—a veritable drop in the bucket. What is more, the majority of inhabitants in the provinces of the Red Sea and South Sinai are men, indicating weak prospects for long-term development in these areas dedicated to international tourism (in the Red Sea capital, Hurghada, there are 106,000 men and only 54,000 women). For the majority of male migrant workers, the desert is only a temporary relocation—either in the service of capital accumulation, or for the benefit of families in the Nile Valley or the Delta.

More than 98 percent of the population of Egypt lives in the Delta and the Nile Valley, as it always has done. Moreover, the provinces where the government focused its land reclamation projects, such as Sharqiyya and Buhayra, are seeing reductions in their rates of population growth as compared to the previous decade. The provinces' large plots of irrigated land attract just a temporary influx of workers at harvest time. Only the region of Port Said can lay claim to a noticeable acceleration in its rate of population growth, due to the improvement projects on the lakes to the west and east of the Suez Canal with the opening of the Peace Canal. Ismailiyya has also maintained a relatively elevated rate of growth.

The densification of the Delta and the Nile Valley, therefore, remains the norm. The average density is currently 2,000 inhabitants per square kilometer, compared with 1,700 in 1996. Outside of urban governorates, the average density is 1,630 in the Delta and 1,830 in the Nile Valley. In ten years' time, an average of 300 more people will inhabit each square kilometer—an Asiatic geographic distribution rather than a Middle Eastern one.

For the first time in 150 years, the provinces to the south of Greater Cairo are experiencing marked growth. In the mid-nineteenth century, almost half of the population lived in Upper Egypt, but since the 1960s less than 30 percent have lived there. Between 1996 and 2006, however, the percentage has gone from 28.4 percent to 28.7 percent, a sign of a more slowly declining birth rate (if not a stagnating one), a falling mortality rate and a slowdown in emigration. On the other hand, the percentage of the population in the Delta continued to decrease, moving from 42.4 percent to 41.6 percent, while the Canal Zone returned to numbers it had not seen since the 1967 war, with 2.8 percent of the Egyptian population.

The percentage of the Egyptian population living in Greater Cairo, which includes the governorates of Cairo, Giza, and Qalyoubiyya, had risen to 25.2 percent by 2006, after a slight decrease between 1986 and 1996. This rise can be accounted for by growth in the area's formerly rural outer regions, since the area defined as urban in Greater Cairo remained stable with 18 percent of the Egyptian population. The rate of growth of Greater Cairo, at 2.09 percent, has become markedly stronger than in the rest of Egypt, at 1.9 percent. Satellite cities in the desert, once ghost towns, are quietly showing signs of life, having absorbed some 417,000 inhabitants between 1996 and 2006. They now harbor 13.5 percent of Greater Cairo's population, as compared with 3.1 percent ten years ago, but these "new towns" account for only 10 percent of the total demographic growth of the three governorates. The densely packed informal outskirts house the vast majority.

Interestingly, Cairo's share of the Greater Cairo population continues to diminish in comparison to Giza and Qalyoubiyya. The Cairo governorate did experience a revival of population growth, moving from 1.2 to 1.7 percent, due to the new development in the direction of the Eastern Desert. Nevertheless, its growth remains weak, a sign of continued absolute demographic decline of the ancient city center and increased migration toward Giza and Qalyoubiyya. Central and old Cairo lost approximately 297,000 inhabitants over the last decade.

Alexandria has also experienced a significant revival of population growth. Having dropped to 1.2 percent per year between 1986 and 1996, the rate rebounded to 2.1 percent during 1996–2006, which translates into more than 780,000 additional inhabitants, mostly through a massive enlargement and densification of the informal outskirts.

It is noteworthy that official figures measuring urban population continue to drop, down to 42.6 percent from 44 percent in 1986. From the official perspective, Egypt has grown ever less urbanized over the last twenty years. The administrative definition of an urban region, which has remained fixed with the exception of several reclassifications in the region of Greater Cairo, is obsolete. It does not account for the dynamic urbanization of areas that, like the villages of Greater Cairo, are outside of the traditional city limits.

More detailed data is needed to determine the extent of this urbanization from below. In 1996, the rate of urbanization in Egypt (defined as the part of the population living in the 800 agglomerations greater than 10,000 inhabitants) was calculated at 70 percent. Today, that figure is around 80 percent. Most of those neo-urbanites, no longer engaged in agriculture, have to earn their living and make their settlements habitable by themselves—without services from the state and, indeed, without its recognition.

CHAPTER 20

Mining for Fish: Privatization of the "Commons" Along Egypt's Northern Coastline

Ray Bush and Amal Sabri

Around 10,000 of the estimated one million people employed in Egypt's fishing sector are based in 'Izbat al-Burg, situated at the northernmost tip of the Nile's Damietta Branch and bordered on the east by the vast Lake Manzala. As recently as 1990, Lake Manzala was a major fishing area and a collective asset for this community. Small-scale fishers using simple, cheap boats and equipment fared well alongside larger operators, working in both lake and sea fishing. But by the turn of the century, the lake was no longer regarded as *rizq* (a source of livelihood). Increasingly, local fishers were prevented from fishing in Manzala by state-licensed private enclosures that virtually sealed off access to the lake's northwestern shorelines. Armed employees of the fish farm owners—known locally as the "Manzala Mafia"—commonly guarded the enclosures. Meanwhile, industrial, agricultural, and municipal wastes, including over 1.5 million cubic meters per day of Cairo sewage, continue to drain into the lake, negatively affecting the health of fish stocks.

The undermining of small-scale fishers' livelihoods in 'Izbat al-Burg is emblematic of the complex interplay between state policies and aquatic resources under stress along the Nile Delta littoral. Through privatization of access to common property resources, rising costs, removal of subsidies, and inappropriately regulated fishing and enforcement, state policies forced small fishers out of their way of life even as overall fish production rose. Policy concern with more efficient management effectively concentrated access to aquatic resource wealth into fewer and fewer hands. This process increased hardship for small-scale fishers and intensified the unequal struggles for the very environmental assets the state claimed to be protecting. Says Husni, a forty-five-year-old father of six who has fished the lake for thirty-two years: "In 1993, Manzala was a source of income for all fishermen of 'Izbat al-Burg. Now the farms have destroyed everything."

POLICY WITHOUT PEOPLE

Egyptian environmental policy discussion focuses almost exclusively on the relationship between population pressure, scarce water resources, and limited cultivable land, echoing the neo-Malthusian sense of crisis in much development discourse on Egypt. This simplistic focus fails to address unequal access to environmental entitlements and fails to include people in policy formulation. Characterizations of environmental crisis centered around resource shortage also provide the rationale for big development projects like the Toshka megaproject in the southwestern desert, which the government hoped would relieve the population pressure in the Nile Valley. Persistent neo-Malthusian beliefs—blaming the poor for lifestyles that undermine the environment and suggesting that fewer people would *ipso facto* mean more efficient resource use—generate a crisis management mentality that distracts attention from actual processes of impoverishment of people and their environments, and the differential impacts of environmental change on different social groups.

Accurate understanding of environmental pressures in Egypt requires moving away from the Malthusian perspectives of planners, and examining actual patterns of livelihood in fishing communities. In addition to pollution, the key issues of environmental sustainability addressed here are the distribution of available resources, government decisions about resource allocation, and the increasing privatization of historically collective assets.

EGYPT'S POLLUTANT "SINKS"

The four northern lakes of Manzala, Burullus, Edku, and Maryout provide a rich and vital habitat for estuarine and marine fish and their regeneration, and have always been major areas of fish production in Egypt. The Four Sisters, as they are called locally, contributed 34 percent of national production in 1976, and still provided 28 percent of the total harvest in 1998, in spite of severe environmental pressures. All have been affected by pollution, declining fish quality, and significant reduction in size due to land reclamation.

Egypt relies almost exclusively on the Nile as a water source, and its intricate water conveyance system eventually delivers the vast bulk of outflows from across Egypt to the northern lakes and coastline. As a result, the Mediterranean Delta coastline and the four lakes act as pollutant "sinks," receiving a large proportion of persistent pollutants generated throughout the Nile Valley and flowing through the Delta's terminal drainage network. Water pollution from local and upstream wastes has steadily increased as a result of the intensified multipurpose use of Nile waters, and the once-annual Nile flood no longer flushes the entire system. This has meant fewer fish, fewer kinds of fish, and lower fish quality.

Of the Four Sisters, Maryout and Manzala are by far the most polluted. Lake Maryout receives a large proportion of Alexandria's industrial and sewage effluent and is undergoing an extreme state of anaerobic decomposition. The largest and most productive lake, Manzala, reportedly still provides about 50 percent of total Delta lake production. Yet the lake receives flows from five major terminal drains carrying pollutants from agricultural, industrial, and municipal discharges, including the Cairo sewage mentioned above. Water quality is further declining because the Salam or Peace Canal project diverts Nile water (mixed with drainage water originally flowing to Manzala) for land reclamation in Sinai. The water diversion reduces the dilution of pollutants in the lake. A UN Development Program and Ministry of Environment report on the lake's environmental health noted increased pollution, causing damage to fish stocks and fishers' livelihoods, tourism, and the habitats of migratory birds.

According to surveys of fish in the 1980s, over 60 percent of fish sampled in the four Delta lakes contained DDT and benzene chloride. Numerous other investigations in the four lakes have shown high levels of heavy metals, pesticides, and PCBs in fish. Fishers themselves are usually the highest consumers of fish; they are the most exposed to the health hazards posed by fish contaminated by heavy metals, pesticides, and sewage. Large numbers of Manzala fishers and their families have worm infestations, while incidences of salmonella, shigella, and viral hepatitis are also high. Fishers know of the dangers, Husni says: "The water in the lake is sluggish and the smell is bad . . . like something dead."

Physical changes in the landscape also affect fish yields and species composition along the Nile Delta littoral. Land reclamation decreased overall lake surface area, and fish yields were reduced by the closure of sea-lake inlets through siltation. The reduction of the river's outflow, which once deflected offshore currents, together with a lessened silt load reaching the sea, means that sea currents produce net erosion along the delta's coastline, altering coastal configuration and wetland channels to the sea. These processes have affected water circulation within the lakes and fish habitats, and obstructed vital migratory routes both within the lakes and between the lakes and the Mediterranean Sea. As early as 1977, prior to the dramatic increase in private fish farming enclosures, lake surface areas lost to land reclamation were already 60 percent in Maryout, 29 percent in Edku, and 11 percent in Manzala. By 1988, losses had risen to 30 percent in Manzala and 62 percent in Edku. By 2000, *al-Ahram* reported that Manzala's surface area was down to a mere one third of its original expanse of 327,000 *feddans* (one feddan equals about one acre).

Fishermen from Lake Maryout demonstrated along the Cairo–Alexandria highway bordering the lake several times during the early 1980s, to protest the degradation of the "commons" due to pollution and landscape change. The demonstrations were quickly quashed. In the mid-1990s, the Lake Maryout Fishers' Federation began a long, difficult, and thus far unpublicized lawsuit seeking compensation for loss of livelihood. In Lake Manzala, fishers met numerous times with various authorities to voice their complaints about pollution and the authorities' neglect of the closed sea-lake inlets. The meetings followed a predictable pattern: the government promised remedial action, and the problems remained unsolved.

"FREE-MARKET" FISH FARMING

Adopting USAID recommendations, over the last twenty years the Egyptian government has promoted privately run intensive fish farming along the Delta Lake shorelines—imposing exclusive access upon areas that were originally public domain, and especially hurting small-scale subsistence and artisanal fishers. Private fish farms proliferated so rapidly that they reportedly contributed 76 percent of total aquaculture production in 1998. These farms raise rather than breed fish: farm operators simply rear the young fish known as fish fries and fingerlings to market size, harvest them, and restock the farms for each cycle. In contrast, fish-breeding farms, which are presently rare in Egypt, breed fish and raise the fry.

A lucrative market for fish fries now exists. Entrepreneurs who have purchased exclusive rights of access to plots along lake shorelines buy the young fish from the General Authority for Fishery Resources Development (GAFRD) and transport them to their farms. A huge percentage of fries— as much as 40 to 50 percent—die during handling and transport to the farms. The fish fry "industry" that arose in response to the steep increase in demand is a drastic example of unsustainable fish resource "mining."

The GAFRD developed hatcheries to respond to the growing demand for fish fries and fingerlings to stock the fish farms, but the establishment and management of hatcheries is complex and difficult. Capital costs are relatively high and they require special inputs like imported hormones. In practice, the GAFRD, at least in Damietta, relies strongly on fish fry collection centers (referred to locally as the *mugamma'at al-wilda*) rather than hatcheries to supply young fish to the private farms. The collection centers draw their supply from open waters, and therefore directly promote the "mining" of fish fries. These practices effectively deplete the lakes' natural fish stocks.

Despite evidence that current techniques encourage unsustainable depletion of Egypt's fish resources, USAID continued to push for privatization. The erstwhile Mubarak regime did not change a policy that had "efficiently" increased aquaculture's annual fish harvest from 300 tons in 1972–73 to as much as 136,500 tons in 1998—a figure exceeding 25 percent of Egypt's domestic fish harvest.

THE MANZALA MAFIA

During the mid-1980s, in line with national policy, the governorate of Damietta (where 'Izbat al-Burg is located) began extending five-year, renewable leases on areas along the northwestern shorelines of Lake Manzala to private fish farmers for the establishment of enclosures. The farmers pay an annual rental fee, in addition to selling their first 100 kilograms of fish per feddan at government-imposed prices. By the 1990s, over 5,000 feddans in Damietta were leased for fish culture. Small-scale fishers operating from sailboats or rowboats, or fishing from the shore with a simple hook and line, used to provide cheap fish for poorer sectors of 'Izbat al-Burg. But the new enclosures have denied small-scale fishers access to large areas of the lake.

According to respondents in 'Izbat al-Burg and media accounts, a spoils system dictates the allocation of licenses for both fishing fries and for fish farms from Manzala to Edku. Veteran fisher Husni explains: "Now there are hundreds of feddans of farms that belong to the elite. For every farm, there are armed guards and vicious dogs." The Manzala Mafia—comprising government officials, bureaucrats, and local elites—sometimes expands the area of enclosures beyond their allocated sizes, and their armed guards have been known to ward off fishers outside of the enclosures' perimeters.

Ironically, Article 48 of the Fisheries Law 124 promulgated in 1983 specifically prohibited the establishment of fish farms within lake waters. A decree of the Ministry of Agriculture and Land Reclamation in 1997 ordered all encroachments onto lake surface areas removed. But the authorities did not implement either of these provisions, at least on Lake Manzala and Lake Edku further west. The Agriculture Ministry's Fisheries Committee, and the Proposals and Complaints Committee of the People's Assembly, complained that fish farmers' encroachments, along with pollution, constitute the "assassination of Lake Manzala." Meanwhile, the livelihoods of small fishers hang in the balance.

The hunting of fish in open waters involves the catching, processing, preserving, and sale of hauls, and the manufacture, repair, and maintenance of boats and auxiliary gear such as nets. Fishing communities have a complex set of customary rights and social conventions to regulate their fishing and allow sufficient time for fish to breed and grow before harvesting, but these processes have all been altered by policies and practices beyond their control.

As in every other Delta region, fishers in 'Izbat al-Burg are bound by a web of government fishery regulations designed to conserve aquatic resources, yet they are continually exasperated by the open flouting of the regulations by powerful interests. The government further confounded fishers by exempting the capture of young fish fries from a range of prohibitions on fishing. Those with licenses to catch fries and fingerlings can do so all year long, and use of prohibited fine-mesh trammel nets and purse seine (*shanshulla*) fishing continues during the night.

Reduced access to the lake pushes local owners of simple boats and rafts, and rod-and-line anglers, permanently out of their original livelihoods. They try to obtain licenses to catch fish fry, or work as crew members on others' boats. Boat owners still fishing from 'Izbat al-Burg fish at sea in large motorized wooden or high-tech ferro-cement boats. Social differentiation between motorized boat owners and owners of non-motorized vessels has increased apace. Seventy-eight year-old Sa'id, a fisher since he was seven, puts it this way: "Now he who suffers, suffers a lot, and he who is well-off is extremely well-off. There is no place to put a foot in Manzala anymore."

Boat owners, fish laborers, and their families complain about pollution, declining catches, reduced access to fishing areas, and increased costs of fishing inputs and of fish. The increase in the price of fish is not passed on to fish workers, but appropriated by fish merchants. Fishers must cope with increases in loan interest rates and the rising costs of boats and various fishing inputs. The latter include supplies for fishing trips, spare parts, maintenance, and repair works. In 'Izbat al-Burg, the cost of motorized wooden boats increased from between £E 70,000 and £E 100,000 in the late 1980s to more than £E 400,000 (about $120,000) today. The price of fuel and maintenance has also risen. Essential cotton yarn for net manufacture and repair costs 300 percent more than it did eight years ago. These increased costs encourage owners to engage in boat shareholding, often between as many as eight partners.

The people hardest hit by the transformation of fishing in Egypt are the *'arraqa*—literally "those who sweat"—who work for boat owners. On a typical boat of 152 horsepower, the supply of diesel, grease, ice, and food for a fishing trip at sea normally costs £E 2,000–3,000, while the total revenue from a good catch on such a trip is about £E 4,000 (about $1,200). Since the owners are chronically short on cash, they find it difficult to finance the costs of the trip. If they do make the trip, the crew of six or more splits the profit after the owner's share. Each crewman's share amounts to £E 100–150 (roughly $30–$50), and often less.

In these dire circumstances, some small fishers resort to indiscriminate fishing practices that lead to overharvesting, including the use of illegal fine-mesh nets and the catching of fish fry, fishing during spawning or breeding seasons, and the use of dynamite or poisons. But, as demonstrated above, the increased demand for fish fry, at least, is stimulated by fishery policy rather than fishers' recklessness. One fisher expressed the dilemma as follows: "This is destroying our tomorrow, but my family has to eat today."

When the price of fuel was raised sharply to £E 80 per barrel in July 1983, fishers from 'Izbat al-Burg and neighboring areas sailed together up the Nile to demonstrate in front of the Damietta governorate headquarters. More recently, the 1996 prohibition on fishing during the prime summer months prompted similar demonstrations. But in numerous other coastal areas where fishers live in informal settlements, protest is avoided for fear of eviction. As more and more shoreline is privatized for fish farming enclosures or tourist and other coastal developments, officials call more frequently for evictions, and sometimes issue the warrants.

A major obstacle to organized actions among small-scale fishers in Egypt is that existing fisher cooperatives must belong to the Federation of Fisher Cooperatives, run under the auspices of the GAFRD. Membership in almost all of these cooperatives is restricted to boat owners, the most influential of whom are "elected" to administer the cooperatives. Attempts continue to register alternative cooperative societies to better represent the demands of small-scale fishers, both boat owners and 'arraqa, for more favorable terms of work. Meanwhile, some fishing communities have registered "community development associations" with the Ministry of Social Affairs to provide basic social services: insurance against work-related injuries and death at sea, general health insurance, and monthly retirement pensions. Given the crisis in fishers' livelihoods, more and stronger alternative grassroots associations are likely.

LOSS OF THE COMMONS

Despite grassroots efforts, small fishers on Egypt's northern coastline suffer from mounting debt and reduced employment opportunities. To cope with the changes, women intensify and diversify their productive activities—manufacturing nets for sale, working long hours in paid fish processing, and engaging in petty trading of fish. Many households face the costs of increasing household debt: longer working hours for those who can get work, declining use of expensive medical services, and hard choices about which children—if any—will receive or continue education. The outcome of these "choices" is likely to be increased social differentiation between those who can remain in the fishing industry and those who lead a marginal existence. Simply feeding a family has become a major drain on fishing families' income. Bahiyya, whose husband works as a partner on a wooden boat, says living standards in Manzala have declined "because it has become a private farm. The whole town is in a bad condition. We only eat fish twice a week, instead of every day."

In Egypt, "efficient" management of fish resources has meant privatization of the commons, concentrating access to fish resources in fewer and fewer hands. The GAFRD aims to increase annual per capita consumption of fish by intensifying fish farming, improving fish management, and developing cooperation with neighboring countries. But unless the needs and strategies of small fishers in places like 'Izbat al-Burg are included in these plans, Egypt's aquatic resource management policy will continue to marginalize the fishing communities around which fish production should be centered. From the perspective of policymakers, small-scale fishers are apparently almost invisible. For small fishers, "environmental action" entails standing up to be acknowledged and to defend their lives and livelihoods. Creating a policy context within which fisher lives and livelihoods can be advanced will be a major challenge for any "post-revolutionary" government of Egypt.

CHAPTER 21

Damietta Mobilizes for Its Environment

Sharif Elmusa and Jeannie Sowers

In 2008, Egypt's Mediterranean port city of Damietta saw escalating protest against EAgrium, a Canadian consortium building a large fertilizer complex in Ras al-Barr. Ras al-Barr sits at the end of an estuary, where the Damietta branch of the Nile River joins the Mediterranean. It is a prime destination for vacationing Egyptians in the summertime and the location of the year-round residences of the Damiettan elite. Fishermen ply the waters offshore. When plans for the fertilizer complex were announced, a coalition of locals feared that all three sources of income—tourism, real estate, and fishing—would be jeopardized by pollution. As summer temperatures climbed and the protests mounted, the government found itself caught between its contractual obligations to international investors and a well-organized local movement opposed to the project on both environmental and developmental grounds.

The Damietta protests marked a watershed for environmental mobilization in Egypt. The coalition that emerged to oppose the EAgrium plant crossed class and occupational lines, and included representatives of voluntary associations, members of Parliament, businessmen, university professors, landowners, and members of unions and professional syndicates. These groups employed a diverse repertoire of protest tactics and mobilizing strategies, including coordinated statements, petitions, marches, vigils, litigation, and strikes. The coalition also framed its concerns in ways that resonated with the vast majority of Egyptians struggling to cope with the rapidly deteriorating conditions in the Delta. Mobilization against the factory emphasized the health threats posed by polluting industries, the subsidy of foreign investors, pervasive government corruption, and the lack of environmental enforcement. These concerns were diffused through Egypt's increasingly lively public and media sphere, including new

Author's note: Our thanks to Karim Kasim, the UN Development Program representative in Damietta, and the students in Sharif Elmusa's sustainable development seminar at the American University in Cairo. Our thanks also to Hoda Baraka for her research and interview assistance; and 'Umar 'Abd al-Salam and Gamal Mareya for their insights and observations.

independent newspapers, private TV stations, and well-known regional satellite channels such as Al Jazeera.

The diverse protest tactics employed in Damietta were part of a larger wave of social protest that washed over Egypt during the 2000s. A dizzying array of actors, including textile workers, ambulance drivers, public-sector employees, syndicate members, farmers, and others conducted strikes, sit-ins, petitions, road closures, and demonstrations of all kinds. The Mubarak regime responded with a mixture of repression and accommodation. While the regime ringed striking workers with security personnel, often leading to arrests and skirmishes, it also sought to placate them with wage increases, bonuses, and other economic benefits. In stark contrast, protesters making political demands were invariably met with force.

The Damietta protests proved effective in part because they did not simply pit civil society against the state. Local economic elites and politicians played key roles in articulating a different developmental vision for the city and its environs than that promoted by the central government. Local elites argued that the area's economic development should rest on its natural advantages of sun and surf, capitalizing on the traditional status of Damietta and Ras al-Barr as premier summer resorts for Egyptians. This case was bolstered by the input of respected environmental scientists, whose opinion was solicited as part of a broader government commission of inquiry. And the movement was not merely local. When the idea of relocating the plant to Suez or Port Said surfaced in the press, protests erupted in these cities as well.

The protesters, however, won the battle and not the war to compel the state to reorder its priorities for development in Damietta and the country. The eventual "solution" reached by the government in August 2008 was to offer the foreign investors equity stakes in the Misr Oil Processing Company (MOPCO), mostly owned by the state and located right next door to the EAgrium construction site, with assurances that MOPCO would double its production capacity by 2011.

ATTRACTING INVESTORS

The Damietta protests must be situated within Egypt's broader attempt to attract foreign investment, particularly in the petrochemical sector, by underpricing its energy resources. The proposed fertilizer complex in Damietta was one of the largest in Egypt, including two ammonia plants producing 1,200 tons per day, and two urea plants that would produce 1,925 tons per day, along with handling and storage facilities. The consortium backing the project was 60 percent held by the Canadian firm Agrium, one of the largest global producers of fertilizer, with minority shares in the hands of Egyptian state-owned petrochemical and natural gas companies and an inter-government Arab petroleum investment corporation. The Agrium facility was to be the seventh identical fertilizer complex designed and constructed in Egypt by the German engineering firm Uhde since 2002, except that EAgrium (E stands for Egypt) was to have double the production capacity. Other turnkey complexes by Uhde have been completed in Abu Qir near Alexandria, 'Ayn al-Sukhna on the Red Sea coast, Helwan south of Cairo, and the Damietta free trade zone directly adjacent to the proposed new site, where the state-owned MOPCO is located.

Like many energy producers, Egypt set the price for natural gas, the primary input to urea and ammonia plants, below those that emerged in futures markets or prevailing long-term contracts. Energy-exporting countries face powerful incentives to underprice domestic energy resources in order to attract investment in secondary processing industries such as petrochemicals, fertilizers, steel, and other energy-intensive industries. The Cairo daily *al-Masry al-Youm* reported that the Egyptian government would supply the consortium with natural gas at a price of $1 per million British Thermal Units (MMBtu) for five years. This price was set at a time when natural gas had become more expensive on the world market, and the government was planning to raise it to $2.65 by 2010.[1] Even after the anticipated increase, the price was far below the level then prevalent on the New York mercantile exchange—the so-called Henry Hub price—which climbed above $11 per MMBtu in May 2008.

By keeping prices on energy inputs low, the government effectively created a rent that state-owned companies and private investors alike were quick to exploit. Most foreign direct investment was earmarked for sectors related to oil and natural gas. Petrochemicals and fertilizers, reliant on energy inputs, emerged as two of the fastest-growing sectors in the Egyptian economy. The period 2002–07 saw industrial investments worth $9.8 billion. Egypt exported over $1.1 billion worth of fertilizers in 2005, and that figure more than doubled to $2.5 billion by 2007, according to the Ministry of Trade and Industry. The government, eager to retain foreign direct investment, was thus reluctant to interfere with the EAgrium project.

The revenues from these investments, however, accrued only to the operating and investing firms. The government's contracts with consortiums have not included revenue sharing for local communities, or offset funds to invest in remediation of the impact upon public health and the environment. In addition, these capital-intensive plants generated relatively

---

1   *Daily News* (Egypt), August 20, 2008.

little employment, particularly when compared to the privately owned workshops that constitute the backbone of Damietta's economy.

Investors in Egypt prefer to locate in Special Economic Zones (SEZs) geared mainly to exports, where they enjoy long-term tax holidays, release from customs duties, expedited permits, and guarantees against expropriation by the state. These enclaves are often close to large towns as well as other industrial facilities. Minimally regulated by Law 83/2002, most SEZs are exempt from the nascent systems of environmental management in Egypt. While the Environmental Management Unit of each governorate is responsible for monitoring industrial pollution, industrial investments in these zones fall under the General Authority for Investment and Free Zones, while investments in new cities and settlements are governed by the mandate of the Ministry of Housing. Agrium itself was granted an investment permit under said Law 83.

LOCAL VS. NATIONAL DEVELOPMENT

In Cairo's view, multinational petrochemical plants easily met local environmental standards and contributed to the gross domestic product. According to the committee of inquiry later appointed by Parliament in response to the protests, EAgrium was licensed on two conditions: that it export 75 percent of its annual production, and that it meet environmental and safety standards. By 2007, project approvals had been obtained from the cabinet and the relevant officials in the Ministries of Transport, Environment, Agriculture, Industry, Irrigation, and Investment.

National priorities, however, were in distinct contrast to those of Damietta's elites. The coastal province as a whole depends upon revenue from summer tourism, industry, fisheries, and agriculture. Industry employs 35 percent of the labor force, while agriculture employs 25 percent. Ras al-Barr itself is primarily reliant upon domestic tourism and agriculture. Meanwhile, industrial employment in the province is concentrated in small and midsize workshops, mostly in the furniture, woodworking, and food processing sectors. These workshops account for over a quarter of Egypt's national output in these activities. Workshop production has been expanding: between 1976 and 1996, the state statistical agency CAPMAS reported 400 percent growth in furniture makers and 500 percent growth in food processing operations. Fishing is another important means of livelihood for the people of Damietta. Its boats make up 70 percent of the national fleet, although the increase in aquaculture, or fish farming, means that Damiettans catch only about 14 percent of the total fish eaten in Egypt.

This diverse economy gives Damietta a higher per capita income than most other Nile Valley provinces. The maritime province ranked third countrywide in the latest UN Development Program index of human development; real GDP per capita in 2005–06 was $6,159. But Damietta also suffers from the poverty, poor education, ill health, and lack of access to sanitation that plague other provinces. Bilharzia, a waterborne disease, is endemic, and the problems with water quality and disposal of solid waste are as severe as they are elsewhere in the Nile Delta, if not more so.

The governor, Mohamed Fathy El-Baradi, had pursued several highly visible initiatives to "beautify" Damietta and Ras al-Barr so as to lure more tourists. He issued a decree restricting economic activities in Ras al-Barr to tourism and related enterprises, an action repeatedly invoked by those protesting EAgrium. During the protests, the governor quietly sought to play a mediating role: in April 2008, he met with the man who appointed him, President Husni Mubarak, and emerged to ask for "self-control, solidarity, alertness, and civilized conduct" from the people of Damietta, a theme he reiterated as the protests gathered force.

BLACK BANNERS OVER RAS AL-BARR

The same month, organizers in Damietta formed the Popular Committee Against the Fertilizer Factory. This step came on the heels of a rally in January called by opposition political parties in the city's main square. The rally was quelled by state security forces, leading to a re-evaluation of tactics, according to interviews with participants. Where the initial rally had relied upon "the street" alone, the Popular Committee held conferences and issued communiqués laying out their objections to the factory and calling for presidential intervention. The first communiqué, addressed to Mubarak from the people of Damietta, declared that the Committee represented a collection of civil society organizations, unions, and professional syndicates.

In May, the Committee issued a statement signed by 150 prominent citizens, some representing political parties and the local chamber of commerce. The Committee then sent an open message to the Egyptian delegates at the Davos economic forum, arguing that Egyptians welcomed foreign investment as long as it was compatible with geography. Ras al-Barr, they suggested, needed investment, but not in the petrochemical sector. The Committee also noted that residents were willing to buy the land allocated to EAgrium; several days later, the head of the local housing cooperative formally applied to purchase the plot for a new tourism development. He noted that the land had been sold to EAgrium for about $7.50 per square meter, and that the cooperative could sell it to developers for much more. Other groups, such as the similarly named Popular Committee for the Defense of the Environment, emerged. The original Popular Committee, according to its coordinator, Nasir al-'Umari, was made up of independent lawyers. Opposition parties led the second, and its head, Samih Balah of the Wafd party, claimed it was equally active, though less media-savvy.[2]

Environmental activists and the Popular Committees organized a series of workshops and conferences to educate the public. Among the events were "Black Industries and Their Impact on the Environment," "No to Agrium, No to Dialogue, Yes to Investment in Tourism" and an Earth Day celebration titled "Against Resource Drain and Pollution in Damietta . . . and No to Pollution in Ras al-Barr."

The popular committees strategically timed vigils and demonstrations to coincide with holidays and special events. For Sham al-Nasim, the Egyptian folk holiday celebrated each spring by both Muslims and Copts, thousands of people trooped to Ras al-Barr, where cabins, villas, and apartments were festooned with black flags and anti-factory statements. Children stood at the city gates, carrying black banners emblazoned with the slogan "In sympathy with Ras al-Barr." A day later, an estimated 5,000 citizens marched bearing still more black banners. The governor, after failing to get the crowd to disperse, told the protesters that "Damietta is in the heart and mind of the president" and that the factory would be moved to Suez. As part of the Earth Day events, children marched carrying balloons, flowers, and banners that appealed to "President Mubarak and Mama Suzanne" to "save us from Agrium and grant us the right to a clean life."

Such pleas to the president and his family were intended to distinguish the "legitimate" protests in Damietta from others with an anti-regime flavor. This tactic paid dividends when Mubarak, according to *al-Masry al-Youm*'s local correspondent, announced that the plant would not be built without the approval of the people of Damietta.[3] From then on, it was a leitmotif of the protesters to invoke the president's pledge. For instance, when the members of the Damietta local councils announced they would freeze work if the government did not cancel the project, they reminded the governor of Mubarak's promise. In early June, thousands of protesters held vigils outside mosques, calling directly on the president for a binding decision on the EAgrium project. They chanted slogans (rhyming in Arabic) like: "We want a decision, disaster beckons," "If no one listens to your demands, we'll remove the factory with our own hands," and "Governor, tell the boss,

2   Interviews with Samih Balah and Nasir al-'Umari, Damietta, June 22, 2009.
3   Interview with Nasir al-Kashif, Damietta, June 1, 2009.

Damiettans are good folks."[4] The protesters thus deliberately played upon the paternalist image cultivated by the regime, according to which the president, as head of the family, should intervene directly to resolve disputes.

Strikes, formal complaints to authorities, and lawsuits were further tactics employed by various groups in Damietta, such as professional syndicates and civil servants. The head of the Chamber of Tourist Facilities in the Middle Delta threatened that his affiliates would strike, while Damietta's lawyers did keep their briefcases shut, effectively delaying the hearing of numerous court cases.

Opposition members of Parliament also voiced their concerns, as did the NDP—though only after the campaign had gained momentum, according to Balah and al-'Umari. An NDP deputy from Damietta observed, "The government with its terrible suspicious silence did not move forward and was oblivious to the feeling of the street, which won't be calmed until the matter is resolved."[5] The secretary-general of the NDP Youth in Damietta filed a court case against the Ministries of Housing, Environment, and New Communities for issuing permits for the project.

Charges of corruption were rife. *Al-Masry al-Youm* reported that local council members accused Agrium of fraudulently using their signatures to indicate their approval of the plant, when in fact they had merely signed their names as attendees of a meeting called by the firm. Anti-factory campaigners, including members of Parliament, also alleged that the company had paid various officials $25 million in kickbacks to secure the required permits. These allegations were later found by the parliamentary fact-finding mission to be inaccurate (a finding al-'Umari disputes). It seems that Agrium had donated funds to other projects of the ministries and local official bodies; if the firm bought influence, it did so indirectly. Nonetheless, the accusations of bribery helped fuel the protests.

The fact that the company is foreign did not help its cause. The Popular Committees played upon nationalism and local pride to stoke public opposition. Thus one writer observed that Damiettans had vanquished the Crusaders, and today could defeat the Canadians. Several calls were made to declare a "national Damietta day" on days when decisive moves were made against the project, such as June 19, 2008, when the lower house of Parliament voted to move the proposed factory. In the same vein, appeals were made to native sons to come to Damietta's aid. The secretary-general of Egypt's Lawyers' Syndicate, Sameh Ashour, a Nasserist opposition figure, argued that "the West" refused to build polluting factories within its borders,

---

4   *Al-Masry al-Youm*, June 7, 2008.
5   *Al-Masry al-Youm*, April 26, 2008.

but had no such compunctions in Egypt. The people of Damietta, he wrote, were merely defending their "land, honor, and property."[6]

EXPERTS WEIGH IN

The government's response to the uproar in Damietta was to convene two expert committees, one representing environmental scientists and another composed of authorities from the relevant ministries. Prime Minister Ahmed Nazif, who had come under sharp criticism for his supposedly close relationship to Agrium (he had once lived in Canada), also endorsed a parliamentary fact-finding committee.

Mustafa Kamal Tolba, the highly respected former director of the UN Environment Program, chaired the scientists' committee. His colleague, the equally well-regarded Mohamad Kassas, had headed the International Union for the Conservation of Nature. These men had been instrumental in promoting environmental laws and policies within Egypt, and were widely perceived as authoritative and independent.[7]

The Tolba report, released on June 8, confirmed the central contentions of the project's opponents. As summarized by *al-Masry al-Youm*, the report found that the site of the fertilizer complex had been chosen in the economic interest of EAgrium, without adequate regard for its proximity to population centers. In addition, it noted that Damietta already hosted a large number of polluting factories besides its wood and furniture workshops. The report argued that while the direct outputs of the new complex were not particularly hazardous, fertilizer production was a hazardous activity and must be handled according to well-defined procedures. Tourism was the better option for development for Ras al-Barr and environs. Nevertheless, the report aptly summed up the dilemma of Egypt's cabinet in noting that breaking the contract with EAgrium would be costly in terms of compensation and discouragement of foreign investment.

The parliamentary fact-finding committee report, published on June 9, documented the contract and the permissions obtained by the company from various government agencies. The committee found no evidence of corruption, wrongdoing, or environmental violations, but did not address the central question of whether the proposed location of the complex was appropriate.

---

6   *Al-Masry al-Youm*, May 25, 2008.

7   On the role of Kassas and Tolba in establishing Egypt's legal regime for nature reserves, see Jeannie Sowers, "Nature Reserves and Authoritarian Rule in Egypt: Embedded Autonomy Revisited," *Journal of Environment and Development* 16/4 (2007).

The Tolba report thus provided the seal of scientific authority that parliamentarians needed to vote unanimously against EAgrium on June 19. Although parliamentary decisions are hardly binding in Egypt, where Mubarak and his predecessors have aggrandized the executive at every opportunity, it was widely believed that the government could not pursue the project when its own party roundly rejected it. In what newspapers described as a "carnival" atmosphere, celebrations of the vote continued through the night in Ras al-Barr and Damietta. The following day, Agrium announced it was studying two options put forward by Prime Minister Nazif, whereby the government would either directly purchase the company's investment or offer Agrium stock in the adjacent MOPCO plant. The second alternative eventually prevailed.

This "solution," however, posed new challenges for the Damietta movement. People living in the vicinity of both MOPCO and EAgrium said they had no prior knowledge of the construction of the state-owned MOPCO complex.[8] While press coverage mostly focused on EAgrium, residents and allied activists embarked on actions against MOPCO. Residents complained of smoke, dust, dead fish in the canal, foul odors, skin rashes, and respiratory difficulties. In December 2008, MOPCO was in regular operation and residents reported bitterly that their complaints had produced little response.

The fact that MOPCO continues to operate, and is on track with expansions, highlights the privileged position that well-connected firms maintain in Egypt's economy. Despite an intensified privatization program since the early 1990s, a number of new companies in Egypt incorporate various forms of state ownership, with stakes held by various holding companies, government and military agencies, and influential persons within the regime. As a consequence, these firms remain more insulated from public pressure than foreign investors.

EXCEPTION OR MODEL?

Some have suggested that the opposition to EAgrium in Damietta was an exceptional case, in that the campaign succeeded in pressing its grievances whereas many other environmental protests have failed. But it is misleading to focus on "Damiettan exceptionalism." The Damietta protests reflected the coincidence of the economic interests of the elite with the health fears of the commoners, the foreign identity of the firm, and the previous experience of the residents with a similar fertilizer plant. These factors would

---

8   Interviews with residents, Damietta, November 22, 2008.

have converged in any Egyptian city (as they did in Suez, which also has a massive fertilizer complex nearby). The campaign further had a limited, well-defined, and seemingly apolitical aim: blocking the factory. In its aims, the movement was similar to the strikes that mushroomed across the country since late 2004, where the government often acquiesced, in whole or in part, to concrete, specific demands.

One key dimension of the EAgrium protests was the mobilization of the local elite. From Cairo's perspective, EAgrium was another example of its success in attracting foreign investment, itself a pillar of the regime's efforts to improve the macroeconomic picture. But the provincial elite, in their resistance to the factory, anticipated Cairo's argument and married the environment to the economy. In light of this gambit, neither the government nor the company could afford to be nonchalant about environmental damage—and its associated health and economic costs. In response, they tried to argue that the project was environmentally sound, or offered fixes that they claimed would make it so.

The other striking feature of the Damietta protests was the inclusive nature of the oppositional coalition. Much of the recent protest in Egypt has been carried out by relatively homogenous groups, such as members of unions and syndicates. The Damietta protests, however, mobilized participants across the highly stratified citizenry. The ability to act coherently and tenaciously as a community may well reflect the historical mercantile nature of the city and its diversified economic foundations in private economic activities of tourism, furniture and woodworking, fishing, and real estate. The political opposition, in the form of parties and individuals, was a key player as well. The opposition found in the EAgrium project an effective rallying cry against the government, and were able early on to mobilize civil society organizations, catalyzed in the Popular Committees, as well as local councils and ordinary citizens. The Muslim Brothers—the strongest organized political opposition—were also an important factor, and they and other groups frequently used Friday prayers as occasions to challenge the government. Environmental scientists played a prominent role by providing journalists and parliamentarians with expert assessments of potential risks and environmental impacts.

This relatively broad-based coalition employed a range of creative protest tactics. These included holding rallies on holidays, calling directly upon the governor and the president to intervene, and highlighting how foreign investors would profit at the expense of the health of the locals. Campaigners evoked the historical memory of Damietta as a bulwark against the Crusaders, equating new petrochemical firms and their associated pollution loads with invading armies. Protest leaders also made shrewd use of the independent press, which was eager to enter the fray to demonstrate its centrality and enhance circulation. Sales of *al-Masry al-Youm* in Damietta, according to its local correspondent, more than tripled, from approximately 2,000 to 6,000 copies.[9]

Damietta inspired another environmental campaign in the crowded working-class Cairo district of Shubra al-Khayma against a proposed petrochemical factory in close proximity to residential areas. The campaign—which goes by the name Itkhannaqna, a colloquial expression meaning "We've been suffocated"—has established a Popular Committee modeled after Damietta's, and hopes to be as successful.[10] In Shubra, however, local economic elites are not at the helm of the protest. It remains to be seen whether commoners can force the hand of business and the government on their own.

---

9 Interview with Nasir al-Kashif, Cairo, June 1, 2009.
10 Sharif Elmusa and Hoda Baraka, "Justice for the Environment," *al-Ahram Weekly*, April 9–15, 2009.

Abeer Adel, nineteen years old, and her fiancé Amgad Muhammad, twenty-one years old, shop for rings and engagement jewelry at a shop in Cairo, November 5, 2007. © Shawn Baldwin

Part V

THE CULTURAL POLITICS OF YOUTH, GENDER, AND MARRIAGE

CHAPTER 22

Downveiling: Gender and the Contest over Culture in Cairo

Linda Herrera

Veiling, particularly youth veiling, has captured the rapt attention of the Western media and scholarly community. Whether in France, Iran, Turkey, or Egypt, veiling—the adoption by women of Islamic dress (*al-zayy al-islami*)—is often represented in highly ideological terms. Veiling has been explained as an assertion of cultural authenticity and Islamic feminism; a sign of both resistance and submission to patriarchy; a rejection of modernity, Western imperialism, and corrupt local secular regimes; a genuine desire by women to live more piously; and a practice born out of economic necessity. Especially when taken together, there is a degree of plausibility in all the above interpretations. But these explanations of veiling tend to overlook the ambivalence within cultural-religious practices of which veiling is one. In light of political-cultural changes taking place in Egypt in recent years, another dimension should be added to discussions of contemporary practices of veiling. This is the increasingly observable phenomenon throughout the streets of Cairo of what can be called "downveiling."

Downveiling refers to a subtle and seemingly growing tendency among certain circles of urban Egyptian women toward less concealing and less conservative forms of Islamic dress. Partly, downveiling reflects the struggle between Islamists and the political elite to exert influence over the everyday practices of Egyptians. But more pointedly, downveiling shows how multiple factors, beyond the control or manipulation of any single group, converge to shape the sociocultural terrain where ongoing debates and negotiations over dress, culture, and identity politics play themselves out.

DIVERSITY OF ISLAMIC FASHION

Downveiling in Egypt, while it shares features with the much-touted *bad hejab* in contemporary Iran, differs from it in fundamental ways. In Iran the government stipulates that all women veil from the age of maturity. The standard middle-class urban attire for women in the years following the 1979 Islamic Revolution was a black scarf covering all the hair, thick black stockings, and a loose-fitting ankle-length black *manteau* (overcloak). Growing numbers of female supporters of Iran's reformist movement express a combination of fashion sense and political defiance by flouting the Islamic Republic's dress codes. Young urban women in particular can be seen wearing their scarves pulled high atop their heads to reveal frosted tufts of hair, sporting open-toe sandals, makeup and ever shorter, lighter, and more tailored manteaus.

In Egypt, on the other hand, the "new" veiling was pioneered in large part by Islamist university students in the early 1970s, on a voluntary basis and sometimes in tacit opposition to the nominally secular state. Young women took to manufacturing their own austere, loose-fitting clothing and head covers from dark-colored, low-cost synthetic fabrics.[1] As *al-zayy al-islami* was steadily adopted by a broader spectrum of urban women of various ages and social backgrounds, a certain diversity of Islamic fashion naturally appeared. From the mid-1990s, however, something else began to occur: many women seemed to be moving toward lesser degrees of veiling.

Urban women wear three main types of Islamic dress, within which there are multiple gradations: the *hijab*, a simple headscarf that covers the hair and might be worn with anything from jeans and a T-shirt to a long-sleeve dress; the *khimar*, a substantially longer nylon cloak that drapes over the torso and arms and is usually worn with a long skirt; and the *niqab*, a full face veil ordinarily worn with an ankle-length dress and gloves. A resident of Cairo since 1986, I first became aware of downveiling when a number of acquaintances from diverse social backgrounds and of different ages modified their Islamic dress to less conservative and less concealing forms than they had previously worn. Downveiling women might remove the face cover from their niqab, substitute the hijab for the khimar, wear shorter and snugger clothing with the hijab, or remove their hijab altogether in an act of unveiling.

The practice of downveiling, which appears to be increasing exponentially, can be explained by four independent, yet ultimately interrelated factors: the state's attempts to curb private, embodied expressions of Islamism, the social influence of youth culture and the growth of Islamic urban chic, the practical needs of urban women, and the emergence of new players on Egypt's stage of cultural politics.

---

1   See Fadwa al-Guindi, *Veil: Modesty, Privacy, and Resistance* (London: Berg, 1999).

A pervasive manifestation of the Islamic resurgence in Egypt has been the informal Islamization of public spaces and institutions and the increased adoption of Islamic dress by both women and men. The government initially treated sociocultural expressions of Islamization as benign. But as armed conflict with militant Islamist groups escalated in the late 1980s and early 1990s, the government began to regard *al-zayy al-islami* as an overt display of politics, and even a threat to the state. Since then, the regime has discouraged and even tried to prohibit men and women from wearing particular types of Islamic attire.

Men sporting short beards of the sort said to be worn by the Prophet, for instance, are forbidden from entering government recreational clubs and required to undergo a rigorous security clearance before obtaining a driver's license. Veiled women, with rare exceptions, are not allowed to appear on state-run television as presenters of any sort, whereas women wearing the *niqab* are banned from any number of state and private educational institutions and workplaces.

The biggest crackdown on Islamic dress has come in the area of education, where female students at all levels have been the targets of the state's de-Islamization dress policies. Minister of Education Kamal Baha' al-Din feared that Egypt's gradually Islamizing schools and universities were slipping dangerously out of the state's control and into the hands of "extremists." He posited that extremists were infiltrating the state's education apparatus, spreading anti-government propaganda, and, most alarming of all, gaining access to the ideological and identity formation of the youth. The veiling of schoolgirls, the minister argued, figured prominently in the Islamists' political project.

Having oriented education policy around national security, Baha' al-Din enacted harsh measures. He began purging Islamist teachers and administrators from schools, intensified the screening and surveillance of students in teacher training colleges, and pushed highly controversial legislation on school uniforms. Ministerial Order 113/1994 on the Unification of School Uniforms legally forbids girls in grades 1 to 5 from wearing the *hijab*, and requires that girls in middle school (grades 6–8) have written permission from a guardian if they wear the hijab, thereby giving parents rather than teachers authority over their schoolgirl's attire. The law prohibits the niqab at all educational levels, arguing that it presents a security risk at schools and university campuses because it conceals the wearer's identity.

In the wake of the ministerial order, dozens of students were suspended from schools and universities, largely for refusing to remove their niqab.

Aside from being strongly contested in the press, the uniform legislation triggered a spate of lawsuits against the Ministry of Education. The well-known Islamist lawyer Muntasir al-Zayyat alone tried and won over twenty-five niqab-related cases in the lower courts. However, in a 1996 appeal that reached the Supreme Constitutional Court—Egypt's highest court—Ministerial Order 113 was ruled constitutional, and therefore enforceable. To ensure that schools complied with the disputed decree, Ministry of Education inspectors and state security force units were dispatched to schools throughout the country. Guards blocked any students dressed in defiance of the regulations from entering their schools. Many school communities reacted to the state's actions with outrage, and some unveiled students even took the veil in protest. But the new regulation also served as a powerful catalyst for downveiling.

SCHOOLGIRL FASHION

The most immediate and visible change in the wake of Ministerial Order 113 was that most primary school girls in Cairo took off their scarves. At more conservative schools that had previously enforced the hijab, adolescent girls continued to veil. Influenced by urban fashion trends, however, schoolgirls found ways of making what they considered their dowdy school uniforms more stylish. At a conservative, private "Islamic" middle school in Cairo—a school that incorporates religious rituals and symbols into its daily life—the pre-1994 uniform consisted of a nylon *khimar* and a shapeless *galabiyya* (a kind of kaftan). Capitalizing on the governmental surveillance at their school following the uniform regulation, students replaced their khimars with shorter cotton scarves and their *galabiyyas* with tailored skirts and blouses. About the student-led uniform rebellion, one schoolgirl remarked, "Can you believe they used to make us wear those old-fashioned clothes? It was embarrassing to be seen walking around in the streets in them!"

Other groups of young women, particularly university students, could be seen in larger numbers in Cairo's public spaces wearing outfits that merged pious Islamic attire with urban chic. They dressed up the hijab by wearing it with designer jeans, pumps, slit skirts, and a range of other snugger, shorter and brighter-colored clothing. These more daring manifestations of *al-zayy al-islami*, while they existed before 1994, increased in the wake of government efforts to curb "extremist" dress. At the same time, a flourishing market developed to cater to the growing fashion trends associated with hijab chic. Clothing boutiques offering the spectrum of Islamic fashions to nearly all social strata now abound in the city. In the upscale district of Muhandisin, a shop called Flash lil-Muhajjabat (Flash for Hijab Wearers) displays an array of embellished and multicolored scarves on heavily made-up face mannequins which line the front window.[2] In the popular, low-income clothing market of Wikalat al-Balah, cheaper imitations of the boutique fashions are for sale.

As the dress choices of students of all ages broaden, many young women express ambiguity over how to comport themselves correctly. Two twelve-year-old girls from the Islamic school mentioned above had the following conversation when, walking home after school with me, they saw an ample woman sporting formfitting pants and a hijab.

> **Girl One:** You see lots of people these days walking in the street with a scarf and tight pants or stretch pants. Pants, anyway, are *haram* for girls.
>
> **Girl Two:** But you yourself wear pants, and stretch pants at that.
>
> **Girl One:** I do, but I'm not veiled. I don't wear a scarf. I'm talking about people who have made the decision to wear the scarf and still wear tight pants. People say that it's *haram* for the woman who wears a scarf to also wear pants.
>
> **Girl Two:** Look, I'm not veiled either, but I don't wear stretch pants and low-cut blouses that expose my chest. I'll wear a blouse, a skirt, something like that. Even girls who don't wear the hijab should still be modest about their clothes.

Like so many young women in Cairo, these schoolgirls are negotiating morality and fashion in the shifting terrain of urban youth culture.

FASHION AND FUNCTIONALITY

In the interest of fashion, but also in pursuit of comfort and functionality, middle- to lower-middle-class urban professional women have opted to downveil as well. A number of women aged thirty to fifty with whom I have spoken acknowledge shifting in recent years to lesser degrees of veiling, for largely utilitarian reasons. Some women explain that the tight nylon khimar caused their hair to thin—in some cases leading to bald patches—so they had substituted it for a lighter and looser-fitting cotton scarf. Other women who routinely walk long distances to and from work complained that the khimar, while perhaps religiously preferable to the hijab, proved too cumbersome. The khimar restricted their movements or caused them to perspire excessively. Some unmarried niqab wearers (*munaqqabat*) removed the face cover of their veil because they felt their prospects for

---

2   Patrick Haenni, "Ils n'en ont pas fini avec l'Orient: de quelques islamisations non islamistes," *Revue des mondes musulmans et de la Méditerranée* 85–86 (Spring 1999).

marriage were diminished when suitors could not see their faces. Those who downveiled or unveiled in the early 1990s recall how they did so at the risk of social exclusion. Now, as the intensity of Egypt's Islamist trend wanes and growing numbers of women engage in downveiling, the risks are fewer.

Despite the increased flexibility in Islamic dress, veiling continues to elicit controversy, involving actors from ever-wider social groups. Two unprecedented recent episodes brought elite, private foreign educational institutions into the public debate over veiling in Egypt. In the fall of 2000, a twelve-year-old girl and her three younger brothers (ages eleven, nine, and four) were expelled from Champollion School in Alexandria, a private school attached to the French Ministry of Education, because the girl wore the hijab to school in contravention of the school's secular policy. It was, in fact, the school's Parent Council that recommended the expulsions, on the familiar grounds that the children represented a security threat. The children's parents initiated a complex lawsuit involving litigation in both France and Egypt.

In January 2001, the American University in Cairo (AUC) officially banned the face veil after an undergraduate student donned the niqab on campus for the first time in the university's eighty-year history. The AUC administration cited security concerns and invoked principles of liberal education to justify the niqab ban.[3] Ardent debates among students and members of the press ensued, many participants decrying the duplicity of a liberalism that restricts personal freedoms and a student's choice to dress as she deems appropriate. Although the student initially threatened the university with a lawsuit, she reluctantly opted instead to downveil. She removed her face veil and continued to study at AUC.

The above cases demonstrate how cultural politics are mediated through disparate local and transnational players and class interests. The foreign elite educational institutions reflect, in part, the policies of the state. By invoking notions of secularism and Western liberalism, these institutions not only further politicize the debates on Islamic dress, but also play their own role in influencing women's choices of dress.

While downveiling may have been triggered by the state's concerns with national security, it has assumed a momentum of its own as factors such as youth culture, fashion, the practical needs of urban women, and the emergence of new players in Egypt's cultural politics have come to the

---

3   A passage from the e-mail message circulated on January 23, 2001 by the AUC administration to the entire AUC community states: "A liberal arts education requires dialogue and intellectual interaction with colleagues and with other members of the University community. Face veiling inhibits this interaction. Students who choose to cover the face should seek another type of education."

fore. Islamic dress, like any socio-religious or cultural practice, has been invested with multiple symbolic meanings and practical functions. The movement of some Egyptian women toward downveiling testifies to the contested and shifting nature of both veiling and the Islamization of society itself.

CHAPTER 23

The Fiction (and Non-Fiction) of Egypt's Marriage Crisis

Hanan Kholoussy

In August 2006, a twenty-seven-year old pharmacist started blogging anonymously about her futile hunt for a husband in Mahalla al-Kubra, an industrial city sixty miles north of Cairo in the Nile Delta. Steeped in satirical humor, the blog of this "wannabe bride" turned into a powerful critique of everything that is wrong with how middle-class Egyptians meet and marry. The author poked fun at every aspect of arranged marriage—from the split-second decisions couples are expected to make about life-time compatibility after hour-long meetings, to the meddling relatives and nosy neighbors who introduce them to each other. She joked about her desperation to marry in a society that stigmatizes single women over the age of thirty. She ridiculed bachelors for their unrealistic expectations and inflated self-images, while sympathizing with the exorbitant financial demands placed on would-be husbands. Four years and thirty suitors later, in 2010 the pharmacist remained proudly single at thirty-two, refusing to settle for just any man.

Ghada Abdel Aal took Egypt by storm—its blogosphere, its literary scene, its television line-up, and even its image abroad. Blogging in collo-quial Egyptian Arabic and peppering her slang with the pop-culture refer-ences of youth, Abdel Aal quickly attracted a large following. By late 2010, the hits on the witty website had surpassed a half million.[1] Her tragicomic tales of matchmaking mishaps had become so popular that Egypt's power-house publisher Dar al-Shorouq tracked her down to offer a book deal. A year and a half after she first posted in cyberspace, *'Ayiza Atgawwiz* (I Want to Get Married) debuted at the Cairo International Book Fair in January 2008. Less than three years later, the book was adapted into an Egyptian television series with the same name. To date, *'Ayiza Atgawwiz* has been translated into Italian, German, Dutch, and, most recently, English.

Divided into twenty-five brief chapters that showcase her best blog entries, the book describes Abdel Aal's encounters with ten different

---

1   The Arabic-language blog is available and occasionally still updated at: wanna-b-a-bride.blogspot.com.

suitors. Each suitor gets his own chapter, with each encounter preceded and followed by a chapter or two of commentary. No subject is sacred: Abdel Aal discusses police brutality, al-Qaeda, and the peccadilloes of politicians, as well as sexual harassment and dating, a phenomenon dimly acknowledged in Egypt beyond Westernized elite circles. Her parade of suitors includes a thief who cons her into loaning him money before making a fast getaway, a polygamist who proposes with his two wives looking on, a detective who checks out her family through a full-blown police investigation, and an avid soccer fan who watches a game during their first meeting and walks out because her family cheers for the opposing team. Most of these episodes are drawn from her own experiences, although Abdel Aal has admitted she occasionally borrowed friends' stories or embellished her own for entertainment's sake. And entertain she did. In a country where books are an increasingly hard sell, 'Ayiza Atgawwiz was an instant bestseller. It had gone through six printings by 2010. The book made such a big splash in Egypt that Western media giants like the BBC and the Washington Post reported on the sensation.

PARODIES WITH A POINT

Throughout her rapid rise to stardom, Abdel Aal ignited controversy. Egyptian literary critics who value formal Arabic were offended that her very vernacular blog was considered a literary contribution worthy of translation. Many men were affronted by her parodies of suitors' behavior, and accused her of being a publicity hound. Many women, too, were uncomfortable with Abdel Aal's expressed anxiety about marrying and her derision at experiences that may be all too familiar. Elders were dismayed by her mockery of matchmaking practices that are deeply embedded in social norms. But the overwhelming majority of her readers, young and middle- to upper-class, found the book hilarious, appreciated the slang, and agreed with her critique of the customs and costs of Egyptian marriage. As a result, the broadcast version of 'Ayiza Atgawwiz was one of the most anticipated shows of Ramadan—the hottest television season in Egypt and the Arab world.

Boasting a famous cast, including Hind Sabri, Sawsan Badr, and Ahmad al-Saqqa, 'Ayiza Atgawwiz was one of the three most watched of the forty-odd new shows that aired during the Islamic holy month, which in 2010 occurred in August and September. Framed as a sitcom, the show reached a much broader audience than the book had, both outside Egypt and inside Egypt, where more than half of the population cannot read or write. Its broadcast as a Ramadan serial cemented the book's status as a cultural watershed—another coup for a small-town blogger from the Delta.

But although half of the sitcom's thirty episodes came straight from the book, and Abdel Aal herself co-wrote the screenplay, the show did not live up to the expectations of many of her readers. Some were disappointed with Hind Sabri, in her first comedic role as the professionally successful but hopelessly single main character 'Ula, a twenty-nine-year-old pharmacist. They faulted Sabri for exaggerated facial expressions, body language, and intonation, and for telegraphing the jokes while failing to provide a sense of character development. Others found 'Ula's aggressiveness in pursuit of marriage unrealistic, and the satire overly broad. In one episode that did not come from the book, for example, 'Ula poisons her best friend and colleague to prevent her from attending a professional conference teeming with potential grooms.

A few readers were upset that the serial did not relay the book's more serious underlying message. In the book, amidst her failures at finding a husband, Abdel Aal pauses to ponder the injustice of the social pressure on women to marry:

> Society needs to stop confining women solely to the role of bride. Because when things fall apart . . . they feel like worthless good-for-nothings, and they sit and complain, like I'm doing to you right now . . . If I don't get married and if I don't have children and if I can't follow society's grand plan, I will always have my independent nature and I will always have my own life and I will never be . . . a good-for-nothing.[2]

By contrast, Abdel Aal's televised persona 'Ula is so swept up in the race to matrimony, at the expense of friendships and dignity, that she offers no such profound reflections in any of her frequent soliloquies to camera.

ANXIETIES UNDERNEATH

These criticisms revealed the underlying discomfort that many Egyptians, regardless of age, gender, or class, feel with the sensitive subject that the show rather shallowly addressed. Some were disquieted by Abdel Aal's more nuanced textual narrative as well. The depiction of a single woman's quest for a partner made many uneasy because Abdel Aal effectively reversed the active–passive binary that has historically dictated the rules of marriage

---

2   All translations are taken from Ghada Abdel Aal, *I Want to Get Married!* (trans. Nora Eltahawy) (Austin, TX: University of Texas Press, 2010).

in Egypt: men choose while women comply. The strict division of gender roles is even reflected in the verbs used to describe the act of marriage in Egyptian dialect: a man marries (*yigawwiz*) while a woman is married off (*titgawwiz*).

In the typical Egyptian marriage, it is the prospective groom who actively pursues a potential bride. If he has not already found one on his own, then it is he, often with his mother, who visits his intended and her family (traditionally in their living room, which is why arranged marriage is referred to as *gawaz al-salonat*, or living-room marriage, in Egyptian argot). It is he who decides if she would make a suitable wife, and he who meets with her father (or male guardian) to negotiate the fiscal provisions of the match. The groom is the one who shoulders almost all of the financial burdens (though rarely without the help of his parents or other economic assistance). His future wife may or may not be present during these negotiations, and may or may not express her opinion about the decisions. But the legal institutions and socio-economic structures that support marriage are set up in a way that reinforces this gendered arrangement across class divisions. Though many Egyptian women, especially among the upper classes, choose their own spouses or at least have much more say in who they marry, few do so without their fathers' consent. Most brides' fathers (or, in their absence, uncles or brothers) sign their marriage contracts as proxies, further reinforcing the degree to which patriarchal norms govern the practice of marriage.

Abdel Aal's fame is due to her sharp and funny writing, to be sure, but just as much to her timing. In 2008, around the time of her book's publication, a spate of articles bemoaning a "marriage crisis" in Egypt appeared in the local and international press. These articles identified a growing number of Egyptian men who could not afford marriage because of its extravagant costs, blaming women and their parents for their unreasonable financial expectations of would-be grooms hit hard by the worldwide economic crisis. Egypt's high rates of inflation and unemployment, matched with unprecedented shortages of affordable housing, took on a more sinister cast: these economic worries were keeping young men from achieving the most basic of rights—the right to marry.

There is no doubt that marriage burdens an Egyptian groom with staggering costs. The pricey wedding celebration, dower,[3] and down payments

---

3   It is customary among many Egyptian Muslims for the groom to offer a dower (*mahr*) to his prospective bride before her family will agree to the match. The *mahr* is intended as financial support for the bride. It most frequently comes as cash, but may be a guarantee of future payments or non-material benefits to the bride. Grooms with the means may also offer a *shabka*, a gift of gold jewelry that the bride usually saves as insurance against

to establish the household are the foretaste of decades of spousal and child support. For many young urban men, particularly from the struggling middle and lower-middle classes, these expenses can be so steep as to deter them from seeking a bride until well into their thirties. But the stream of news coverage offered little insight into how the "marriage crisis" affected women. Nor did it provide convincing evidence that there was a genuine crisis, that is, a significant erosion of the ability to marry. Journalists and analysts initially cited a vague 2007 Brookings Institution statistic that nearly 50 percent of Middle Eastern men aged twenty-five to twenty-nine were single.[4] A year later, however, Navtej Dhillon, who had directed the two-year research project that produced this figure, announced a "noteworthy" reversal in the trend of delayed marriage in Egypt: men born in 1976 were marrying at the median age of twenty-six.[5] Similarly, in 2009, the head of Egypt's Central Agency for Public Mobilization and Statistics retracted his own agency's report that the 2006 census had shown the number of single Egyptian women to be 5.7 million. Amidst the media brouhaha, he revised the estimate to only a few hundred thousand.[6]

More significant than the accuracy of these statistics or their subsequent retraction is the recurring perception that a marriage crisis menaces Egypt. In 2008, Western analysts, Muslim Brothers, academics, and laypeople all weighed in: What are the implications of large numbers of bachelors for national and international security? Might the young men be lured by Islamist groups, which provide interest-free loans and celebrate mass weddings to facilitate marriage? How might they vote in elections in which Islamists and others inveigh against the dearth of legitimate unions? The engagement of these questions in the press revealed a great deal about Egyptian men and women (as well as outside observers): marriage, it seems, is regarded as a barometer of the nation's social progress, political well-being, and economic health. The "marriage crisis" is about much more than matrimony. It serves as a platform for debate about materialism, privatization, social customs, unemployment, gender roles, Islamism, and the performance of the government. Contrary to commentators' beliefs, furthermore, the marriage crisis is not a phenomenon unique to twenty-first-century Egypt. In decades past, anxieties over marriage have spiked whenever Egypt found itself in the midst of socio-economic and political upheaval.

---

widowhood or divorce. There is no concept of dowry, or payment from the bride's family to the groom, in Islam.

4 Navtej Dhillon, "The Wedding Shortage," *Newsweek*, March 5, 2007.

5 Navtej Dhillon and Ragui Assaad, "Light at the End of the Tunnel in Egypt's Marriage Crisis?" *Egyptian Gazette*, November 23, 2008.

6 Ursula Lindsey, "The Marriage Crisis That Wasn't," *Foreign Policy*, March 19, 2010.

TAKING BACK SPINSTERHOOD

What distinguished the late 2000s round of marriage crisis debate was its coincidence with the popularity of *'Ayiza Atgawwiz*, a voice that claimed to speak on behalf of single women. In her blog profile, Abdel Aal identified herself as one of Egypt's 15 million single women between the ages of twenty-five and thirty-five. Though she did not reveal how she obtained this improbable number, she did something far more powerful and provocative than add a statistic to the hubbub. She co-opted the slur "spinster" and proclaimed herself a spokesperson for this constituency. In doing so, Abdel Aal exposed the implicit threat concealed within the discussion of the marriage crisis affecting men: the fate of a nation full of unwed women in a society where marriage is the only legitimate outlet for sexual activity, particularly for women. As throughout the twentieth century, the late 2000s press debates on the marriage crisis focused overwhelmingly on bachelors and their reasons for not marrying. Rather than ask women why they are not marrying, analysts assumed that they must be the main reason for men's abstention from marriage and thus a persistent obstacle to the course of nature. These female thirty-somethings were labeled materialistic, and said to be too career-oriented, educated, or "liberated" to make proper wives— not because they wished it so, but because men could not possibly choose them as partners. A single woman like Abdel Aal, who has made a career of explaining why she is not married, reversed the gender roles that maintain the social order. If throngs of single and not-so-young women like her are actively resisting marriage, they may be more subversive to the nation than the bachelors and their supposedly inadequate pool of potential brides.

Abdel Aal was aware that her simultaneous determination to marry and refusal to settle for just any suitor challenges social conventions. She began her book by acknowledging: "This whole subject of marriage, suitors, and delayed marriage is a really sensitive subject. It's hard to find anyone who talks about it honestly. Especially girls. Because girls who talk about this honestly are either seen as crass and badly raised, or as obsessed with getting married. Either that or as old maids who can't find anyone to marry them." Like her audience, Abdel Aal seemed unaware that she was not the first in Egypt's long history of women's rights activism to castigate the institution of arranged marriage, or advocate for a woman's right to choose her life partner.

Since the inception of a women's press in the 1890s, Egyptian women (and men) have reproached fathers for marrying their daughters off to men without their consent. They have also condemned the custom of arranged marriage for preventing the prospective couple from getting to know one another before marriage. Most of these critical voices framed their arguments as providing a service to the nation and its sons. According to these commentators, men were in dire need of being better acquainted with women so that they might find suitable companions: women who could, for example, assist in giving children (especially boys) a modern education. The colonial nation, in turn, was in need of successful marriages that would serve as a strong base of unity in the anti-colonial struggle against the British, and then form the foundation for independence. Few writers asserted the right of women to choose a mate for their own sakes, like Abdel Aal did. Nor did they suggest that women should marry freely and without their fathers' consent.

Nowhere in her book, however, did Abdel Aal advocate for women's ability to marry against their fathers' will, and never did she condemn marriage itself. As the title of her works made clear, Abdel Aal wanted to get married. She was merely saying that she did not want to settle for the first caller with a furnished flat; she demanded the right to get to know her suitor, to make sure he was the one for her. And if she never did find a partner, she was asking society to respect her nonetheless. She wrote:

A thirties girl has been employed for seven or eight years, seen all sorts of people, understood all sorts of people . . . It has given her experience, a certain outlook on things, and it's made her demand things of a future husband that go beyond the dreams of a girl in her twenties . . . A thirties girl has held down jobs, has made money, and she doesn't need a man to support her financially anymore, so it's not likely that she'll be impressed with an apartment or jewelry or a car . . . Anyone who thinks thirties girls are desperate and will settle for anything needs to read this over again and think again.

While other Egyptian women might not say these things out loud or so forcefully, many agreed with her, judging by her fan mail and the comments on her blog. Abdel Aal even inspired a few, like Yumna Mukhtar and 'Abir Sulayman, to launch Facebook groups and blogs in support of single women.

The various interpreters of Abdel Aal's story seemed to intentionally disguise the unsettling reality about her: she upended everyone's preconceptions about veiled middle-class Egyptian women. To many Egyptians, a woman—especially a middle-class veiled one from the Delta who was a product of the public school system and worked as a government bureaucrat—should not have publicized her desire to marry or condemned Egyptian customs and men for thus far preventing her from finding a true companion. While Egyptians are accustomed to feminists and women's

activists, who have been publicly and harshly rebuking customs and practices they find oppressive for more than a century, such women are easy to
classify (even if incorrectly) in one of two categories—secular Westernized
radicals or conservative Islamist activists. Abdel Aal did not fit neatly
into either mold. While her socio-economic and political critiques were
not new, her tactic of disguising them in tongue-in-cheek slang was original. The satirical mode not only enabled Abdel Aal to get away with her
rather biting criticisms, it also afforded her fortune and fame in doing so,
which she admitted made her prospects of marriage in Egypt even slim-
mer because men feared they would end up as characters in her next book.
Her detractors—among them a commentator on her blog who suggested
someone marry her to shut her up at long last—saw marriage as an institution that disciplines women into submission. Abdel Aal's refusal to shut up
reversed, at least temporarily and in this instance, the conventional hierarchy of marriage. This hierarchy is premised on women's subordination
to—not their disruption of—the normative order in which men seek and
women comply, men provide and women consume, men speak out and
women remain silent.

And Abdel Aal was not unique. She just happened to blog about the
thoughts and experiences that many women before her and around her
shared. Like women everywhere who face the pressure to conform, keep
quiet, or behave passively, Abdel Aal employed subtlety to deliver her
message. The reader was often too busy laughing to realize just how powerful her socio-economic and political critique was, even if she was not the
first or last Egyptian woman to offer one. Ghada Abdel Aal effectively and
brilliantly shifted the spotlight of Egypt's fictional "marriage crisis" from its
male victims to its female critics.

CHAPTER 24

Explaining Egypt's Targeting of Gays

Hossam Bahgat

On July 18, 2001, fifty-two suspected gay men went on trial in Cairo on charges of immorality. The trial signaled an end to long years of discreet and quietly tolerated public activity by the Egyptian gay community. Standing in a cage in a small, crowded courtroom, the defendants were testament to the deep political crisis faced by an insecure regime, a threatened gay community, a mediocre press, and a shattered rights movement.

The fifty-two men, along with three others who were released without being officially charged, were arrested on May 11, 2001 on the Queen Boat, a tourist boat moored on the Nile in Cairo. The boat had long been a known gathering place for the Egyptian gay community. What motivated the sudden crackdown? Although the Mubarak regime has consistently violated human rights, observers agreed that something must have impelled state security forces to raid a tourist discotheque at a time when Egypt's economy, which depends heavily on tourism revenue, was still struggling to overcome the fallout from the 1997 Luxor massacre.

DISTRACTING THE PUBLIC

One motive was certainly to divert public attention from economic recession and the government's liquidity crisis. According to official statistics, in 2001 at least 23 million of Egypt's 65 million people lived under the poverty line. In 2000, poor Egyptians watched their purchasing power sink due to devaluation of the Egyptian pound. The huge media frenzy over the Queen Boat case distracted people while the government introduced additional sales taxes, despite private-sector complaints about a severe drop in sales. Two other sensational cases also crowded out economic issues. Days after the Queen Boat raid, a businessman was referred to the criminal court for having been married to seventeen women. Shortly afterwards, a banned videotape that purportedly showed a former Coptic priest having sex with women who came to his monastery to seek healing was leaked, many think by State Security, to the press, leading to Coptic demonstrations, clashes with security forces, and a series of newspaper articles and state security trials.

According to lawyers for the fifty-two detainees, State Security arbitrarily arrested many men who were not on the Queen Boat on May 11, to inflate the numbers arrested for the press. After the July 18 court session, a beleaguered mother screamed: "He had gone out to buy my medicine when [the police] arrested him." This would explain the almost identical news reports published in the two weeks that followed the raid. The reports, probably issued by state security sources, described rituals of a Satan-worshipping cult and public orgies allegedly taking place on the Queen Boat every Thursday night. By the time the public prosecutor issued a statement denying these reports, the goal had been achieved: the public was agog. "The case involves religious beliefs and morality, two elements that have always succeeded in keeping people engaged for a long time," said Tahir Abu al-Nasr, a lawyer from the Hisham Mubarak Law Center, which represented four of the defendants.

FLASHING CAMERAS

The semiofficial Egyptian media had always shown willingness to be used by the security services in their quest for publicity. The heavy coverage of the Queen Boat case brought to mind a similar case in 1997, when seventy-eight teenage men were arrested on charges of establishing a Satanic cult. They were released after two months of detention, and the case was never brought to the courts. Newspapers came under harsh criticism for printing the names and pictures of the suspected devil-worshippers, tarnishing their images despite their release. But in May 2001, official, opposition, and independent newspapers published the names and professions of the fifty-two Queen Boat defendants; some front pages carried their pictures with the eyes crossed out in black.

On the following July 18, families of the defendants punched and kicked photographers who tried desperately to take pictures of the men before, during, and after the court session. "Filthy press. You fabricated the whole story," relatives shouted at journalists. Fathers and mothers who came to see their sons could not, since the handcuffed defendants were covering their heads with scraps of newspaper, plastic bags, and towels to avoid the flashing cameras. Publishing any details concerning an ongoing investigation or trial that might influence the course of the proceedings was prohibited by the Press Law 96/1996 and the Code of Ethics issued by the Egyptian Journalists' Syndicate.

"ISLAMIC VALUES"

But the state's motivations to raid the Queen Boat may have run deeper than the pursuit of photo opportunities for the police. The May 2001 assault on gay men fit into the Mubarak regime's efforts to present itself as the guardian of public virtue, to deflate an Islamist opposition movement that appeared to be gaining support every day. In November 2000, the outlawed Muslim Brothers sent seventeen new members to Parliament, outnumbering the representatives of all the official opposition parties put together. In 2001, the Brothers' list of candidates swept the elections for the bar association's board. To counter this ascending power, the state resorted to sensational prosecutions, in which the regime stepped in to protect Islam from evil apostates. Article 98 of the Penal Code, which criminalizes "contempt of heavenly religions," was used by the state prosecutor twice in 2000, against writer Salah al-Din Muhsin and female preacher Manal Mani'. In June 2001, prominent feminist writer Nawal El Saadawi was interrogated by the public prosecutor under the same law, regarding views she expressed in a press interview. The charge was dropped, though a maverick Islamist lawyer still tried to divorce El Saadawi from her husband.

June 2001 also saw the front pages of official local newspapers carrying headlines hailing Egypt's position "in defense of Islamic values" at the UN General Assembly Special Session on HIV/AIDS. At the session, Egypt led several other Islamic countries in a failed attempt to ban the only representative from a gay and lesbian organization, the International Gay and Lesbian Human Rights Commission, from taking part in the official roundtable on HIV/AIDS and human rights. Later, the Egyptian delegation to the UN succeeded in deleting a sentence from the final declaration of the session, which mentioned gay men and lesbians as a vulnerable population at high risk of HIV infection. These "Islamic" positions raised the eyebrows of Egyptians accustomed to a foreign policy that had only stressed "Islamic values" at the low-profile, and mostly meaningless, meetings of the Organization of the Islamic Conference. The Mubarak regime seemed to have realized that suppression and persecution of Islamists would not eliminate the Islamist threat unless it was combined with actions that bolstered the state's religious legitimacy.

GOING WITH THE FLOW

Egyptian human rights organizations found themselves in an awkward position during the Queen Boat case. Activists felt bound to take a stand, especially after international groups like Amnesty International and Human

Rights Watch issued statements condemning the Queen Boat arrests. But instead of playing the vanguard role in explaining the rights dimension of the case, most of them chose to go with the flow to avoid being attacked in the local press. Moreover, many human rights activists volunteered their own homophobic views to the press, and attacked the international organizations that took more positive positions (one such individual even decided to write a book about how gay rights are not really human rights). They deliberately chose to ignore reports that the suspects were tortured and ill-treated to extract confessions that they were homosexuals and were on the Queen Boat at the time of the raid. Even the fact that police officers broke into a public place and arrested all the Egyptian men inside, while pointedly leaving foreigners and women alone, did not bring any response from local rights groups.

Most human rights activists in Egypt are former political activists, who took up human rights work when it became clear that legal and illegal opposition groups would not shake the powerful state. Since human rights groups were accused by the Mubarak regime of following a Western agenda, they were often more anxious to gain popular support than to take up controversial rights cases. Asked about his position on the Queen Boat case, a leader of one legal aid association spoke of "red lines" that human rights groups should not cross in their defense of civil liberties. By toeing these self-imposed "red lines," some human rights groups tried to send a message to the regime that the rights movement would stand by the state against foreign pressures.

MORE MONITORING AHEAD

When asked for an explanation of the May 2001 assault, members of the local gay community referred to the establishment of the Internet Crimes Unit at the Interior Ministry. Gay men recounted several incidents that took place in the two months preceding the Queen Boat event, in which gay men were set up for arrest through fake dates from the Internet. Several gay websites were closed down, and most Egyptian gays now avoid gay chat rooms and matchmaking websites. Gay men believed that the government had decided to step in after months of monitoring their sites and clubs. The cyber-interaction of Egyptian gay men with their Western peers seems to have led the former to become more vocal about their rights. Given that any potential for citizen organization was considered a threat to national security by the government, the Queen Boat case seemed to presage greater surveillance of the mounting number of young Egyptians who use the Internet—more than 1.5 million in 2001.

In light of these considerations, the local gay community chose to keep an even lower profile than usual during the trial of the Queen Boat detainees. Initial speculations that the Queen Boat incident would turn into the Egyptian Stonewall proved unwarranted. Egyptian gay men lacked the motivation to challenge this societal and religious taboo, at the risk of losing their jobs, families, friends, and social status, as well as spending up to five years in prison, knowing that nobody would support their struggle.[1]

---

1   *Editor's Note*: Hossam Bahgat, author of this article, was dismissed from his position at the Egyptian Organization for Human Rights (EOHR) two days after this article was originally published in *Middle East Report* on July 23, 2001. EOHR's secretary-general commented in the Egyptian press at the time that he would not defend the fifty-two men arrested on the Queen Boat, because he did not "like the subject of homosexuality."

CHAPTER 25

Imagined Youths

Ted Swedenburg

Youth—what is it? The notion tends to be taken for granted, as a natural stage in human development. But, in fact, "youth" is a socially and culturally determined category, a transitional phase between childhood and adulthood that, in its contemporary form, is a product of modernity. In the pre-modern era, adolescents were usually regarded as troublemakers, and so it was customary to marry them off soon after the onset of puberty, giving them adult responsibilities in order to stave off any social threat and ensure uninterrupted agrarian and pastoral production. The forces of modernity, and in particular the forms of education that capitalist production requires, have greatly extended the period of youth and delayed the age of marriage. Youth today is typically defined as a phase in life between the ages of fifteen and twenty-four, but in practice one's youth knows very fuzzy bounds. Young men in the Middle East may belong to this social category well into their thirties, due to the economic difficulties that many of them face in getting married.

Delayed marriage is one of several socio-economic realities—another being high unemployment—that has had Western observers and regional governments worried about a youth "problem" in the Middle East for decades. Samuel Huntington, for instance, has argued famously that the large number of unemployed males between fifteen and thirty constitute "a natural source of instability and violence." And poor countries are not the only ones thought to have a problem: "Too often Muslims are against physical labor, so they bring in Koreans and Pakistanis while their young people remain unemployed," mused ex–Defense Secretary Donald Rumsfeld in one of his "snowflake" memoranda, referring to the oil-rich countries. "An unemployed population is easy to recruit to radicalism."[1] Such concerns have been felt as urgent because twentieth-century advances in public health have created a "youth bulge" in the region's demographic

---

Author's Note: Thanks to Lori Allen, Arang Keshavarzian, and Paul Silverstein for their helpful and timely suggestions and comments.

1   Robin Wright, "From the Desk of Donald Rumsfeld . . ." *Washington Post*, November 1, 2007.

profile: in most countries of the region, at least 20 percent of the population is between fifteen and twenty-four (though such "bulges" are not unusual in other populous, non-Western countries). The flip side of this coin for Westerners is to see the rising generations, "globalized" by technology and the allure of liberal capitalism, as the agents of inexorable "change" in countries perceived as mired in stagnation or worse.

PROBLEM CHILDREN

It has frequently been claimed that the so-called youth problem of the Middle East is essentially a demographic one: there are simply too many of them. Typically cited as evidence are the high percentages of young people; in Iran in 2005, for instance, 25 percent of the population was aged between fourteen and twenty-five.[2] Others argue, however, that the problem is not so much demographics as the expectations generated by the forces of modernization. The Middle East has witnessed a massive and rapid increase in its educated young population and, in particular, a dramatic growth in the number of educated females. Large numbers are entering the labor market and are unable to find jobs commensurate with their education. High rates of unemployment and underemployment particularly afflict those with higher levels of education, and such problems are exacerbated in countries undergoing "structural adjustment," where employment opportunities are declining in state-owned firms and the bureaucracy. In addition, young people who hope to become financially and socially independent—which means finding suitable employment, leaving home, and setting up a household as part of a married couple—frequently face critical shortages of housing. (Somewhat different problems affect less privileged classes in both urban and rural areas, where many young people enter the workforce at an early age.) And when marriage is, for most, the only sanctioned outlet for sexual activity, the issue of what young people do in their spare time becomes particularly salient for elites.

Youth were not always perceived as a crisis in the making. During the optimistic years that succeeded independence (as in Egypt after 1952) or revolution (as in Iran after 1979), youth symbolized the future of the modern nation that the state hoped to build. Whereas the older, under-educated generation represented backwardness, the youth were imagined

---

2   Farzaneh Roudi-Fahimi and Mary Mederios Kent, "Challenges and Opportunities: The Population of the Middle East and North Africa," *Population Bulletin* 62/2 (June 2007), p. 15. Future generations can expect to encounter different sorts of problems, given that the birth rate in many Middle Eastern countries has declined significantly, in some cases close to European levels.

to be the recipients of a modern, progressive education and the imbibers of state-propagated ideology. In Iran, youth were regarded as the index of the success of the state in creating a true Islamic Republic, until the success of the state's pro-natalist policies prompted a rethinking.[3] In Turkey during the Kemalist era, educated youth were viewed as the main instrument of the state's national civilizational project.

The trajectory of the image of youth in Turkey may be taken as an exemplary case. During the late 1960s and early 1970s, when violent conflict erupted on university campuses between leftist and rightist students, youth came to be reimagined in public discourse as a threat to the national interest.[4] This theme, of "dangerous" youth, has become increasingly common in public discourse in Middle Eastern countries. But in contrast to how the theme is understood in the West, where youth is "dangerous" because the young are self-motivated delinquents, in the Middle East it is more frequent for young people to be seen as vulnerable innocents. The forces that are said to threaten youth are various and changeable, depending on the context, and depending on the political affiliation of the commentator.

Westernization is regarded across the board as one of the greatest sources of danger to susceptible youth. Western culture and its immoral values (related forces include Zionism and globalization) threaten youth with the evils of HIV/AIDS, premarital sex, drugs, suicide, Satanism, and so on. A related threat is the media, held as responsible for relaying corrupting influences to young people, and therefore film, music, radio, and satellite TV broadcasts, as well as the Internet, are all foci of great concern. In Egypt such dangers are usually summed up as the "cultural invasion" (*ghazw thaqafi*), which foists bad morals and "vulgar" culture—the macarena, Madonna, and Michael Jackson—upon youth, leaving them without viable national role models, only alien and decadent ones.[5]

THE DADDY STATE

Symptomatic of such perceptions about the dangerous potentiality of youth and their need for supervision, instruction, and protection is the fact that states explicitly view themselves as surrogate parents (and especially "fathers") for the country's youth. One facet of this assumed parental role

---

3   Roxanne Varzi, *Warring Souls: Youth, Media, and Martyrdom in Post-Revolution Iran* (Durham, NC: Duke University Press, 2006), p. 11.

4   Leyla Neyzi, "Object or Subject? The Paradox of 'Youth' in Turkey," *International Journal of Middle East Studies* 33/3 (August 2001), p. 420.

5   A mild version of this argument appears in Galal Amin, *Whatever Happened to the Egyptians?* (Cairo: Dar al-Hilal, 1998). [Arabic]

has been the establishment of Ministries of Youth and Sports, many set up during the 1990s, for instance, the Palestinian Authority's in 1994 and Egypt's in 1998. (In Tunisia, the equivalent body is known as the Ministry of Youth, Sports, and Physical Education.) The purpose of such ministries is to develop a national youth policy and youth programs.

It is telling, of course, that government policy and discourse links youth and sports so intimately. Sports are regarded as a way of channeling youthful energies into activities that are wholesome and, not coincidentally, serve as means of bringing glory to the nation. Saudi Arabia established the General Presidency of Youth Welfare in 1974, in part with the aim of fostering boys' interest in sports, and by 1994 it reportedly had established strong programs in 18,000 schools throughout the kingdom.[6] The importance that states attach to sports as a youth policy can be gauged by the fact that such ministerial posts are not necessarily honorary sinecures for politically unimportant figures. Algeria's current president, Abdelaziz Bouteflika, got his start in government as minister of youth and sports. 'Ali al-Din Hilal Disouqi, who held a post as Egypt's minister of youth and sports, was formerly touted as one of the main mentors of Gamal Mubarak, when, to all appearances, he was being groomed to succeed his father, Husni, as president.[7] And then there is 'Uday Hussein, son of former Iraqi dictator Saddam Hussein, and his notorious tenure as head of Iraq's Olympic Committee and national soccer team (as well as the youth television network Shabab).

States also make great efforts to guide youth through the ideological work of institutions devoted to education and health, conscription into the military, and the establishment of state-directed youth and student unions. The concern of the state, then, is not simply protection of its youth from danger, but national and social reproduction, the project of ensuring that young people do not deviate from the transcendent goal of maintaining the integrity of the nation.[8]

MARKET NICHE

Dick Hebdige has observed that the two key themes in modern representations of Western youth are "youth as trouble" and "youth as fun."[9] The images of "youth as fun" emerged amidst post–World War II affluence and the development of the category of the teenager. Such images depend on the

---

6   Brian Clark, "A Cupful of Pride," *Saudi Aramco World* (September–October 1994).

7   *New York Times*, October 3, 2002.

8   On this process in Algeria, see Kamel Rarrbo, *L'Algérie et sa jeunesse: Marginalisations sociales et désarroi culturel* (Paris: Harmattan, 1995).

9   Dick Hebdige, *Hiding in the Light* (London: Routledge, 1998).

ability of youth to participate as independent agents in consumer culture and on the growth of market niches targeted at youth. There is evidence to suggest that youth are a growing target for marketers and advertisers, particularly in the more affluent Gulf countries. The Middle East contains some of the globe's fastest-growing ad markets and audiences; Dubai is the advertising hub and Saudi Arabia contains the largest audience, while Lebanon supplies the local creative talent.[10] The State Department has even dipped into these waters, launching a slick lifestyle magazine in 2003 called *Hi*, aimed at the same affluent Arab youth targeted by Dubai's advertising agencies—but apparently failing to gain enough readers, and ad revenue, to sustain itself.[11] The glossy was "suspended" in 2005.

There is abundant evidence to suggest that increasing numbers of Middle Eastern youth are participating, to various degrees and in various ways, in a globalized capitalist youth culture. Although this is good for business, the processes of incorporation of youth as consumers are full of contradictions and pitfalls. In Turkey, for instance, today's youth are regarded as shallow, individualistic, driven by crass desires for consumption, apolitical, and insufficiently nationalist. It is common in Turkish public discourse for young people to be found wanting in comparison to what are regarded as the more heroic previous generations, especially those of the nationalist (Kemalist) or revolutionary ("Sixties") eras.[12] On the other hand, even supposedly apolitical efforts to promote youth as consumers can spin out of control, as when Saudi Arabia suspended publication of the youth-targeted daily newspaper *Shams*, launched in 2005 and circulated widely in Gulf states, after it reprinted some of the cartoons of the prophet Muhammad originally appearing in the Danish newspaper *Jyllands-Posten*, as part of an editorial critical of the paper's action.

One of the most significant signs of the mobilization of images of youth-as-fun and youth consumption is the ubiquity of the clips, or music videos, on Arab satellite TV (and the Internet). As Walter Armbrust shows, hostility to these video clips on the part of pundits and commentators is as omnipresent as the clips themselves. According to Armbrust, typical arguments are that video clips are a form of Western cultural hegemony that "make Arab youth want to become what they can never be" (Palestinian poet Tamim Barghouthi) and that undermine patriarchal society through the marketing of sex, which "makes marriage increasingly difficult as a practical course of

---

10 Tim Burrowes, "Middle Eastern Promise," *Campaign*, May 26, 2006.
11 Elliott Colla and Chris Toensing, "Never Too Soon to Say Goodbye to *Hi*," *Middle East Report Online* (May 2003).
12 Neyzi, "Object or Subject?" p. 424.

action" (Egyptian professor 'Abd al-Wahhab al-Massiri).[13] Mass consumption, therefore, even when it involves local products, can also be regarded as posing dangers to youth or producing "youth as trouble." One peril is said to be that Arab youth will be tantalized by the offerings of global culture, yet unable to afford the commodities of their dreams or get access to public spaces in which to enjoy the pleasures associated with such products.

LIMITS OF DISAFFECTION

The discourses of the state, the mass media, pundits, and professional commentators tend, on the whole, to position Middle Eastern youth as lacking in agency, needing protection, and requiring the tutelage of state institutions, experts, and the nationalist intelligentsia. While such discourses are correct in their understanding that youth are in a position of dependency on their elders and the institutions they control, what about youths' own motivations and desires?

One of the countries whose youth have received the most attention is Iran. Roxanne Varzi, in her important ethnography on Iranian youth, finds widespread disaffection for the ideology of the Islamic Republic among the middle-class youth of northern Tehran. While showing how such youth deploy various features of Western popular culture in expressing their dissent, Varzi is careful to avoid the trap of many Western observers who see such Iranian youth as so intensely disaffected that they are unanimously secular and Westernized. Varzi demonstrates, on the contrary, that middle-class youth have been molded by the Iranian state project of religiosity. Religion is very much a part of their lives and their expressions of resistance, rather than being external to them. For instance, one of the modes of disaffection is an embrace of what Varzi labels "Sufi cool" by long-haired, bohemian Iranian youth. The state has responded by producing its own brand of mystical pop music in an effort to appropriate and compete with Islamic practices outside its control.[14] In addition, young people in Tehran's northern suburbs typically use Shi'i religious rituals like 'Ashura as occasions to mingle freely and publicly with the opposite sex, turning such events into street parties. Similar things occur at *mulids* (saints' days) in Cairo, in this case, among youth of working-class and lower-middle-class backgrounds, as depicted in Yousry Nasrallah's 1995 documentary, *On Boys, Girls, and the Veil*.

---

13   See Walter Armbrust, "What Would Sayyid Qutb Say? Some Reflections on Video Clips," *Transnational Broadcasting Studies* 14 (Spring 2005).

14   Varzi, *Warring Souls*, pp. 21, 133, 136.

Marc Schade-Poulsen's important ethnographic work in Oran, Algeria in the early 1990s likewise avoids the errors made by many Western observers of raï music, who tend to view it, like rock 'n' roll, as a youth-based cultural movement striking blows against the puritanical and conservative practices supported by an authoritarian state and backward, intolerant religious mandarins. Schade-Poulsen demonstrates that there is no inherent contradiction between listening to raï music and being a believing Muslim, despite the violent antagonism toward raï artists on the part of some militant Islamists. And while raï music is associated with youth in Oran, it is by no means exclusively consumed by them, but, in different ways, by all generations—especially, and collectively, at weddings. Moreover, raï music is not "authored" by young musicians but by older producers and established studio musicians, and is mostly performed in nightclubs frequented by well-off adults, rather than young people who have little disposable cash. For young men in Oran, raï is not exactly "rebel music" *à la* punk or reggae; rather, its lyrics represent a means by which they negotiate the difficulties they face in meeting and dealing with young women, at a time when women, as a result of modern education and employment, wield more social power than in the past.[15]

Armbrust's examination of the discourses surrounding video clips likewise demonstrates the importance of avoiding simplistic stereotypes when it comes to youth culture and consumption. While many local observers condemn the clips as corrupting, and Western observers often view them as sticking it to the man (through depictions of liberated sexuality), Armbrust shows that the reality is much more complicated. The video flow includes not only the celebrated (and maligned) gyrations of sexpots Haifa Wehbe and Elissa, but also the "family values" clips of 'Ali Gawhar and clips of the massively popular Sami Yusuf, which use pop conventions to articulate messages of Islamic piety and devotion.

All this suggests the need for careful study of the daily lives of young people, but also a caution against focusing on the spectacular or relying overly upon Western models. A spate of articles and books, for instance, has suggested that Iran's young people are overwhelmingly secular and thirsty for Western commodities and lifestyles. These youth are believed to represent the best hope that Iran will abandon its fundamentalist ways and rejoin the civilized community of nations. An analytical focus on Iranian rappers and young women wearing makeup and allowing their headscarves to slip to reveal frosted hair obscures a more complicated reality. Young

---

15   Marc Schade-Poulsen, *Men and Popular Music in Algeria: The Social Significance of Raï* (Austin, TX: University of Texas Press, 1999).

volunteers man the paramilitary Basij, which is on the front lines of the Islamic Republic's struggle against "immoral" behavior, particularly on the part of privileged youth. This is one indicator of the regime's continued support among many lower- and working-class youth. Moreover, Iranian university students may be disenchanted, but they are essentially apolitical. They are mostly concerned with quotidian goals such as landing a job or getting admitted to graduate school. In fact, 150,000 Iranian professionals leave the country each year, giving Iran one of the highest rates of brain drain in the Middle East.[16]

In view of the severe limitations on youth incomes, the paucity of public spaces for youth leisure, and the nervousness on the part of authoritarian states about congregations of young people, "oppositional" youth movements are unlikely to take the same forms as youth subcultures in the West. Other Western frames of analysis of youth, such as the notion of the generation gap, can likewise be misleading. As Varzi shows, for instance, secular youth in upscale precincts of Tehran rely on the discretion and permission of their parents when they organize private parties in their homes that sometimes involve mixed-gender socializing, live music, and consumption of alcohol.[17] Claims that mass consumption and access to the trappings of globalized youth culture will necessarily make young people materialistic, individualistic, apolitical, and lacking in social consciousness are equally dubious. Palestinian youth who have embraced rap music, for instance, have typically deployed this art form to articulate fiercely nationalistic political concerns. And Turkish youth, widely criticized for their selfish consumerism, turned out to be at the forefront of relief efforts in the wake of the Marmara earthquake of 1999.[18]

LIBERATORS IN TROUBLE

The theme of "youth as trouble" emerges most clearly—and the fears of Western observers and Middle Eastern states converge—with regard to militant Islamism, the supreme ill from which young people must be protected (or else). In the minds of Westerners prone to "clash of civilizations" thinking, the supposed susceptibility of Middle Eastern youth to radical Islam is the factor that most calls into question the belief that youth will set the region free. If not even the new generation can be trusted to

---

16   Kaveh Basmenji, *Tehran Blues: How Iranian Youth Rebelled Against Iran's Founding Fathers* (London: Saqi Books, 2005), p. 316.
17   Varzi, *Warring Souls*, p. 166.
18   Neyzi, "Object or Subject?" p. 426.

embrace "moderation"—that is, to acquiesce in the US-sponsored liberal capitalist order—then there is no hope of coexistence. In the words of Thomas Friedman, "Young Israelis dream of being inventors, and their role models are the Israeli innovators who made it to the Nasdaq. Hizballah youth dream of being martyrs, and their role models are Islamic militants who made it to the Next World."[19] In the Middle East, the young may not be seen as irredeemable, but they are no less at risk: the success of Muslim "extremists" is often attributed to their ability to prey on youth, in particular, underprivileged young men who are sexually frustrated due to their inability to afford the costs of marriage. A paradigmatic example of such representation in Egypt is the 1994 hit film *al-Irhabi* (The Terrorist), in which the young terrorist (played by the not-so-young 'Adil Imam) is recruited when the Islamist group promises him a wife in return for fulfilling an assassination mission.

More broadly, there is a tension in dominant discourses about youth between seeing them as victims or perpetrators of violence. Consider the great outrage and distress in the West over Palestinians' "use" of children in the first year of the second *intifada*, forcing Palestinian spokespeople to explain that Palestinian mothers actually love their children, and do not send them out to compel the Israeli army to shoot them. On the one hand, the denial of agency to the youngest stone-throwers allowed Westerners (and Israelis) to locate the cause of the children's victimhood in a flaw of Palestinian culture, rather than in the occupation. On the other hand, the older "stone-throwing youths" of a thousand wire photos—having acquired agency by virtue of their age—were regarded as purveyors of violence, not victims. This episode also serves as a reminder that, for Middle Eastern states worried about their youth problem, the project of national reproduction has always been managed within an international arena of (Euro-American) expectation that judges the modernity of other countries by how those deemed vulnerable are treated. The category of the vulnerable in the Middle East includes women and ethnic minorities (Jews, Berbers, Kurds), but also the young. When Middle Eastern states are judged incompetent in their care for youth, the response of the West may be to assert surrogate parental rights of its own, intervening directly to save the *madrasa*-bound boys and unschooled girls of Afghanistan, or encouraging the students of Iranian universities to rebel against their elders.

In the post–September 11 era, indeed, the sheer numbers of Middle Eastern youth have been cited as the Achilles' heel of the existing non-democratic order in the region. It has become a media truism, for instance,

---

19   Thomas Friedman, "Buffett and Hezbollah," *New York Times*, August 9, 2006.

that 60 percent of Iran's population of 70 million is under thirty years of age, including a substantial cohort born well after the 1979 revolution. This fact is frequently adduced to imply that hard-line clerical rule has no future.[20] In a sign that such hopes have not faded in Foggy Bottom, the State Department has lately employed one Jared Cohen, twenty-six, author of *Children of Jihad: A Young American's Travels Among the Youth of the Middle East*, to advise its policy planning staff on how to "divert the world's impressionable youth away from 'illicit actors.'" Cohen told a *New Yorker* profiler: "I always say that the largest party in every country—the largest opposition group in every country—is the youth party."[21] Yet following the 2005 election of President Mahmoud Ahmadinejad, which consolidated all the branches of the Iranian government under conservative control, Iranian youth have largely been relegated to the role of victim in Western discourse. "Iran's youth are as talented as young Indians and Chinese, but they have no chance to show it," the ever-quotable Friedman has lamented. "Iran has been reduced to selling its natural resources to India and China—so Chinese and Indian youth can invent the future, while Iran's young people are trapped in the past."[22] It is a short distance from this avuncular solicitude to the proposition that Iranian youth could reclaim their agency—with a helpful nudge from outside.

Youth in the Middle East are burdened with authoritarian states, corruption, and nepotism that circumscribe their life chances, as well as structural socio-economic crisis stemming from the failures of state-led development and the systemic inequalities of global capitalism. Not the least of their burdens, however, are the expectations and imprecations generated by the "youth" of the elite imagination. In the manner of their peers everywhere, young Middle Easterners can be expected to heed the paternalism of their governments and the projections of outsiders unevenly at best, as they strive to fulfill their own aspirations, whether these be eman-cipatory, mundane, or somewhere in between.

---

20   See, for example, *Christian Science Monitor*, June 16, 2003.
21   Jesse Lichtenstein, "Condi's Party Starter," *New Yorker*, November 5, 2007.
22   Thomas Friedman, "A Shah with a Turban," *New York Times*, December 23, 2005.

Contributors

Asef Bayat is Professor of Sociology and Middle East Studies at the University of Illinois at Urbana-Champaign. His books include *Workers and Revolution in Iran* (Zed Books, 1987), *Street Politics: Poor Peoples' Movements in Iran* (Columbia University Press, 1997), *Making Islam Democratic: Social Movements and the Post-Islamist Turn* (Stanford University Press, 2007), *Life as Politics: How Ordinary People Change the Middle East* (Stanford University Press, 2010), and *Being Young and Muslim: New Cultural Politics in the Global South and North* (co-edited with L. Herrera, Oxford University Press, 2010).

Hossam Bahgat is the founder and director of the Egyptian Initiative for Personal Rights (EIPR), a Cairo-based independent human rights organization established in 2002 to promote and defend the rights to privacy, health, religious freedom, and bodily integrity, through research, advocacy, and strategic litigation. Bahgat is also the vice president of the Egyptian Association Against Torture, an Advisory Board member of the New Woman Foundation and a Steering Committee member of Sexuality Policy Watch.

Joel Beinin is the Donald J. McLachlan Professor in History and Professor of Middle Eastern History at Stanford University. From 2006 to 2008 he served as Director of Middle East Studies and Professor of History at the American University in Cairo. In 2001–02 he served as president of the Middle East Studies Association of North America. His recent books include *The Struggle for Worker Rights in Egypt* (Solidarity Center, 2010); *Social Movements, Mobilization, and Contestation in the Middle East and North Africa* (Stanford University Press, 2011), co-edited with Frédéric Vairel; and *Workers and Peasants in the Modern Middle East* (Cambridge University Press, 2001).

Ray Bush is Professor of African Studies and Development Politics at the University of Leeds, UK. His research focuses on the political economy of Africa and the Near East. His recent book is *Poverty and Neoliberalism: Persistence and Reproduction in the Global South* (Pluto Press, 2007), and editor with Habib Ayeb, *Marginality in Egypt and the Middle East* (Zed Books, 2012). He is deputy chair of *The Review of African Political Economy*.

Elliott Colla is Associate Professor and Chair of the Department of Arabic and Islamic Studies at Georgetown University. The author of *Conflicted Antiquities: Egyptology, Egyptomania, Egyptian Modernity* (Duke University Press, 2007), he has translated a number of works of Arabic literature, including Ibrahim Al-Koni's *Gold Dust* (Arabia Books, 2008).

Eric Denis is Senior Researcher in Geography at the Centre National de la Recherche Scientifique (CNRS) in France. He is presently heading the Department of Social Sciences at the French Institute of Pondicherry (India), and formerly directed the Urban Observatory of Cairo at CEDEJ research center in Egypt (1997–2002). His publications focus upon metropolitan and real estate dynamics, illegal settlements, and access to services in Egypt, Sudan, and India.

Issandr El Amrani is a Cairo-based writer and consultant. His reporting and commentary on the Middle East and North Africa has appeared in *The Economist*, *London Review of Books*, *The Financial Times*, *The National*, *The Guardian*, *Time*, and other publications. He blogs at arabist.net.

Mona El-Ghobashy is Assistant Professor of Political Science at Barnard College. Her articles on political mobilization in contemporary Egypt have appeared in *American Behavioral Scientist*, the *International Journal of Middle East Studies*, and *Middle East Report*. In 2009, she was named a Carnegie Scholar to support a research project on Egyptian citizens' use of street protests and court petitions to reclaim their rights.

Sharif Elmusa is Associate Professor of Political Science at the American University in Cairo. His books include *A Harvest of Technology: The Super-Green Revolution in the Jordan Valley* (Georgetown University Press, 1994), *Water Conflict: Economics, Politics, Law, and Palestinian–Israeli Water Resources* (Institute for Palestine Studies, 1998), and *Flawed Landscapes: Poems, 1987–2008* (Interlink Press, 2008).

Linda Herrera is Associate Professor in the Department of Education Policy, Organization, and Leadership at the University of Illinois at Urbana–Champaign. A social anthropologist, she is currently working on youth, new media, and the Arab revolutions. She has co-edited two volumes, *Being Young and Muslim: New Cultural Politics in the Global South and North* (Oxford University Press, 2010, with Asef Bayat) and *Cultures of Arab Schooling: Critical Ethnographies from Egypt* (SUNY Press, 2006, with C. A. Torres).

Hanan Kholoussy is Assistant Professor of History at the American University in Cairo. She is the author of *For Better, For Worse: The Marriage Crisis That Made Modern Egypt* (Stanford University Press, 2010) and several articles on gender, law, and nationalism in Egypt.

Ursula Lindsey is a journalist and writer who has lived in Cairo since 2002. She is the Middle East correspondent of *The Chronicle of Higher Education* and she writes about politics, media, and culture in the Arab world for a variety of publications. She covered the Egyptian revolution for Public Radio International's *The World* and *Newsweek* and is a regular contributor to *The Arabist* blog (www.arabist.net).

Timothy Mitchell is Professor and Chair of the Department of Middle Eastern, South Asian, and African Studies at Columbia University. He joined Columbia in 2008 after teaching for twenty-five years at New York University, where he served as Director of the Center for Near Eastern Studies. His books include *Colonising Egypt* (University of California Press, 1991), *Rule of Experts: Egypt, Techno-Politics, Modernity* (University of California Press, 2002), and *Carbon Democracy: Political Power in the Age of Oil* (Verso, 2011).

Karen Pfeifer is Professor Emerita of Economics at Smith College. She has published numerous articles and book chapters, and was named a Fulbright Senior Scholar twice. Her current scholarly projects focus on the relation between the discipline of economics and Middle East area studies.

Amal Sabri was director of the environment and development program of the Association for Health and Environmental Development, an Egyptian NGO. She previously worked in the Middle East office of Oxfam in Cairo.

Paul Schemm is chief correspondent in North Africa for the Associated Press. He joined AP in 2007 in Cairo as an editor for the Middle East regional editing desk. Previously he worked as a reporter for Agence France-Presse in Baghdad and Cairo. He has written for a number of publications including the *Middle East Times, Cairo Times*, the *San Francisco Chronicle, Christian Science Monitor*, and the *Boston Globe*, among others.

Samer S. Shehata is Assistant Professor of Arab Politics at Georgetown University's Center for Contemporary Arab Studies. He is author of *Shop Floor Culture and Politics in Egypt* (SUNY Press, 2009) and editor of *Islamist Politics in the Middle East: Movements and Change* (forthcoming, Routledge, 2012).

Ahmad Shokr is a doctoral candidate in Middle East history at New York University and a senior editor at the English edition of *al-Masry al-Youm*, Egypt's best-selling private newspaper. His articles have been published in *Arab Studies Journal, Economic and Political Weekly*, and *Middle East Report*.

Jeannie Sowers is Assistant Professor of Political Science at the University of New Hampshire. She has published in *Climatic Change, Journal of Environment and Development, Development and Change*, and *Middle East Report*. Her book *Environmental Politics in Egypt* is forthcoming from Routledge.

Joshua Stacher is Assistant Professor of Political Science at Kent State University. He has published articles in *Middle East Journal* and *History Compass* (among others), as well as frequently contributed to *Middle East Report*. His book *Adaptable Autocrats: Regime Power in Egypt and Syria* is forthcoming from Stanford University Press (expected Spring 2012).

Ewan Stein is Lecturer in International Relations at the University of Edinburgh. His forthcoming book is *Representing Israel in Modern Egypt: Ideas, Intellectuals, and Foreign Policy from Nasser to Mubarak* (IB Tauris). He has published articles in *International Studies Quarterly, Review of International Studies, Third World Quarterly*, and *Middle East Report*.

Ted Swedenburg is Professor of Anthropology at the University of Arkansas. His books include *Memories of Revolt: The 1936–1939 Rebellion and the Palestinian National Past* (University of Minnesota Press, 1995); *Displacement, Diaspora, and Geographies of Identity* (co-edited with Smadar Lavie, Duke University Press, 1996); and *Palestine, Israel, and the Politics of Popular Culture* (coedited with Rebecca Stein, Duke, 2005).

Mariz Tadros is a fellow with the Institute for Development Studies at the University of Sussex. Her publications include an article in *Journal of Security, Conflict, and Development* (March 2011), an edited volume, "Gender,

Rights, and Religion at the Crossroads" (*IDS Bulletin*, January 2011), and a forthcoming book on the Muslim Brothers (Routledge, 2012).

Chris Toensing is Executive Director of the Middle East Research and Information Project and editor of *Middle East Report*. An Arabic speaker, he lived in Egypt for three years in the 1990s. He is co-editor, with Mimi Kirk, of *Uncovering Iraq: Trajectories of Disintegration and Transformation* (Center for Contemporary Arab Studies, Georgetown University, 2011). He has written for *The Nation*, *The Progressive* and other US newspapers and magazines, and frequently appears on radio and TV to discuss Middle East affairs and US Middle East policy.

Jessica Winegar is Associate Professor of Anthropology at Northwestern University. She is the author of *Creative Reckonings: The Politics of Art and Culture in Contemporary Egypt* (Stanford University Press, 2006), which won the Albert Hourani Book Award for best book in Middle East studies. Her articles have appeared in *Cultural Anthropology*, *Anthropological Quarterly*, *Review of Middle East Studies*, *Contemporary Practices*, and online at *Jadaliyya* and *ArteEast*.

Index

Page numbers in **bold** refer to illustrations, page numbers in *italic* refer to tables.